PETER
Supplem
and writes on modern politics and ancient literature. His previous book, *30 Days: A Month at the Heart of Blair's War*, is a diary of his time observing the direction of the 2003 conflict with Iraq.

From the reviews of *On the Spartacus Road*:

'*On the Spartacus Road* makes for a wonderfully rich and endlessly thought-provoking brew, part ancient history, part modern travelogue, part personal memoir, with a distinctly philosophical strain . . . reminiscent of the writing of W G Sebald. Beautifully written, musing and far-sighted . . . Here is Stothard not just as a fine and engaging historian, but a historian with an imagination that can vault with ease over two millennia . . . An outstanding success'

CHRISTOPHER HART, *Literary Review*

'Stothard puts his literary knowledge, journalistic skills and classical erudition to powerful use . . . An astonishing tale of men fighting against the odds for reasons they themselves hardly understand, and by using a mix of personal travel narrative and historical re-enactment, Stothard brings it to life triumphantly.'
GILES FODEN

'Haunting, erudite and beautifully written . . . It is proudly and defiantly, the very opposite of journalism: a fusion of memoir, history and travelogue that is unlike any other book ever written about Spartacus, and all the more precious for being quite so unexpected'
TOM HOLLAND, *Spectator*

'Moving . . . for an empathising moment, the past become now'
Independent

By the same author

30 Days: A Month at the Heart of Blair's War
The Best of The Times:
Words and Images from the Year 2000 (editor)

ON THE
SPARTACUS ROAD

A SPECTACULAR JOURNEY THROUGH
ANCIENT ITALY

Peter Stothard

Harper
Press

Harper*Press*
An imprint of HarperCollins*Publishers*
77–85 Fulham Palace Road
Hammersmith, London W6 8JB

Visit our authors' blog: www.fifthestate.co.uk

This Harper*Press* paperback edition published 2011
1

First published in Great Britain by Harper*Press* in 2010

A catalogue record for this book is available
from the British Library

ISBN 978-0-00-734080-4

Typeset by Terence Caven

Printed and bound in Great Britain by Clays Ltd, St Ives plc

To Anna and Michael

Contents

Prologue

In the final century of the first Roman Republic an army of slaves brought a peculiar terror to the people of Italy. Its leaders were gladiators. Its purpose was incomprehensible. Its success was something no one had ever known. Never before had the world's greatest state been threatened from the lowest places that its citizens could imagine, from inside its own kitchens, laundries, mines, fields and theatres. Never again, the victors said when Spartacus was dead and his war was over.

The Spartacus Road is the route along which the slave army fought its Roman enemies between 73 and 71 BC. It is a road much travelled then and since by poets and philosophers, politicians and teachers, torturers and terrorisers of different times, those living today and those long ago dead, innovative thinkers about fear and death, some with truths to teach us, others whom we can try to forget. It stretches through 2,000 miles of Italian countryside and out into 2,000 years of world history. From Sicily to the Alps and from Paris to Hollywood, it has never wholly left the modern mind.

This book is a diary of a journey on that Spartacus Road. It is, in part, a journalist's notebook because I have been a journalist – a newspaper reporter and editor – for most of my life. It is a classicist's notebook, written with half-remembered classical books for company, because while reporting politics in our own time I have so often felt the beat of ancient feet. It is also the notebook of a grateful survivor: ten years ago

I was given no chance of living to make this trip and, on the Spartacus Road, the memory of a fatal cancer and its fortuitous cure shone stronger, and stranger, than I ever thought it could.

Little of this book is as I thought it might be. It began as notes written night by night, on bar tables and brick walls, in the places where the Spartacus War was fought. It became a history of that war, the best that I could write, and the history of how I came to know anything about that war, other wars, and many other things.

Thanks are owed to Greek and Roman writers whom I thought I knew when I was young and know differently now. Returning to old books is like returning to old friends. They have changed, both the familiar characters studied at school and some of the less read ancients, a director of Roman water supplies, a historian who was a lovable tabloid hack, a pioneer writer on interior décor and on the apocalypse. Thanks too to some equally little-known twenty-first-century travellers, a pair of Koreans, an actor seeking centurion roles, a Pole selling DVDs and a bibulous priest.

The barest facts about Spartacus, like the road itself, are often hard to find. They disappear and reappear – in the landscape and in the memory of succeeding centuries. They have been twisted in the service of cinema, politics and art. There is Spartacus the romantic gladiator from Thrace, the fighter for freedom, the man who lives on in the memory of emulators; and there is Spartacus the terrorist and threat to life, the one who survives in others' fears. There is the hidden man and the man of the Spectacular, the word which appeared on the first page of my first notes and is left still in the subtitle of this book, the Romans' own name for the theatrical games and aesthetic of death that so powerfully defined both their lives and our memories of them.

I

ROME to ARICCIA

Via di S. Stefano Rotondo, Rome

This Spartacus Road begins high on Rome's most south-easterly hill, the Caelian, with questions that were asked here first some five hundred years after the great slave revolt. How could twenty-nine gladiators have strangled themselves in their underground pens? How did they dare to do it? How had they succeeded in doing it? There was no rope, no cloth, nothing to make a noose. The games had barely begun and twenty-nine men had suddenly been their own stranglers. Somehow it had happened. How?

These were not the questions which Quintus Aurelius Symmachus most wanted to ask. A power-broker of an age when his city had lost so much power liked to think of better

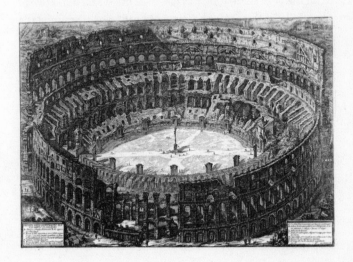

things. Life was too short, its needs too great, for anyone, let alone him, to agonise over some ingeniously suicidal Saxons.

He had his duties as ambassador between the old Rome and the new, the pagan and the Christian. Rome's rulers in Constantinople and Milan were militant leaders of the new ruling faith. Many of their subjects, his own people here among the empty barracks and neglected temples, were more relaxed in their religious commitments. Symmachus needed all his old Roman's diplomatic skills to mediate between the two.

He had serious private interests as a writer and intellectual, a word he would happily have used of himself had he known it. He was self-important, self-reliant, subtle in his own cause, fond of focusing on himself in every way. Now one of the least read writers of ancient Rome, his nine hundred surviving letters and forty-nine reports to the rulers of his world are reminders of a time when he could demand to be read.

In the year AD 393, he was just over fifty years old. He had already held the thousand-year-old office of city prefect, a title whose antiquity was of some importance to him. True, he had not held the city prefecture very long: but brief tenures in office were nothing now of which to be ashamed. Holding on to any job, or even any consistent line of thought, was difficult when commands and signals came from two imperial courts, in east and west, so very far away and apart.

At least he had added a prefect's distinction to his family line. Symmachus was still a Roman senator, a senior priest whose sway extended from Vestal virgins to omens of war, a man of wealth in gold and land to protect against what sometimes seemed the end of his world. On this troubled Roman morning, four centuries after the death of the first Caesar, he had greater anxieties to express in his letter to his brother

4

than a mass immolation of twenty-nine men from the cold, dank north.

How much did he or anyone really care how the gladiators had died? They were captives condemned to appear in the Colosseum arena. He could see down to their last killing place from up here at his Caelian home. Their miserable heads had been unable to save their miserable necks. Those same heads had decided to break those necks. How had they done it? Who could tell?

He could see silvery streaks in the southern Roman sky, the first morning lights on the high arches built by great warrior emperors of old. This was only the second day of his games, only the start of his latest personal offering for the entertainment of the Roman people. Yesterday had been disastrous but there was much more still to come. Above the soaring marble was the fading array of stars at dawn. Symmachus, like many in uncertain times, found much contemplative comfort in the stars.

His first thought? No one had directly killed himself. Not even the toughest gladiator is tough enough to be his own strangler. All human grip fails before the body is dead. Second thought. Maybe the Saxons had a leader, an elected executioner or one chosen by lot, who stood behind each prisoner in line, choking the breath of one, then another, breaking the bones, stopping the blood. That was possible but not likely. Leadership of such an enterprising kind would surely have been detected – and corrected – before they arrived.

Third thought. Maybe the twenty-nine formed themselves up in pairs, as they should have done in the arena on this second day of his spectacular. Fourteen against fourteen. Or rather fourteen *for* fourteen, since they seemed to have agreed on their suicide, with one of them just watching from the wooden beams or wet brick walls. Then fifteen left in the cells, seven on seven, with a different one watching. Seven against seven, the most mythical numbers. Strangling a strong man is hard work, even if the strong man wants to die. It could have taken thirty seconds before each death came.

Then four on four, with no one sitting out the show. It was strange how odd numbers eventually divided into even. The chance of a three-on-three fight, once one of the most prized gifts for the Emperor and people of Rome, was gone for ever. In the cramped, low-ceilinged darkness, the blue-fleshed faces would by now have had hardly a place to fall. Then two on two. Another great spectacle he had paid for. The finest moment of a double duel in the arena brought two simultaneous sets of dying eyes, one to remind the spectator that he was still alive, the second to tell him that one day he too had death to face. But this time the eyes had been seen by no one.

Till one on one, the final, but a pathetic parody of what he had hoped to offer to the puppet-man on the imperial balcony. A gladiator who died in the dark need never have lived. Symmachus was this week celebrating the latest promotion of his son, a boy who one day might follow his father to the rank of consul. It was important to remind everyone that, while Christianity had its place in this new Rome, there were old Roman traditions which needed patronage and protection too.

And after that? Surely at least one of the men would be left at the end. That was the troubling question, though none of his household slaves had mentioned a survivor. Had the Saxons cast lots for who that survivor would be? Had they decided for themselves who would be the one to fall, feeling the other's thumbs at his throat, and who would be left alive as the last gladiator in this shameful night's work? Symmachus

was someone who liked a long, tendentious, apparently logical, mildly melodramatic question like that. He was famed throughout the city as a man of many words. Had one of the bastards fixed to cheat his fellows? Had the last man held some last hope of escape, of fighting in the games, of pretending to die, of avoiding the hooks of the body-clearers, of hiding in the wagon that, every hour or so during a week like this, hauled the corpses outside the walls? Who could tell?

Perhaps the two last determined men, knowledgeable in all the ways to kill and be killed, could have arranged that each died almost simultaneously. Possible again. But only in the old story books. Symmachus was beginning to be impatient with the whole bloody business. Words piled upon words until even the man who could demand that listeners hear him was doubtful whether he wanted an audience.

It was a brutal truth that the awakening city he could see from his home was little more now than a city of words.

Deeds were not done in Rome as deeds had been done before. For more than half a century the city that had defined the world's centre had been pushed to its edge. He had once described the Senate, his Senate, as the 'better part of human-kind'. But being 'better' was not the same as making anything happen. Easterners, northerners and even southerners did that now. Goths, Gauls and Saxons did that. Even Saxons – especially so now, it seemed.

The names of the emperor in charge of Rome changed at challenging speeds. Thugs and puppets of thugs followed one after the other. Six years before, Symmachus had made a dangerous mistake, publicly pouring one of his famous speeches of praise over a chancer who did not last very long. He hoped not to make that kind of error again.

The best emperor now would have been the very general who had captured those Saxons. His name was Arbogast. He had the military muscle but was not acceptable to traditionalists despite being a great traditionalist in spirit. So Arbogast had chosen someone else instead, a Christian schoolteacher called Eugenius who had a reputation for tolerance but little else to recommend his claim.

Why had so much of the world ended with the so-called Christ, with that bureaucratic incompetent Pontius Pilate and the gullible fools who felt guilt for a single crucifixion? A good ruler was now a Christian who tolerated the gods that had made Rome great, one who respected the pieties that had thrived before. A bad ruler was a Christian fanatic who did not tolerate even variants in his own religion.

Symmachus remembered the Eastern Emperor Theodosius from when he had been a lucky Spanish warlord, one of dozens: now the man sat on a throne at Constantinople as a single God's sole representative on earth. To see him or to see any emperor ever in Rome itself was a rarity. Even the Western court was up north in Milan. The last time that Theodosius came to the one-time capital of the world was when he wanted support from the Senate for the succession plans of his son. That was how Symmachus had won his consulship, a victory showing either that his virtue and status were suddenly and inexplicably valued (he tried to be as optimistic as he could) or how unpredictable all life had become.

During his long career, Symmachus had spent millions on Colosseum shows. The family coffers had given up uncountable gold to gladiator-sellers, some of the greediest tradesmen he had ever known. He had imported bears and paid extortionate customs duty. He had paraded leopards, antelopes and lions, recalling those great occasions of the past when the Emperor himself might shoot arrows at the neck of an ostrich and when prisoners fought wild boars and wild witches as well as each other.

In his short time as city prefect he had written to his masters in rapture at the arrival in Rome of real prisoners-of-war for a real gladiatorial event. 'No longer are we inferior to our ancient fathers. We have seen for ourselves the sights we used to read about with wonder: the lines of the conquered led in chains, those pallid faces that were once so savage, their hands, well used to barbarian arms, trembling at our gladiators' weapons.' The amphitheatre stars on that occasion were the descendants of exotic nomads from the eastern deserts, famed for a thousand years for deploying women among men as archers and cavalry. This week Symmachus had planned to be more modest. This present time was one when modesty was often best.

He had bought some splendid wolfhounds from Scotland: all Rome viewed them with wonder, he told his brother. But this present show was still indisputably inferior to the great examples of antiquity. A dog was still only a dog. 'I did not want my display to be in any way gaudy,' he wrote. He had an extravagant present ready for when Emperor Eugenius made his appearance before the crowd, a carved ivory panel in two hinged parts each framed in gold. But excessive theatrical extravagance might easily be frowned upon. Even tolerant Christians could be sensitive on the subject of the Colosseum, believing, quite wrongly, that thousands of their saintly predecessors had perished on its sands. It was probably only a few hundred, Syrians, Jews and other riff-raff, vicious, violent people for the most part, their agonies and their numbers absurdly exaggerated by religious propaganda.

The loss of twenty-nine Saxons, a few hours before their lives were meant to be lost, had depleted his cast. There was no denying that. The alien soldiers had broken every rule of their Roman school. Trained to kill in front of the country's sharpest critics, in the open, on stage, they had chosen to die the unseen death of the untrained criminal. He could hardly fault his own behaviour. Even if he had paid the best of private guards, how could such reckless idiots have been stopped?

Who needed gladiators anyway? There was still time to add more African animals to his games. He would do it without a thought. He had spent too much effort already on this wretched gang of slaves who were, he told his brother with a flourish, 'worse than Spartacus'. There was nothing for it but to use the experience to make himself a better person. The philosopher Socrates, one of the better Greeks, had taught that disappointment brought its own rewards, that failure to attain one's cherished goals was a lesson in itself. Failure was so often better than success; there was so much more to be learnt from it.

Via San Giovanni in Laterano, Rome

The name of Spartacus sounds Roman enough to those who are tourists in the city today. But the distinguished senator of the elderly Roman Empire was using a word which his fellow countrymen had for centuries preferred not to use.

In many places, including here among the rats and recycling bins of the Via San Giovanni, Spartacus is among the most notable Romans of them all. In these streets around the Colosseum you can pay fifteen euros to a bulky Bulgarian in fancy dress and have your photograph taken with him. Behind the doorways of the bookshops where the tourist-trapping gladiators lurk, you can buy videos of Kirk Douglas in the role, DVDs of mini-series successors to what was once the most expensive film ever made, postcards of Spartacus from Pompeii, even the 'worse than Spartacus' letter of Quintus Aurelius Symmachus, though not translated into English.

To the ancient Romans who lived in 73 BC, and their successors for a long time after 73 BC, the rebel leader of the Third Servile War, as modern history books describe him, was an obscenity. To Marcus Tullius Cicero, greatest orator of the Republic, his name was a term of abuse to be used against the vilest of state enemies. To such as Symmachus he stood somewhere between gnawing vermin and rotting vegetables, to use the classification of the natural world that was then so fashionably a part of an intellectual gentleman's life.

The events of that year in which a Thracian slave had escaped from his gladiator school, turned on his captors, summoned a rebellion and terrorised the country were a blot on the city record even though the battles had taken place almost half a millennium before. A very successful Socrates might be able to explain it away as a lesson for the future. But Symmachus and his fellow scholars were not easily philosophical about memories such as this. Socratic justifications were little comfort. Slave wars formed a nasty part of Rome's narrative of decline – when greed overcame good sense, when the governable became ungovernable, when the rubbish rose to the top of the heap. Rome was rotten from the inside. There was always the nagging question of when the rot had set in. The Spartacus devastation (only the common herd called it a war) was one such moment.

This bit of the city is almost awake now. The actor gladiators are creeping out of their beds. The plastic gladiators are back on the tables where they will best attract trade. The light rises on Colosseum ivy, its ancestors as old as the Colosseum itself, and over a mass of Mexican daisies, more recent arrivals who love the same damp, dark places as the rats. A coffee outside the creperia costs fifty cents, the pre-tourist, beggars' breakfast rate.

Why bother with the mind of Symmachus? Not because of his charm or his prose but because he was here close to the end. Within a few decades of the date of his letter to his

brother the Western Roman Empire would be dead. The homes on the Caelian Hill would be razed by Visigoths from around the forests where Spartacus was born. Gladiatorial games would not just be difficult, they would be history. Symmachus does not know any of that. Characters from the past never know what is coming next. That is one of the less acknowledged reasons we like to think about them.

Today's traveller to Rome may know that gladiatorial combat – and much else that Symmachus loved in Roman life – was already as doomed in AD 393 as its combatants had mostly been. The public fight-to-the-death was by then a peculiar old custom, ready to begin its journey into the history books of a different age, a 'dark age' to a classical scholar, an age of light to a lover of the gospels.

Modern historians know Symmachus' personal future after his year of the dead Saxons – that he would live for about another decade, still indulging his guilty *morbum fabricatoris*, his passion for building houses; that he would still be importing crocodiles, leopards, men and bears, for one last pagan extravaganza in 401, before one last and fatal ambassadorial trip, to a besieged and snowbound Milan, in 402. What Symmachus could claim to know was only his own and his city's past.

This was a Rome which had struggled from the muddy banks of the Tiber river at a time when Greeks already had their Olympic Games. There were thick-packed oak forests on the Caelian when Greek city statesmen were inventing modern politics. Rome's leaders, however, had prospered quickly, creating their own young state by sharing a little power with their people, first conquering their near neighbours, Latins, Sabines and Samnites, and soon afterwards their far neighbours, dark Sicilians and Italian Greeks. Romans had next defeated their Mediterranean rivals, Hannibal's Carthage and Greece itself, then the Syrians (a name for every servile eastern type) and finally, after nine hundred years, almost the whole of the known world.

Roman rulers had built their own extraordinary structures of stone, not just killing grounds and temples but stages for history and horror stories, tragedy and laughter. Even now, one of the prides of the capital was the theatre of Pompey the Great, soaring tiers of red and grey arcades, stage-sets with secret doors into painted forests, seats for 10,000 living spectators and hundreds of the bronze and marble dead. So how come that Rome was now beset by Goths and by other human garbage it had imported once to shift its scenery, clean its water closets and do all its most menial tasks?

This was a common question then. It is always a common question for civilisations of a certain age. Some spectators looked up at Pompey's theatre, saw the statues of bisexuals, transsexuals, hermaphrodites, sex pets, sex pests, mothers of thirty children, mothers of elephant men, and wondered. Had these been their ancestors? Had Roman lives been less pious and pure than their teachers told? Had foreign decadence and magic been Roman from the beginning? Much old Roman practice was now seen by Christians as evil mysticism, unacceptable adultery, unnatural crudity, the kind of behaviour that got senators killed by the state. Was there justification for such a view?

When did the rot really set in? Some remembered Pompey's war with Caesar, one of those many civil wars between ambitious warlords that ended the Roman Republic. Afterwards had come other civil wars and the Empire – with just one warlord who ruled for life – until that system too had broken into West and East under its own colossal weight. There were now Roman citizens so remote that they had never known a Roman, neither past nor present. Their masters might just as well have been a mythical hero as a modern thug, a Theodosius or an Aeneas, a Caesar or an Agamemnon, mere names spread indiscriminately through a space as vast as time.

On this dirty Roman sidestreet south of the Colosseum, with 1,900-year-old prison cells down below and a shopfront of books and statues behind, there is a wide range of spurs to the modern imagination of what went right and wrong. There are stone slabs here, 2,500 years old, antiquities in Symmachus' time and kept to mourn the best of the ancient past; there are others, designed by Mussolini's Fascists some seventy years ago, to keep alive that same past. Often an ancient mourning stone has been used for a second time or a third. It has become a modern monument, losing most of its original force but maintaining a little momentum still; most monuments here keep something of their mourning origins.

It is not so hard, in the grey start of a city day, to imagine these men of ancient Rome who saw their own past so clearly. There is no need ourselves to mourn their lost grandeur as Symmachus did. We are more likely to mourn those desperate Saxons, driven to suicide by an impending fate in an arena so repugnant to us now. But we can imagine old Symmachus mourning without sharing his anxieties. He has left enough monuments in stones and words to let us do that.

He seems a modern politician in many ways, someone we can identify, for better or worse, with our own. He was practical. He preached tolerance. He cited Socrates more enthusiastically than he attempted to understand him. He wheeled and dealed. He played his bad hands of cards as best he could. He took his wife away to the seaside when times were too hard. He talked about more wars than he fought, seeing action only in a skirmish against the Germans, an unusually one-sided show that had been staged for visiting dignitaries almost as in an arena. He was pleased that there was no rape

15

of sleeping tribeswomen on that occasion – not while he, the man of sensibility, was watching the show. He wrote carefully about how pleased he was.

He was conscious of his image. He was famed during his short time as city prefect for rejecting the new foreign extravagance of a silver-panelled carriage paid for by the state. Like a British prime minister pointedly refusing a private jet, he chose the drabbest and most traditional means for his transport, running into trouble only when the Emperor wanted back the money for the silver panels. He told his story in letters, always keeping a copy so that he might have history's last word. If we can imagine Symmachus – not a well-known figure and from a time that most of us do not know well – we can picture other builders and writers, and through them those who did not build or write but who, like the Saxons, still inspire our feelings. We can see both the terrorisers from ancient Rome and those who were terrorised and how sometimes, very often, they were the same people.

Spartacus and his armies had been a special part of that terror. Civil wars were always catastrophic. But when a slave army was rampaging through Italy, no one could trust the very men or women on whom they depended for everything, the foreigners whom they had brought into their houses and fields and who might suddenly, despite every threat to their own lives, slaughter the masters in their beds.

A slave war placed doubts over so much. Pessimism about decline was a necessary part of Symmachus' old Roman way of seeing the world. It was one of his and his kind's great legacies to later minds. Pessimism had been at the root of Rome even in the good times. There had always been an earlier and better golden age, even when this had been a city of success, when barbarians were routinely routed in battle rather than regularly victorious. There was much now to be properly and

justifiably pessimistic about. Where had it started? That was the common and weary question, spat out from angry mouths, a wholly understandable reason, in AD 393, to abuse a pile of Saxons 'worse than Spartacus'.

The tour-guides are arriving now with their Evian-powered flocks, tiny children from China, towering women from the Caribbean, Americans, Africans. Coffee prices are advancing with the clock. Two linen-clad English tourists, with a BlackBerry and an 1890 *Baedeker* and little enthusiasm for using either, ask the way to the 'Ludus Magnus, the school where the gladiators were trained'. The husband, in beige from brow to shoelace, begins the question and his wife, grey from head to sock, completes it, making 'school' sound 'preparatory' and 'trained' as though it means the same as 'taught their manners'. The Ludus that they are looking for is a small semi-excavated arena with a surround of prisoner pens, standing now a dirty yard of pavement from where they ask their question. In one sense this was both a 'prep school' and a 'finishing school'; doubtless there were bad pupils who were 'worse than Spartacus' and better ones who were not.

When Symmachus used those words he was himself being a bit of an old buffer, a fish-out-of-water and proud of it, boldly but self-consciously conservative, loose-lipped in the aristocratic tradition, like Prince Philip speaking of the 'slitty-eyed' or George V saying 'Bugger Bognor.' It was a spit-away, throw-away line. But let us imagine Symmachus without company outside his house that morning as he first formed the syllables in his mind.

How did others see Spartacus in the crumbling years of the Western Empire? Traditional Romans had tried to forget him – and had mostly succeeded. Christians might have been sympathetic in their own rebel days but to the new masters of the world a rebel was the worst of creatures. Symmachus' wayward protégé St Augustine, sitting in Africa twenty years later contemplating the City of God and his own shift to faith from reason, wondered how so 'very few' gladiators had come to lead 'such a very large number of fierce and cruel slaves'. Augustine's Spanish disciple Orosius wrote of 'the universal fear' that Spartacus had spread among the civilised people of his time. Historians had found no satisfactory explanation for the defeats of Roman armies and the devastation of so many Italian cities. Neither had the new princes of the Church.

The last major poet of classical Rome, the Egyptian syco-phant known as Claudian, arrived from Alexandria at around the same time as the suicidal Saxons. He had a more vicious verbal wit than the senator whose pagan cause and windbag reputation he shared. The name of Spartacus appears just once in his works – in his abuse of one of Symmachus' contacts at the Eastern court, a Christian fanatic who deploys 'racks and whips, chains and windowless cells, before putting his opponents to the sword: *cruciatus, vincla, tenebras Dilato mucrone parat*'. This cruel Rufinus, claims Claudian, kills wives and children, tortures small boys in front of their fathers and 'labours to exterminate the very race and name of Rome: *exscindere cives Funditus et nomen gentis delere laborat*'. Compared with this monster, screams the poet, 'even you, Spartacus, will be seen as a do-nothing: *iam Spartace segnis Rufino collatus eris*'.

There would have been some clever Greek slave to whom Symmachus dictated his letters. A trained secretary would probably have known of Spartacus – either as a problematic question like Augustine's, perhaps as a noble hero or a bio-graphical model, or very likely as another bit of human trash.

Those who still enjoyed the poetry of Horace, that genius son of a freed slave in the time of the first Emperor, Augustus, might also remember the slave general. Horace used the name only twice – the first with the boldness of youth in pos-sibly his earliest poem, written thirty years after the revolt, in which 'fierce Spartacus: *Spartacus acer*' is high on the list of fresh horrors for Rome. In a much later poem Horace wonders with a weary hauteur (or is that a mock-weary hau-teur?) whether there is any decent wine left in the cellar from the years before Spartacus and his bands passed by. That question was posed about fifty years after the event. The wit even then still held a chill.

Four centuries later, Symmachus had a good knowledge of what had happened in all the slave wars against Rome, in the Spartacus scandal and in two earlier revolts that had raged through Sicily. He knew of their colourful leaders and chaotic ends. There had once been another mass suicide, not unlike his own disaster, when a bunch of defeated Sicilian slaves, thirty years before Spartacus, had been brought to Rome as lion-kill and had preferred to kill each other. On that occasion, as he recalled, the last slave left standing had succeeded also in killing himself. Perhaps that was what had happened to his Saxons. It was hard to say.

Symmachus had read studiously in the Histories of Livy, that master of Roman morality in the age of the first Emperor. His library held all the other books by writers who had told of the Spartacus War, as well as poems dedicated to himself by his friends. *The Riddle of the Number Three* was not perhaps the finest work by the imperial tutor, Ausonius of Bordeaux: 'Three the Graces, Three the Fates, Three the corners of Sicily . . .', a wearying list of Threes including 'Three the pairs of Thracians at Rome's first gladiatorial games'. But the poem was his and his alone. There was true magic in the number three. Or perhaps there was. Anyway, how else would any books survive if rich men did not inspire and keep them?

The Christians, of course, had made their own Trinity an obsession. They fought bitterly between themselves over how their Father, Son and Holy Spirit could fit together to make a single object of worship. These were absurd disputes. But why did any man's belief in the unknowable have to stop the public practice of what Romans had always known? Bishop Ambrose, the local strongman whom Symmachus hated with a passion, was a master bully in the battles to show that three could be equally one. Ambrose had a peculiar policy too of persuading women to remain virgins. None of Symmachus' fellow priests of Vesta, at any time in a thousand years, had ever suggested that what was right for Vestal virgins was necessary for everyone else. The Bishop was both brutal and absurd.

Romans were inexorably losing the battle for their own minds. There had been many self-styled historians since the first century BC but not much history in Latin worth the name since the death of Tacitus three hundred years before. The real Roman historians had always written to praise Rome, to prove that Rome was just as smart as any foreigner as well as infinitely mightier. All their Roman wars had been just wars. In recent years there had been ever less to praise and to rival. The diplomat and politician who mourned his lost gladiators that morning in AD 393 was a proud scholar – with not quite enough to be proud about.

He made no claims himself to be historian or poet. There had never been any Roman poets of real account, none born here in this city. The Romans made other peoples' poets their subjects – and then gave them their subjects. That was the mission – to turn Neapolitans, Greeks, Spaniards and Gauls into artists of Rome. Symmachus himself was more a man of rhetoric, of words that led to actions, a man well known in his time as a physical protector of Roman values, most gloriously and dangerously against Christians who a few years before had torn the goddess Victory out of his Senate chamber. A mob had smashed her statue to pieces. That was one of his finest rhetorical hours.

He had, however, edited some of the texts of Livy, the books that began with the myths of Troy and Romulus and went on to tell of the great Republican days before the generals began fighting among themselves, before the common people got above themselves and everything went wrong.

21

'One history' was to be preferred to any 'one god'. He could relate the history of Rome from before there were emperors, from before there was an empire, from before his society, as he saw it, had been suffused by the peculiar imaginations of Greeks and Jews, gladiators and other slaves from everywhere on earth. He had read many fine words – as well as speaking and writing some of the weariest words to have survived for us from the whole of the ancient world.

How exactly did his Saxons die? Where? Was it under this street, where the sun rises every day over the Colosseum to form sickle-shaped shadows on holding pens and cells? Was it in the larger of the semi-excavated rooms, the one where the sewer smell also rises? Take away the pink drinking-straws and Red Bull cans. Imagine the place as it once was, dark, piled with corpses, cloacal then as now.

Via Sacra, Rome

These are the first days on my Spartacus Road. This is where an English newspaperman, after four decades of interrupted love for the language of ancient Rome, tries to understand what he has sometimes glimpsed. I could have chosen the roads of many different men, Hannibal or a Caesar, Horace or a Symmachus. But Spartacus has got the call. He has form. He has worked for me before, in pictures and in words, not always when or how I was expecting him, but reliably enough over the years for this to be his journey as well as mine.

First there was the film. In the 1960s Spartacus was there for everyone, even on the wall of our Essex school science room where the light of only improving films was shone. Through toxic whiffs of sulphur dioxide, hydrogen sulphide and whatever our sixth-form manufacturers of hallucinogens were cooking up that week there emerged the words 'SPARTACUS, the most spectacular movie ever made', Kirk Douglas, pathfinder for the liberating power of Christ, his face projected over equations of organic chemistry, the famous dimple on his chin dipping up and down like a light-pen over the formulae for oxides on the wall.

The second engagement was in the shabbier classics class-rooms, with a smaller scholastic band. Spartacus was then a reduced figure in the massive sweep of Roman history, a rebel nuisance in others' careers. The third time was just before I became a student at Oxford – through the enthusiasm of an eccentric Italian milk-salesman, pursuing the ghosts of clas-sical heroes on the shores of Lake Como. These Como months were the high point of my life as a Latinist. For years texts had poured into my seventeen-year-old brain and stayed there, a help not just in passing exams but in promoting a peculiar innocence that I might be with Rome's writers and fighters myself, a witness to what I was reading. Like many gifts, I barely knew I had it till it was gone. Neither the naivety nor the receptive memory for Roman detail survived much beyond my eighteenth birthday.

The last and least expected sight of Spartacus was thirty years of journalism later, when I had become a newspaper editor, suf-fering occasional but peculiarly vicious pain, then suddenly dis-covering that I was as good as dead from a cancer, then looking to see if somehow that sentence might not be true. In those days many characters from my past reappeared in different lights, the fictional and historical as well as the personal. There are moments of horror when a mind does not choose its subject, when the subject chooses its mind. Spartacus has not just a faded childhood claim on this trip but a vivid adult one.

Back at home there are hundreds of books that might be useful guides for the coming weeks. With me here beside the

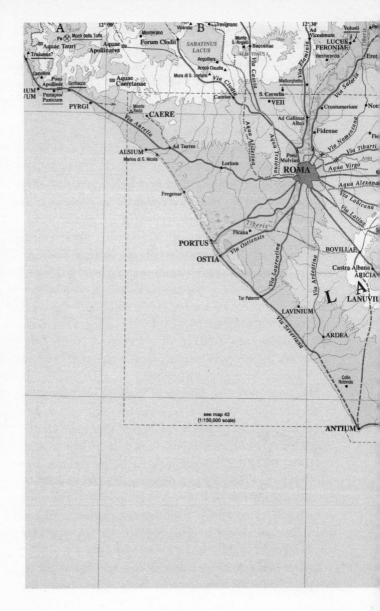

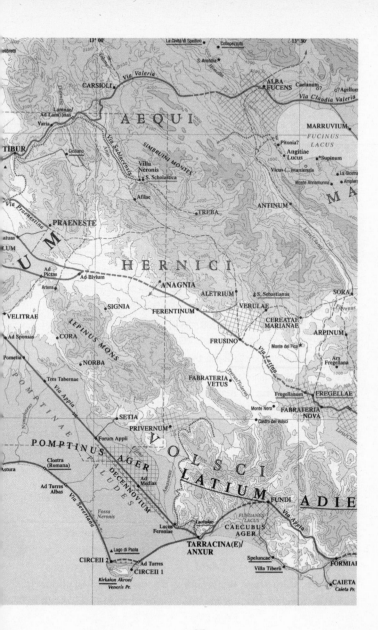

gift shop at the Roman Forum there are just a few. Most are soft-backed classroom texts with the name P. M. Stothard and an Essex address in tumbling Quink-blue italics on the inside cover. In 1964, the year of Harold Wilson's first Labour government, Spartacus, the bit-part player of Roman history, was not only the easiest ancient to imagine but also, in our patch of brick-box houses, the closest thing to a socialist. A green-backed Brentwood School edition of *Parallel Lives* by the Greek biographer Plutarch is my reminder now of that time – with greasy-thumbed pages in the chapter where the great slave-leader rose and fell.

Other books in the road-bag date from the early 1970s, the handwriting of their ownership inscriptions deliberately disjointed in an attempt to throw off childhood. One of these, a book of Latin letters, is still smeared with the wine and butter of the milkman who sold his wares in the Italian hotel where I worked for a while. Others seem little read at all. I appeared to have stopped studying the classics at the very moment I was supposed to be studying them the most. At Oxford there was so much else – bad theatre and worse newspapers. Spartacus was one of many ancients who could no longer compete. Next to some Livy, here now with a Trinity Oxford dateline and wholly unsullied by any human hand, there is the poet known as Statius, a favourite of one of my schoolmasters, derided then in most textbooks as a 'lackey' and lick-spittle to tyrants. Each of his pages, purchased dearly when money was short, came from my old undergraduate boxes fresh, stiff and never-been-read.

Now Statius is one of the writers who has set me on this present road. He was not a contemporary of Spartacus. He never wrote directly about him. He is not always easy to read at all. But, from a new beginning in the cancer days of about a decade ago, the strange metallic verse of Statius has done much to get me to this sewer-perfumed corner of the Forum with a plan to report on 2,000 miles of travel. Statius of Naples was a weirdly wonderful poet, a life-giver to dead things, a flatterer and inflater of the powerful, a prophet of the end of the world, a man who might lead us somehow to the end of this journey too.

But he has to share his place. There is also a brown file of extracts from Sallust, an Italian politician, historian and extortionist, probably the first to write about Spartacus in any systematic way. There are pages by Florus, a less remembered popularising hack from Africa; and some pieces by Frontinus, a military scourge of the Welsh and the literary master of his Emperor's waterworks; photocopies too from Frontinus' best-known protégé, the hero of the Como milk-salesman, the Pliny who is doomed always to be called 'the Younger'. Then there are Greeks, in variously Roman garb with contrastingly Greek ambitions.

There are pictures by artists who tried to preserve their views of ancient Rome, by the eighteenth-century Venetian master Piranesi more than any other. There are disconnected words from many centuries in many styles, from Claudian, the forgotten Egyptian who hailed Spartacus as a torturer and child murderer, to Catullus of Verona, the ever popular poet who wrote on love as well as hate. Claudian wrote lengthily on warlords and briefly, bizarrely and more readably on the water inside crystal balls. Catullus wrote long poems on eastern cults and short ones on sodomy. In Symmachus' time, as now, these and others, big and small, are the men whose minds we can summon to bring Spartacus to life.

Old books will not tell us everything. They will not even tell precisely either where or how Symmachus lost his gladiators. They do contain all sorts of other strange details – about a games promoter in the age of Nero, fifth Emperor of

Rome. He too found one of his German fighters dead by his own hand before the games began, this time on the seat of the school latrine, dead from a sponge-on-a-stick that he had stuck down his throat. 'What a brave man, well worth his chosen fate,' remarked the philosopher who recorded the story, 'and how boldly he would have used a sword.'

There was another suicidal gladiator from around the same time, one being drawn by cart for the morning spectacular, one who pretended to be asleep, who let his head fall low towards one of the wheels and pushed it through the spokes. Do we not see how 'even the lowest of slaves, when pain is the spur, may rise to the moment?' The teller of this story concludes that 'he is a truly great man who not only orders his own death but also finds the death by which to die'.

Ways of dying were a Roman obsession which a traveller on this Spartacus Road struggles to understand but he cannot understand Rome without confronting them. Ways of dying are some of many aspects of ancient life that are a mystery to those who study only when young. My own fiercest confrontations – with Roman rituals, beliefs and much else besides – all came in that year a decade ago when I was forced away from my newspaper office, aged forty-nine, experiencing the twin peculiarities of a killing cancer and its then barely plausible cures.

Memories from that time have since then come and gone. While most have vanished and others have long ago faded, a few seem redefined now by distance, like the foundations of a destroyed house when seen from the air above a field. Pain, it seems, produces permanent pictures which pleasure cannot. Chemotherapy pulls different images from parts of life that the patient has long forgotten, from places he can scarcely remember and books he thought he had never opened. My mind in the days of cancer-cure would swing back and forward, forward and back, day after day, a slow-mo version of what happens fast when a man is about to hang, or lose his head or see a sword slit his stomach. How the Romans died became then a bigger part of their story for me than how they lived. The virtue of a 'good death', or so the Romans thought, gave greatness to any man. That thought had meant nothing in the classroom or the chemistry lab.

Was Spartacus a great man? Many have argued so. Karl Marx considered him one of his favourite heroes of all time. Garibaldi made him his model for uniting and freeing Italy. For Voltaire the Spartacus war was the only 'just war' in all history. Kirk Douglas and other film-makers and novelists agreed, attributing to him their own passions and ideas, seeing seeds of the future that may or may not have been there, creating myths and legends on an epic scale.

Others have either gently or violently disagreed. For Symmachus and his friends in the former capital of an empire, Spartacus was still an expletive. The only benefit in the Saxons strangling themselves was they did not do that much more dangerous thing, escape. Gladiators were there to be symbols and mirrors, symbols and mirrors of Rome itself, stage-stars, even sometimes celebrities, stage-extras if they could do nothing else. In the southern Italian city of Capua, in 73 BC, a group of them got out into the real world.

Via Labicana, Rome

Some imitations of ancient Rome are easy to see in the modern city. Around the Colosseum and the Forum they are almost everywhere. Carlo is just one of them. He is from Capua. He is six feet tall, taller in his tinny helmet, taller still if he has tied on his red-feathered crest. He is tight-wired in his thighs, thick-shouldered, dark-skinned to an intensity more southern Greek than sub-Saharan and looks in every inch what a gladiator was supposed to be when Spartacus wore his own costume-armour.

Carlo speaks twenty-first-century AD Italian and English, not first-century BC Latin and Greek. But only the most pedantic hirer of 'photo-me fighters' would hold that against him. His plumes are dyed in a shimmering crimson that did not feature much in the training schools of Republican Rome, more cup-cake chemical than crushed shellfish. But that is hardly Carlo's fault. Every other hired swordsman flashing his mirrored shield for the flashing cellphones has the same fancy dress.

Carlo would rather be in Capua than where he stands now, on the pavement outside Rome's Hotel Gladiatori. He would rather be at home than looking up at the high-priced bedroom balconies, the ones that overlook the Ludus Magnus, the school for the Roman games. Instead he is stuck here breathing sunlit dust and smog with me. In Santa Maria Capua Vetere (to give his home town its full name today) there is another Colosseum, not as big as the one we are looking at this afternoon, but the one which covers 'the real gladiator school from which Spartacus escaped'. There are tourists there too, always a few tourists, but not enough of the sort that pay fifteen euros to be photographed. He would still prefer to be at home.

Carlo is not even working as a tourist attraction here this afternoon. His costume is in a bundle by his side. Instead, he is 'managing' Cristina. He points her out on the other side of the metal-packed roundabout. She is not a Roman matron or slave girl or gladiator's moll. She 'does La Vergine', he says proudly. She does, indeed, 'do La Vergine' – as though it were her profession from birth. It is impossible to describe Cristina precisely. Her skin colour is hidden. It may be close to that of

Carlo or closer to mine. She is a human statue, her face made up in gold, with a golden halo of hair and a casino-gold dress which falls in folds past the platform on which she stands, mute, still, moving only as often as her most determined photographers and her own comfort require.

It is apparently more difficult to play the part of a marble mother of Christ than that of a walking, posing, preening gladiator. Virgin Marys bring in more money. It takes more skill, he says, to keep silent, to make only the smallest and sharpest moves, to signal some special dissent when a trussed-and-belted Dane has all his daughters photographed with La Vergine and leaves behind one of those half-breed silver-bronze coins that are less than your advertised euro-tariff.

Carlo says that Cristina is the mistress of her art. Or I think that is what he says. His language cocktail of Neapolitan and New Yorker, a verbal Negroni of bitters and gin, gets cloudier as he moves from being glum to being angry. It seems that he ought rightly, at this very moment, to be a professional gladiator here in Rome, slapping his sword and shield for the Colosseum trade at the same time as Cristina is keeping the pilgrims content. But he is prevented by the trades union, or some unofficial form of it.

There is, it seems, a tighter 'syndicalist' grip on Thracian-swordsmen jobs than there is on Virgin Marys or Mary Magdalenes or mute mimics of St Francis. A few weeks before, when he had tried to adopt a regular place in a busy sidestreet, the broadswords had become raw swords, the fake weapons all too realistically deployed. He had needed some sort of document that he did not have. Somehow the immigrant Poles and Roms could disregard this requirement. It was a disgrace. Many Italians agreed with him. There had been a nasty rape and murder of a respectable woman by Romanians – and talk of sending every one of them back home. But it had not seemed to make any difference on the ground where Carlo stood.

The night on which he found himself clashing with a legionary, blunt blade to blunt blade, was when he felt all too much like the gladiators of his home town 2,000 years before. The better he understood the part the more irritating it was to be banned from playing it. He takes off his helmet and offers his unofficial 'Spartacus tour'. From Vestal virgins to Pompey's theatre, from the slave markets to the Appian Way, he will explain it all.

We agree terms. He points my head up towards the Colosseum's high arches with an air of proprietorship, like an estate agent selling a historic house. 'This is where Spartacus would have fought and died if he had not escaped from Capua first.' Every time one of his sentences contains the word 'Capua', the stress falls on that word. 'Spartacus was a Thracian, a tough northern Greek, trained as a Roman soldier, punished for crimes that no one knows and retrained as a gladiator. In the lifetime of Julius Caesar and Cicero, he led the first slave armies to threaten Rome itself.' Carlo stops and places a leather-bound thumb next to his forefinger. 'He came this close to walking down this road as a conquering hero. From Capua he could have changed the world.'

Two Americans who have heard the last part of this peroration applaud. They want to know whether this is the place for paying respects to the latest gladiator movie, the one starring the Australian actor Russell Crowe. Carlo nods. The great stone bowl of the Roman Colosseum, one of the best-known monuments in the world, was not open for business until 150 years after Spartacus' death. But it is perfect for imagining the arena of the second century AD, with Crowe the hero in single combat against a deranged Emperor Commodus.

The stones in front of us were dragged into place by thousands of men enslaved after the fall of Jerusalem in AD 70. They heralded the high days of gladiator displays, not their low BC beginning. The underground cells of the Ludus Magnus, which the Gladiatori guests can see from their expensive balconies, were built even later than that. They are not at all useful for pitting Kirk Douglas against Laurence Olivier in their battles of the first century BC. But that does not matter to Carlo. On the Spartacus Road I should stop worrying. 'Time here is nothing.'

So where do I want to go? This guide has not been here for long enough to get dogmatic. We trudge up to the far end of the Republican Forum, a half a mile or so away, past the house of the Vergine of ancient Rome, the Vestals, with a quick glance at the flowers that are still left every week or so on the supposed site of Julius Caesar's cremation. That had been a 'good death' for him, for anyone, stabbed on the nearby theatre steps, sudden, almost painless, spectacularly public.

At the furthest point, a Chicago tour group with its professorial guide is looking up to the hall where the Senate met, up to the Rostra platform where politicians fought for votes, up to the temple treasuries where the profits of victory were dedicated and kept safe. But we two, Carlo proudly points out, have our own agenda, looking down through the metal grilles which break up the slabs of the Forum floor.

There were twelve shafts down to this old Roman underworld. We can still see the edges of the stones which, in every sense, were the manhole covers. Some of the shafts descend more than ten feet below and archaeologists a hundred years ago found remains of wooden lifts which once brought men or animals, like hot food on a dumb waiter, to the waiting sands. Underneath the grey leaves and trees, beneath a layer of smashed mirrors which bizarrely has replaced the grass in patches, perhaps for some stunt of art, there is a chamber with ceilings high enough for men to swing a sword in practice play and for beasts to be stacked one above the other as in a giant pet-shop. All the performers could be kept there secure and ready until the winch was ready to hoist them into the arena above. Under here, says Carlo, is the short tunnel to Rome's first prison, the torture chambers (he says the words with a dark flourish), the places of secret execution. There is a church of the saintly Joseph, the Vergine's husband, on top of it now. Somewhere near by, Spartacus was sold as a slave in the Roman markets. His wife is said to have remembered

miraculous snakes curling round his head as he slept. This was also where Spartacus 'might have died in combat' – if he had been good enough to be worth bringing back here from Capua and if he had not escaped first.

There are many 'ifs' in this history, not all of them made clear by the guides or their books. Only one major structure in the Forum has been standing since the time that Spartacus 'might have died' here – Rome's public record office, the Tabularium, which lowers above its visitors like luxury caves in a rock face. Nothing at all has survived above ground of the first arenas in Rome where gladiators fought. The seats for the spectators were not even meant to survive. They were set up and taken down for every separate display. To have a permanent place might have offended some of the gods and ancestors whose spirits, like everything else, became heavily concentrated here in the centre of the centre of the world.

Once merely a swamp between the hills of Rome, the Forum was drained early in the City's history so that it could be a place of trade, worship, politics, sacrifice. It was built and rebuilt by Roman emperors, foreign emperors and triumphant popes. Its ground is still drained by the same Cloaca Maxima, the primal sewer that made it habitable 2,500 years ago. This was the site of gladiatorial fights in the city for at least two centuries: a modern equivalent in London, a very tepid approximation, would be to have heavyweight boxing, Victorian-style without Queensberry Rules, between Westminster Abbey and Whitehall.

What exactly was the fighting like? For all the attention that the sport of the gladiators has attracted since, no contemporary accounts from the arena come even close to a sports-writer's version of what used to happen here. The Spanish poet Martial, the man chosen to mark the opening of the Colosseum, produced a single short scene in which a pair called Old and Reliable fight to a draw in which neither dies. Lucian, a Syrian writing in Greek a few decades later, describes a more diverting day: wild beasts let loose on men in chains followed by a 'fight-the-gladiator-and-win-a-fortune' competition for the audience.

Lucian's afternoon seems the more diverting occasion. While Martial's pair slug it out for survival, Lucian's hero, Sisennes, aims for stardom. With his eye fixed on the 10,000-drachma prize, he jumps out of the crowd, takes the wager, declines his safety helmet, suffers a setback with an undercut to the back of his thighs and triumphs with a straight stroke through the gladiator's chest. Whether this gallant blade or the plodding Old and Reliable were the normal fare, no one knows. Some men fought by the *dictata*, the numbered rules of the training school. Others aimed for stardom. There was probably a broad variety of death on offer. Few in Rome ever cared if public slogging and killing interfered with politics or trade. The gladiatorial contest was bigger than both, a burial ritual that became an entertainment, an entertainment that became a vote-buyer and a vote-buyer that became big business, a business which eventually summed up so much of what was Rome and what Rome would be remembered for.

There is a buzz of hip-hop from Carlo's belt. He finds his mobile phone and frowns. Cristina has a problem. Or rather Cristina's co-worker, Carlo's second street artist, so far unmentioned, has a problem. This man is a Tutankhamun, a task of imitation that is easier, it seems, than being a Vergine. This new King Tut, despite relying on a fixed face mask and needing no powers of mime or movement, has been doing well – too well. Euros have been showering on this ill-sited symbol of pre-Roman Egypt. The official gladiators' shop-steward has been getting nasty. The Mummy was getting nervous. What was Carlo going to do about it?

First, he was going to get rid of his new client. There was no time for Pompey's theatre or an explanation of why precisely we should go there. You should get down the Appian Way to Capua Vetere (he stressed the 'Vetere' even more strongly than the 'Capua'), the place from which Spartacus escaped, the place from which the road can truly begin.

II

ARICCIA to BENEVENTO

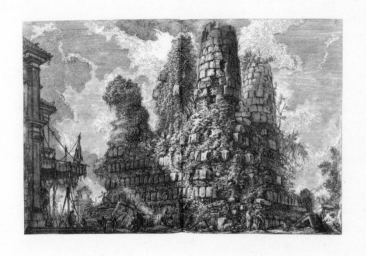

Via Appia, Ariccia

I am trying to stop the car as little as possible before Capua. The old Appian Way sets off like a stone arrow and makes the ancient route as easy as an autostrada. One by one the sites drop away in the rear-view mirror. Pine trees and monuments flash by. The Scipios' tombs, rock-cut reminders of glories from before Spartacus was born, are a smudge of mural rouge. The memorial to Paezusa, beautician to the court of Nero, is the merest blur. The tower of Caecilia Metella, daughter-in-law of the richest man of the Republic, is a shadow. Far back in the distance is the Quo Vadis church and its marble footprints where St Peter saw his disembodied Christ. Just as ignored are the niches of brick where statues once contemplated the embalming of Priscilla, a former slave whose 'modesty remained constant as her fortunes rose'. Priscilla and her mourning husband had a good friend in their poet Statius.

The bridge here at Ariccia is a traditional first resting place for travellers hurrying out of Rome. There is a domed church modelled on the Pantheon. There is a palace packed with the blackest paintings from the blood-and-suffering age of the Roman baroque. The surrounding monuments are of Julius Caesar's family. For a traveller on the Spartacus Road the main attractions are memorials to the Horatii and Curatii brothers, Roman boys and plucky locals who fought a famous triple duel, three-on-three, in the mystic era of the Roman kings.

That 'Horatii vs Curatii' affair is the first spectacular of this route, a tiny spark from 250 years before the building of the Appian Way, one of the earliest Italian contests that became more than just a street brawl, a match with some significance and rules, one that meant more than other fights because so many people kept talking about it. No one knows the names of anyone who was there.

Even Livy, Symmachus' favourite traditionalist, was not certain which side had been Roman and which for the opposition. There were no written records. The Romans later pretended that invading Gauls had burnt the sources of their history; but the words had probably never existed. No one knows if King Tullus of Rome was there or whether he ever was Rome's king. But for centuries afterwards there were tourists at competing sites who felt that they had seen the fight between the three brothers Horatius and the three brothers Curatius. Their lives were somehow linked to its outcome.

What, more exactly, is a spectacular? From the Latin, *spectaculum*, say the dictionaries, a show, usually a public show, an attraction for the 'carnal mind', an object of public curiosity, contempt or admiration, often of blood but also of song and dance. Or a means of seeing, an opportunity, a front-row seat, a window, a mirror. Or a standard, an example to watchers of an event. Or an example to be passed on to those who have not seen it for themselves, a means of teaching, to angels or to men. Or a sport, a wonder, one of the world's seven wonders, and then, descending blearily down columns of tiny type, something about phonographs and railway engines, a transparent shield over the eyes of certain snakes.

Spectacular is to spectacle as oracular is to oracle – lavish, amazing, strikingly large, addicted, addicted to spectacle. It is a figure in painted marble up high somewhere, the higher the better, in the *oculatissimo*, the place with specularity, the place most eyed. It is a play with actors in boots and ballooning togas, declaiming to the sound of flutes, disappearing down trapdoors, rope-walking between columns of red stone while scented water-streams cool and decorate the aisles. Roman politicians long distrusted the theatre; the first building in stone had been dismantled under pressure from the pious while it was still under construction; an edict was passed that one should never be built; but permanent theatre eventually came to Rome.

Castel Gandolfo, Ariccia

Or, to choose another version of the spectacular, the performing poet's version: semi-naked women who knew nothing of the sword condemned to fight one another in the arena, Amazons playing the parts of men, pregnant dancers from the kingdom of Croesus, fist-fighting dwarfs, local girls for sale, corpse-eating cranes, dough-balls raining down on to

the crowd. These sights are the first on the Spartacus Road to come from the pen of Statius. One of his own showiest triumphs took place a few hundred yards from here up the hill towards the summer house of the Pope.

The poet was writing about the Kalends of December, spectacular, bizarre games given by the homicidal god-emperor Domitian, successor and brother to the Emperor Titus who inaugurated the Colosseum. Killer freaks, killer birds, food to die for: 'amid noise and novelties a spectator's pleasure flies lightly by: *hos inter fremitus novosque luxus Spectandi levis effugit voluptas*'. There were Roman spectaculars for all tastes and times. The Alban literary games, celebrated here 1,900 years ago beside the mountain lake where the Pope has his holiday palace, included a poetry competition, an opportunity for highbrow performance art. On a games day the competitors would vie to impress the Emperor with carefully prepared improvisations while the statesmen of Rome would picnic on the steep banks of the crater, each with one eye on the poet and the other (their better eye if they were wise) on their master.

The less literary spectaculars were always the more popular. Statius was one of the grateful winners of that Alban poetry prize but gives us a vivid version of a people's stadium show, a lower-brow occasion for birds to eat small but expensive men, for men to eat small but expensive cakes, and for slave-women of the Black Sea to take up gladiatorial swords in a snuff-movie mixture of female mud-wrestling and *Rocky IV*. Here too it was wise for spectators to watch the Emperor as closely as they watched the slave-dwarfs and duellistes. Were pregnant Lydians funny or not? Only one man at that time could safely say.

Statius was born around AD 45 near Capua in a Greek ghetto of Naples, one of the tiny parts of Italy where the

44

pure Greek language survived. The Romans had mixed their Latin into most of the colonies that Athens, Corinth and Sparta had centuries before sent to Italy. Greek thought was deeply dyed into Rome from the earliest times, whatever Symmachus and his friends might have later tried to pretend. But a few neighbourhoods of the Italian south remained exclusively and resolutely Greek.

Poplios Papinios Statios, in the native version of his name, was a child poet star, son of a poet scholar who ran a Greek school for Roman grandees. Statius' literacy and learning were not the classroom-acquired kind of his father's pupils. The poetry of Homer and the philosophy of Plato were in his first language. Statius was married to a fellow performer's widow, a woman who looked after her daughter and the literary interests of both her husbands. He was a professional's professional who personified the spectacular idea in art.

His main rival, the Spaniard Martial, is the poet of this time who is the more often read today. Martial wrote short, sharp sex scenes as well as paeans to the great, some pithy abuse of his enemies, and his turgid match commentary to open the Colosseum. He gives a dutiful account in his *De spectaculis* of how the greatest beasts of the natural world must kneel and fall before the Emperor. But his treatment of spectator sport was happiest when he moaned that his mistress liked to be watched while they were making love: 'a spectator pleases you more than a lover since joys unseen are no joys at all: *et plus spectator quam te delectat adulter; Nec sunt grata tibi gaudia si qua latent*'.

Statius preferred the longer style. The extra words gave him more opportunities and surfaces to shine, and more cover for his back. He was a writer who polished every possible superficiality in an age when it was dangerous to dig too deep. A few hours with Statius is like a mind-sharpening shot of chemical in the skull. His subjects shine out from sharply lit edges. His golden crown for poetry, given to him in Ariccia by his emperor, was his perfect reward. The smallest jewels, fragments of marble, mosaic, metal, flash as though on giant screens.

Reliable about what happened in the Colosseum? Not wholly. He would not have quite understood what we meant had we asked him that. The knotted dwarfs and semi-naked swordswomen are there in his poem on the Kalends of December show, and then they are gone. They may have existed 'in the flesh'. They may not. Women did fight as gladiators. Laws were passed to stop them, then ignored and passed again. No one knows how often they fought.

Sexual exhibitionism, random couplings in the street, beatings as an alternative or preliminary to sex: all were part of the earliest Roman games, however much anxious Romans tried

to deny it. When the licence became too political, too radical, too encouraging to the disorderly, it was curbed, sometimes stopped, but never wholly lost. How amusing were those pregnant Lydians? It was perilous to predict. Domitian was not the first politician to want both to recall the past and to control it.

In the theatre there were favoured subjects for history plays: the 'rape of the Sabine women' was always popular, a foundation myth that was itself set at an early Roman gladiator show. Favourites for mythological dramas were the stories of beautiful Andromeda tied to her rock and other tales of naked nymphs pursued by gods and monsters. When did the rot set in? With Greeks and Celts and other alien imports or was it there at the start? Symmachus' historians and their successors have every opportunity to argue among themselves on this Spartacus Road. Library disciplines need not always apply.

Statius would have had his own answers while being careful to whom he gave them. He was the great performer and the great spectator, ever on the lookout for new ways of describing the present and the past, a new show or statue, a new road or swimming pool, a pet eunuch or pet parrot. His listeners loved him. He had the crooner's sweet voice. He toured like a rock star, competed like a sports star and, in reward for his skills, was stared at like all stars are stared at. His appearances were sell-outs. As soon as he had fixed a date, the tickets were gone. He sold his poems as party pieces to the Emperor's favourite actors. He never made as much money as he had expected. But he was a success in his career and in his art.

Later readers looking for grand Roman ideals have never much liked Statius. He was a 'silver age' artist, an imitator and flatterer. He wrote quickly like a journalist, and was proud of his speed as a journalist is. He sometimes took longer in writing than he pretended to take, again like a journalist. For Chaucer, Shakespeare, Dante and countless lesser writers he was a mine to be plundered. For travellers today who appreciate an artist's eye on how their ancient road was built, on the statues in the roadside tombs, on what the gardens might have looked like, on what we might have seen when entertainers were killing each other, he is still a literary star.

'See those untrained swordswomen, standing their ground, holding their lines, shameless in the battle roles of men: *Stat sexus rudis insciusque ferri: Et pugnas capit improbus viriles.*' Statius was an especially self-conscious expert in the literature of fighting and killing, in death and in sport. His literary hero, Homer, had been first to put words to the world of war, Greek words. Statius knew about fist-fights, track-sweat and the butcher's knife. He knew the jargon and used it. He had learnt at his father's knee.

Killing was absolutely an art. It was a subject for argument and expert appreciation, for commentary and verbal conflict. At the Kalends we can imagine problems with those women fighters. Might they be a bit 'amateur-night' with their blades? Were they totally untrained or only half trained? As deadly as the male? Maybe. Their odds were harder to call. There was not the usual form book. It was all mere holiday-betting.

Death-dealing women were mythical monsters: 'Like Amazons at war by rivers faraway: *Credas ad Tanain ferumque Phasin Thermodontiacas calere turmas*'. At games like this the fighters were not on show to be inspirational. A man could hardly look into a female face for spurs to his own courage. A dying Amazon or dwarf was something different from the standard fare, an alternative type of spectacular pleasure, a reminder of what would never happen to Romans, only to other people. 'Other people' were always needed to be looked down on and laughed at. When women fought in the stadium every man could be a know-all as well as a see-all. The feeblest fellow in the stands could puff up some critique of how the blonde from the Don blocked and parried, how the face of the River Rion missed her best chance to kill in the opening moments of the bout. Amazon style? Black Sea bravado? Enough to keep the men on the benches bantering for hours.

Those same male spectators could have argued too about the technique of the *retiarius*, the net-wielding fighter who battled without a helmet and whose eyes were always satisfyingly on show. He was one of the more traditional games characters. His art was to entwine sword and shield with yards of enveloping rope, to neutralise the gladiator in the same way that a fisherman netted carp or a hunter neutered the claws of a bear. But, in a few words about the warrior women, Statius projects more vivid possibilities than from any ordinary blood-on-the-sand bout. There was no point in the ordinary in the best of art or the best of death. A skilled pikeman was formidable but commonplace. Women with swords, some of them hardly knowing which end to hold, were different, much easier on male egos, not spectacular in the purest sense but potent.

When gladiatorial games began in Rome, most of the spectators had their own experience in wielding sword and shield: these first spectaculars were mere added education for the army. Then came the theatre of naval battles, fought by gladiator marines, designed to show to land-loving Roman citizens the new techniques of war at sea. The Romans used to flood stadia to make artificial lakes or use natural ones like those in the hills around here. Thousands of prisoners died in these demonstrations, and there are reports of at least one who killed himself, like Symmachus' Saxons, to avoid his death by drowning.

DOMITIAN PUTS ON A SHOW

Silvae I VI

Out of the way, all you unwanted gods.
(That's how a good poem should begin).
I'm going to tell the story of Caesar's party,
How even early in the morning,
When hardly had the first light of dawn appeared,
(That's another line the greatest poet liked)
There were luxury foodstuffs
Falling from the wires across the stadium,
Damsons and dates,
Ibiza's best figs, apples and pears,
Pastries to die for.

Do we fear the thunderbolts of Jupiter?
Not while our emperor, our own king of the gods,
Sends blasts like these.
Hey, here come the Ganymedes with gleaming napkins,
Pouring potent wine for everyone,
Not just for those in the best seats.
There was nothing like this in the Golden Age.
All now are the Emperor's guests.

Amid noise and novelties,
A spectator's pleasures fly lightly by.
See those untrained swordswomen,
Standing their ground, holding their lines,
Shameless in the battle roles of men
Like Amazons at war by rivers faraway.

Then look at the dwarfs, those knotted lumps,
Whose little fists pack such a bloody punch.
Do I see somewhere a flight of vicious cranes,
Just like in Homer, birds who take small bodies
When they're dead?

It's getting dark now. Enter the girls.
You have to pay for those but they don't cost much,
Pregnant Lydians who play the cymbals,
(How funny is that?)
Noisy Syrians, actresses and match-sellers,
Whoosh! There are flamingos flying in now,
pheasants and fowl, all free, to take home
If you can catch one.
Everyone wants to hail their Emperor as their god.
But that is the only liberty he does not allow.

Look! A globe of fire has arisen in the arena,
Flickering light to every darkest place.
Who can sing of such a spectacular as this?
Not I, not in the state I'm in.
Next time maybe.
To recall a boast of that great poet, Horace,
For as long as the Tiber flows and the Capitol stands,
This festival will be Caesar's.

By the time that Statius was writing, the need for mass military education had passed. Roman citizens now preferred other peoples to win their wars, concentrating on how to survive their own rulers as best they could. The known seas were uncontested except by the occasional pirate band. The spectaculars of Rome had found other purposes.

The most famous legacy of the age of Domitian is his invitation to terrified senators for a dinner party in total darkness, with coffins for tables, charcoaled slaves in naked attendance and silence except from the host. In the mid-twentieth century it became fashionable to offer Domitian a little rehabilitation, to see him as a Roman King John, a decent administrator who had 'his little ways' but was forced to wait too long for the deaths of Vespasian and Titus, his Colosseum-building father and brother. One of his remembered good deeds was to ban the castration of boy slaves; he was exemplary in his modest intake of food and drink. He collected statues of subjects other than himself: a violent mythological blinding and a vicious female monster survive from his gardens. He wrote poetry of his own and a textbook on hair care. 'Able and intelligent' was the mischievous verdict of an Oxford admirer in the 1920s. Statius' vision takes us, cautiously, to the more traditional view, to the first of Rome's self-styled gods on earth, to an erratic tyrant who filled every corner of the screen and was never quite satisfied with his exposure.

Domitian plays the divinely generous host on the Kalends of December. When his spectator guests grow bored with the female swordfights, there are other attractions, the parade of the pregnant Lydians, musicians and match-sellers, and those pot-bellied dwarf cohorts, so very keen to stop themselves becoming bird-food or kebabs. Even if these men and women of stunted growth did not have swords, they could throw a few good punches before the net-carriers scooped them up like forest pigs.

There are the most delicious items of food, some of it cooked and some of it, the pheasants and guinea fowl, still alive and flapping, available, like home-run baseballs, to be taken home by the lucky ones in the crowd who caught them. Domitian delivers everything – from the women-for-hire to the free figs from Ibiza. Popularity-seeking politicians once staged games to get the highest Republican offices. By this point in the imperial era only an emperor could produce anything as spectacular as this. He asks nothing in return. His sole intervention is to stop the crowd hailing him as their lord – while at the same time wanting them to do so.

Statius was a subtle man of this literary theatre, flexible and imaginative in projecting his images. Domitian's beautiful boy favourite, Earinus, has his picture fixed shut in Cupid's mirror ('*et speculum seclusit imagine rapta*'), the first camera lens in literature. A statue of Hercules is small but a giant in its appearance: '*parvusque videri, sentirique ingens*'. A statue of Domitian on horseback exceeds the wooden horse of Troy in every way. Domitian was notoriously fussy about the weight of the statues of himself in gold. The poet knew that. He knew his emperor personally. The elder Statius had tutored them both. They had villas close by in these Alban hillsides that Pompey once owned. They even shared a water-supply connection, not a small matter when one of the heights of civilisation was the hottest bath. For his prize-winning Alban poem Statius stuck to the safest of all subjects, the glories of grinding down the Germans.

This town of Ariccia, scene of that triumph, is only a first and very short stop on this Spartacus Road. There are some massive ivy-covered remains here of the Via Appia, the first great Roman highway, the one that slave-wagons, armies and fleeing poets all once took. There are no signposts to it now. Only the irregular limestone blocks, with the marks of thousands of chisels still on them, place it at the beginning of the age of roads. By climbing over fences into tomato fields, by vaulting over a rusted tractor and pushing down the barbed wire over the Valvoline grease guns in the grass, the traveller can get some small sense of how solidly and menacingly it once stood.

The father of anthropology, James Frazer, began and ended *The Golden Bough* near here at Lake Nemi, Diana's mirror as it was known, her *speculum*. In his twelve volumes of comparative myth he likened the local worship of the goddess to ceremonies of South Sea islanders, camel-herders and Aztecs. Long before Spartacus and long after Statius there was a killer priest here who lived a sleepless life in fear of the successor who had to fight and kill him in turn.

At the bottom of Diana's mirror-lake two large ancient ships were found by Mussolini's archaeologists in the 1920s, to the excitement of scholars who had doubted whether Rome's naval architecture had ever quite matched its road-building. These were true floating palaces and well proved their makers' prowess with lead and timber. No local tribes had sunk them in a naval battle. These imperial vantage places – for blood-in-the-water sports and other pleasures – would have been a worthwhile destination in themselves had not German soldiers on 1 June 1944, exacting who knows what kind of Saxon revenge, burnt them to black ash.

Via Appia, Foro Appio

Ariccia long ago rose above its low origins. Domitian set a tone for his childhood and imperial home which lasted into the era of Symmachus, his Christian foes and beyond. The townscape in the rear-view mirror is papal, grand, palatial, baroque – with almost nothing left but the tomato-plantation bridge and a chalk grotto in its Chigi Palace to bring back the days when travellers, fresh out of dying Republican Rome, found only a single modest inn. Ask where that inn originally was, and the answer now is either a traffic island or the Flavio factory producing *porchetta*, the local pig delicacy. The *porchetta* option appears to have the greater support.

This next stop, the gateway town into what for 1,500 years after the fall of Rome were the vast and open Pomptine Marshes, is less changed by time. Bernini and his seventeenth-century designer friends did none of their business here in Foro Appio – which was wild in Roman times and is still wild today. A single bizarre 'boutique hotel' sits within a reclaimed swamp of agri-businesses, surrounded by telegraph poles, lead-blue sky and yelping birds. Only a few of the ancient watery paths remain: Mussolini removed most of the region's stagnant mud when the creation of new Italian land became easier than conquering bits of Africa. But this small part can speak loudly and clearly enough for what has gone.

The sludge beside the restaurant here passes under another bridge of the old Via Appia, smaller than that in Ariccia, equally unappreciated, noticed or cared for but clearly there. On the surface of the bright-green chemical slime squat frogs and turtles. There are comatose catfish in the watercress below, which the local boys catch as easily as from a tank of pets. Dragonflies dart above them. In the sky are crop-sprayers and herons; an owl flutters over the metal barn.

On the other side of the road there is a granite-grey monument, a ring of prisoners in stone, a man with hands and a heavy weight behind his neck, a woman with a curved and crippled child whose head is not quite where a head should be. It is dedicated to victims of terrorism and cowers appropriately behind a garden hedge of bamboo, crowded by beer bottles, condoms and red-and-yellow vouchers for shoes. The Via Appia encourages long looks forward and back while distracting sideways or downwards glances. Behind is Rome. Ahead is Campania. That is all it needs to say. The man who built it was called Appius Claudius Caecus, one of the pioneering aristocrats who empowered Rome by giving power to its people, the first Roman with a firm place where myth without history merges into history with myths. He is a genuine founder and father of the city, the earliest individual of whom some sort of picture can plausibly be made: he promoted sons of freed slaves to the Senate and made the demigod Hercules the public hero of this Spartacus Road. In his later years he lost his sight. Today his most solid legacy still straddles the ancient waters here, rising barely perceptibly and barrelling on – past signs for mozzarella, palm trees and spruce, murdered innocents and size-three sandals, as though none of these newcomers were there, or would be there for long.

Statius passed through Foro Appio on his trips between Naples and Rome without, as far as anyone knows, writing a word here. Perhaps there was no one to pay him or he was always in too much of a hurry. The conceit of his Silvae, as he called them, his 'little bits of wood', his 'uncultivated forest', was that they were rapid sketches, first drafts, and did not require an epic stay. The reality, as so often, was of longer, harder work.

The subjects here could have tempted him. The clearing of muddy rivers was a favourite theme. He liked to write about the latest styles in villas and the means of making swimming pools. But he preferred imperial properties (a safer study for praise than any other) and a river not like the dirty Cavata here but the one closer to Capua itself, the Volturnus, whose

Prospetto del Lastricato e de' margini dell' antica via Appia, delineato così come si vede verso Roma poco più in quà della città d'Albano.

very cleanliness he could credit to Domitian. The greatest road-building scheme of his emperor, 'He who puts Peace back in place and inspects Heaven's street-lights', is also further south, the Via Domitiana.

Foro Appio is better known for that earlier poet who lived closer to Spartacus' shadow, Horace, pioneer in precise description as in so much else, who set here the first of his classic 'why are we in this flea-pit anyway?' passages – a later theme of many a grumbling Grand Tourist. Horace's fifth satire, the 'Journey to Brundisium', is the world's first piece of recognisably modern travel-writing, packed with dirt and discomfort, asides on food and sex, all against a background of big events to which he alludes without much confronting them. William Cowper is one of many English poets who have enjoyed translating it.

'*Egressum magna me accepit Aricia Roma*', Horace begins, escaping from a Rome still terrorised by the murder of Julius Caesar with an almost audible Latin shout of 'I'm out of here: *egressum*'. Only a few years before, he had been on the wrong side of a civil war, fighting for Caesar's killers. In what was probably his first poem, one of the two in which Spartacus appears, he deplored the horrific civil disasters that had befallen the whole idea of Rome. He had even suggested a mass exodus of good men to the mythic 'Islands of the Blessed', a paradise of nostalgia ruled by gods older than Jupiter, the volcanic Atlantic rocks of Tenerife and Lanzarote today.

By the time of his journey to Brundisium he has found the right side, the side of Caesar's adopted son. He is more relaxed about the future. He is adapting himself to the new official doctrine of progress – a fresh start for history. Ariccia 'receives' him in its 'modest inn' as he begins this much more agreeable poetic enterprise, sketching postcard pictures of places and people, irritations and ejaculations, bad bread and better wine.

The poet and his diplomatic companions take their canal barge towards Capua from Foro Appio. The immediate destination is the town of Anxur, perched ahead on its widely shining rocks: '*impositum saxis late candentibus Anxur*' were Horace's few sharp words, 'perhaps the first time in the history of European poetry that so faithful and suggestive a picture was given', the Oxford maestro professor, Eduard Fraenkel, wrote in one of my few well-used student textbooks. The whole trip of eyes-wide wonder would have been fine if the passengers and boatmen had not got sourly drunk, if the frogs and mosquitoes had allowed the poet some sleep and if the horse had actually moved the boat. In Horace's day the town was crammed with cheating innkeepers and sailors, '*differtum nautis, cauponibus atque malignis*', a verdict which requires a certain confidence if one is to inscribe it in large Latin letters around the walls of a chic designer bedroom. The owner of the single hotel in the town today has taken the risk. A celebrity Roman is better for a 'boutique destination' than no celebrity at all.

This is my first time in this place where Horace set his scene of pioneer satire in around 38 BC, even though its familiarity from words and pictures makes that hard to believe. This has become a great *egressum* for me too. When I was a student in the 1970s, distracted into journalism, terrified of Fraenkel and awed by the massive quantity of classical literature, I read the Roman poets without ever travelling to where they lived and wrote. That was somehow what we were encouraged to do: to stick to the text and to the texts behind the texts; to note that Statius wrote an affecting and affectionate poem about his father, just as Horace had; to know that when Statius was cleaning rivers he was writing with Greek models in his mind; to note, with appropriate examples, how Statius wrote as a luxury-lover and Horace as an apostle of simplicity. No one needed to visit Naples or Rome to do any of that.

Later, as a newspaper journalist, I travelled without reading or, at least, without reading anything much in Latin or Greek. The decent 'classicist', when I could call myself such a thing, concentrated on the elaborately interlocking words

HORACE'S JOURNEY TO BRUNDISIUM.

BY WILLIAM COWPER

'Twas a long journey lay before us,
When I and honest Heliodorus,
Who far in point of rhetoric,
Surpasses every living Greek,
Each leaving our respective home,
Together sallied forth from Rome.
First at Aricia we alight,
And there refresh, and pass the night;
Our entertainment rather coarse
Than sumptuous, but I've met with worse.
Thence o'er the causeway soft and fair
To Appii Forum we repair...
Now o'er the spangled hemisphere
Diffused the starry train appear,
When there arose a desperate brawl;
The slaves and bargemen, one and all
Rending their throats (have mercy on us!)
As if they were resolved to stun us.

'Steer the barge this way to the shore;
I tell you we'll admit no more;
Plague! Will you never be content?'
Thus a whole hour at least is spent,
While they receive the several fares,
And kick the mule into his gears.
Happy, these difficulties past,
Could we have fallen asleep at last!
But, what with humming, croaking, biting,
Gnats, frogs and all their plagues uniting,
These tuneful natives of the lake
Conspired to keep us broad awake.

on his page. The reporter looks primarily for what no one has yet written at all. Between these two extremes of seriousness was a space I had never much visited, certainly not visited enough, a past in part impossibly alien but recognisable in flashes, a space now to make pictures out of words and faces out of diagrams and fragments.

Horace and Spartacus both passed by here, some forty years apart. The poet, whose father had been a slave, was on a sensitive peace mission on behalf of the man who would soon become the first Roman emperor. The Thracian slave, whose father is wholly unknown, a nomad or a man from the Maedi tribe depending on how a particular piece of Greek is understood, was on his way to gladiator school in Capua from the auction blocks of the Roman Republic.

The superficial symmetry of a thought like that appeals to the reporter more than the scholar. How does the scholar know that Horace was not imagining his stop in Foro Appio when he wrote his satire, or copying it almost completely from a literary model now lost? How does he know that Spartacus' slave-wagon took the shortest and best road from Rome to Capua? He does not. But there are clues, in words as well as stones, more survivors from this age and place than from many that are nearer and closer. There is good material for imagination here. For all the proper historical scepticism in its proper place, some certainties can be sought and celebrated too.

Tourists from London in the eighteenth and nineteenth centuries loved to read Horace, who was modest, witty, bold, almost British. They were not so keen on Statius, who was toady, terrified, too glossy, dangerously continental. Readers of ancient poetry then had, and still have, different perspectives, some based on places and others on time. The young have sometimes the better facility in reading the language, the greater naivety of imagination; the older have the better experience of what the writers were writing about. The best travellers have always looked to understand as much as they could from different ages in the past and their own different ages, a bit of linguistic argument here, a bit of imagination and compression there. This is a small experiment in doing the same, with the expectation that neither the scholar nor the reporter in me will be fully satisfied but with the feeling that both those masters have been served already quite enough.

There is the lure of the gladiator on this trip too, not just the ghost of Spartacus but all the men and women like him who made the spectaculars of Rome. Like the best newspaper stories, the gladiator is always a 'story'. Like every 'good story' in a newspaper it is good in both what is there and what is not there, what is known of it and what is not known. The idea of the gladiator has been squeezed into so many clichés over the centuries, rung in, wrung out, alien to modern experiences like so much of the ancient world, but somehow, once approached, perversely close.

Curiosity about dying in its most visible forms is curiously addictive. Most of us face death before we are ready to face it. A fatal disease is a gladiatorial experience of a kind, a final appointment with a certain end at a near but not quite specified time. Cancer patients learn of bodily organs that they never knew they had, body parts that will kill them none the less. We imagine those deadly pieces of ourselves. We sometimes call them names. When I had a cancer, I called it Nero.

At Foro Appio today the sludge beneath the bridge over the Cavata flows on. A white nutria rat climbs out beside a giant Australian eucalyptus, flicking the slime from its back. The fields on the banks are full of potatoes and artichokes and kiwi fruit. Below all these imports from around the world are relics that once bore the weight of thousands of Romans, tiles and amphorae, pots and plates, baked earth with sparks of shining silica, double panhandles in the shape of crouching dogs: hardcore for the first Via Appia, fresh erosions reaching daily from the river mud like limbs of the newly drowned.

Piazza della Vittoria, Formia

Seaside Formia, a few miles past gleaming Anxur on the Appian Way, was known 2,000 years ago as a wine-maker (only the most expensive wines) and as the home of Mamurra, an exceptional sexual and financial predator even by the standards of Julius Caesar's engineering staff. Today fine wines are still grown from the pale sparkling sands, and drunk here over long lunchtimes like today's when nothing stirs bar yellow-legged gulls, bees the size of meat-balls and a single harassed priest, sweating under a black cowl, muttering, shading his face in response to a request for directions. Mamurra? Yes, that bastard knew how to live. His house was still standing when the Germans came in 1943 and smashed it, marble by marble, to the ground.

The churchman waits. We talk. He wants to show me the town's tiny museum. When will it open? Maybe 4.00 p.m., maybe 5.00 p.m. He cannot wait. He suggests we share some Falernian later, the only original Roman grape in the world, he says. Avoid any wine from Sorrento, he warns, 'noble vinegar' an emperor once called it, a 'very wise emperor'.

At 5.30 p.m., when any of Italy's vintages would be much more welcome than its antiquities, the museum door opens and then immediately closes, as though evening sun and evening tourists are equally unwelcome. Inside stand ill-lit statues of heavy Roman men, wary hosts with thick hands and hard lips, slender shadowed women with swinging hips and hands high in ritual greeting. Theirs is the only welcome. There is no sound at all. It is not so hard to imagine Julius Caesar's road-man here, the local hero Mamurra who brought his billions home from Britain, Spain and Gaul (he had a fancy Caelian Hill house too), without doing much more for the cash than building a few bridges and, so the poet Catullus tells us, buggering his boss from time to time.

Mamurra, I am thinking, would have been paunchy, puffy-eyed, imperious, snapping his fingers, striking blows and poses alike. Here he is: a sodomite Romulus *'superbus et super-fluens* . . . striding from bed to bed . . . swallower of anything he can see'. Sex with anything, sex with everything: that is the state your reputation reaches if you offend a poet like Catullus.

It is not so very hard to imagine others who lived here too when Spartacus passed by on his journey to Capua from Rome. It was the fashion then to carve men and women as they were, with warts and worse-than-warts and all. Families chose to remember their dead as they had lived, with chicken-necks, bat-ears, hack-saw teeth, sandpaper complexions. Local sculptors may have exaggerated some of the grotes-queries: if the art market seemed to favour thick lips and boss eyes, there will be some lips more thickened and some eyes more bossed. But a visible truth remains.

Curators claim to date quite precisely some of the centre-parted hairstyles here. Some of the facial expressions in the busts, while they defy anyone's precise dating, are recognis-ably those of the southern Italian rich of the Republican age, those like Mamurra, soft-faced men who did well out of the wars. Others look angrier, suggesting somewhat humbler citizens, a junior religious official like my new friend or a small farmer, faces of a fragile provincial community, not quite worthy of a life-sized statue. Even after so many centuries a man with fat eyes and hair over his ears seems still ablaze and outraged – at some slight or scandal perhaps, a murder, an uppity slave, a lost contract, or merely that he himself is so undeniably dead.

There is a certain sense of parsimony in the faces of the buyers preserved here in stone. This is not a museum of great art but a place to meet the ordinary, the men and women who were spectators of Spartacus and his kind. As well as images of themselves, they collected lamps and ornaments decorated with gladiator motifs. Thousands survive of these pottery figures – some in silver and bronze – with their spears, nets, emblazoned helmets and blank faces. A carved or moulded head of any individual? Only the most ambitious imagination

could find such a thing in Formia or anywhere else. What did the soon-to-be famous gladiator look like in his Capua school? There was no demand at all for statues of rebel slaves.

A window briefly opens, wafting a dust-cloud of light along the dark marble lines. The statues here with fewer flaws, or no flaws at all, are from a later time, the imperial age when Greek ideals of beauty were preferred, when the youthful body became more important than the characterful face. Local sculptors had then to carve what the conquerors could not bring back from Greece itself. There were copies made of ancient masterpieces and gradual adaptations to meet the needs of this different market – with a sharply varying eye on quality and only at prices that careful buyers were prepared to pay.

In every phase of fashion most of the artists of Rome originated far away from Rome. Sculptors from other places carved the Romans' statues just as they wrote the Romans' poems. They produced what was wanted. It was to become firmly fixed in the city's founding mythology that only other peoples breathed life into bronze and stone. Roman men and women had altogether different duties.

The most famous image of Spartacus before the age of the movies, the one most commonly seen on books and postcards, was inspired by this later classical style. It came from the chisel of a nineteenth-century French sculptor, six foot six inches of the whitest Carrara marble, a hero made to be seen not in death but at the bright moment of his first freedom. This naked Greek, naked in his best Greek pose, is leaning back in anticipation of his glories to come, with his hands still crossed in the shape of the straitjacket of chains he has cast away.

Its creator, Denis Foyatier, was a fortunate man in finding his own small place on the Spartacus Road. He completed his statue just at the right time, in 1830, when a more liberal imperial regime was taking over in France. His seriously thoughtful freed slave was just the sort of soft white symbol required. Foyatier had conceived his glowing contribution to garden furnishings, and even carved much of the rock, long before Louis-Philippe's coup. But the romance of the King's July Monarchy made the work an instant masterpiece, neither the first nor the last time at which Spartacus has swayed to the demands of changing times.

My clerical friend returns filled with wine, wakefulness and local pride that the museum ever opened and that his visitor is still here. Spartacus? His black eyes wrinkle like drying olives. He frowns knowingly before a broken limb that could be a Hercules or a sea-monster. He measures its circumference as though some deep secret lay in the answer. He then says suddenly that, if we are thinking of the hours before the break-out from Capua, Foyatier's nakedness may be just about right, though not, he whispers with distaste, the whiteness nor the cleanliness nor even the uprightness of his statue.

This priest knows about Spartacus: 'the killer would have smelt like a rat'. His torso would have been striped like the back of a game bird and ticked and crossed like a stone column of tax accounts. The cells that he has seen under the local amphitheatres do not show many spaces where a tall man could stand. The Frenchman's choice of physique was 'probably right'. Spartacus was a big man, a slave from the east, selected for strength, schooled in violence and probably not much more. He would have been a closely confined prisoner both in Capua and before, precisely because of his physical power, a more knotted, muscled, scar-corrugated power than Foyatier shows. He was one of those men who thrive and become a hard man among prison hard men.

'Immense strength' was an accolade not given lightly in the ancient world. 'Muscle' was important for an owner of men: slavery was the energy industry of its time. In prison life the same muscle meant the power to press the blood out of an adversary's arm or neck; it meant the power to enforce will and to will the force of others. The French sculptor of the Romantic age captured too the sense of self-discipline, the sort that other strong men recognise as necessary sometimes even though they lack it themselves, the ability to focus strength and be one of those men who thrive in leadership, prisms able to direct the scattered beams of others into a single hot line.

Romantic admirers of Spartacus inspired Foyatier to make him more like an Athenian Greek than a Thracian one, two types which were very different in ancient eyes. Athenians were philosophers and artists, with a potential Socrates or stupendous vase-painter at their every street corner. Spartacus came from northern Greek tribes in Thrace, people whom the Romans, echoing local neighbours as well as their own experience, recognised as the most savage in the world.

A good gladiator for a games promoter had to be a 'barbarian's barbarian', a title something like our modern respect for the 'professional's professional', the 'criminal's criminal'. He could be and would be the object of fascinated observation – but only if he were firmly in his place. If Spartacus had been loose tonight in this room full of thugs and molls in Formia, even the most military Roman would have been hiding behind the pillars, calling out the guard. My man in Catholic black has no doubts about that. Spartacus was a trained assassin, master of the stabbing sword, the push to the throat, the rip of the face. If he had not been a slave, an object of sympathy now, we could call him a professional killer, with the certain respect we allow for that group too.

Spartacus was one of many. He was never marked out by the Romans for anything very special. Capuan gladiator shows in 73 BC were mere scraps in dustbowls when compared to the spectaculars that were commoner later and the more remembered ever since. There might already have been 'rare wild beasts' on the play-bill that Spartacus would miss by his escape. There might not. Many in the audience would hardly have expected or seen much difference between Spartacus and a beast.

There was also a 'sophisticated set' in the city of Capua, some of whom watched the gladiators in training and looked forward to the chance of being there for the kill, for the moment when a dying man's eyes became a dead man's. This was not mere sadism but a kind of therapy. The Romans cared deeply how they died, how they might look to others when they looked out themselves for the last time. But could anyone ever properly imagine himself when dying turned to death? It was very hard. The more one thought about it the harder it became. To watch others die was a training for the imagination, important training because a Roman man's whole life depended on others seeing his death well.

It is becoming darker now in the Formia museum. The ropes are gradually falling in front of the galleries so that only one of these ancient party rooms is now open, the place of the minor tradesmen, the lesser men and women of the old town of Mamurra, the types with the most to lose in a slave revolt, the almost prosperous, the always vulnerable. Time is nearly up. The curators of these antiquities, chatting softly beside their predatory sea-snake, cluck-cluck as though the very chastity of their marble Roman matrons might be at risk before the English intruder. It is as well he has a priest to keep an eye on him.

We are guessing further and faster now – whether Spartacus had the square face and red hair of the Celtic upper class in Thrace or the longer facial features of the lesser locals, lupine and slow. Did that matter? However smoothly his image has emerged in the minds of a modern priest, sympathetic ancient

Greeks and a mildly liberal Frenchman of the 1820s, Spartacus himself would have been the most dangerous of animals in this room beside the Appian Way.

The gladiator had once had, and maybe in 73 BC possessed still – his Dionysiac priestess wife who had seen snakes twisted around his head, a sure sign of something mysterious to any Roman eyes who cared to see such things. Spartacus carried all manner of alien marks from the east. Whether these were marks of very good or very ill fortune, even the best Greek texts are unclear. It depended on who was copying them down.

The ropes close the last room. Outside in the street, there is a choice of tours to two local tombs. The first, in a bright-green taxi, is to that of Munatius Plancus, a military adventurer who backed almost every side in the Republican civil wars but won his immortality in a drinking poem by Horace. The second, in a minibus, is to that attributed to one of many politi-cians betrayed by Plancus, Marcus Tullius Cicero, a man who won his enduring reputation from literary works of his own.

Cicero had the boldness once to compare his enemy Mark Antony to Spartacus, a fatal enmity as it proved. But neither Cicero's tomb nor that of Plancus is a necessary diversion on this road. There is instead a golden choice of wine in the bars here, both for the off-duty churchman and for his dinner com-panion who, following the reporter's discipline he long ago set for himself, has first to write down these notes on the day.

Piazza Orazio Flacco, Benevento

The priest said that he could meet me again in this next town along the Appian Way. Benevento's Leproso Bridge is the most visible relic here of Spartacus' time, lizard-like arches of low-lying stone and long grass. The only living things in the Piazza Orazio are feral cats, prowling through the polythene sheets of long-absent archaeologists. When Horace came to Beneventum on his journey to Brundisium he complained of getting nothing to eat but burnt thrushes from a burning kitchen. This abandoned piazza of deep empty pits, corrugated iron barricades and peeling dance-school posters is the town's appropriate revenge.

My new friend is comfortable talking about Spartacus, a man whom he has somehow accepted into his own faith. There are certain pagans whom followers of Jesus Christ have long seen as honorary Christians. Spartacus finally won his place thanks to Kirk Douglas and the Hollywood money men. There was big box-office appeal in a saintly rebel who had lived just too early to be a saint. Statius had won the accolade somewhat earlier and was thus available to lead his Renaissance admirer Dante along paths through Paradise.

Horace has not been so blessed by the Church, being no sort of freedom fighter and a religious sceptic too. But before the black-eyed priest begins his explanation of all this he wants to know more about the traveller he is talking to. He does not care about newspapers or politics, about Britain or the possibilities of my notebook becoming a more permanent book. He believes in origins. Very precisely he wants to know who my father was, where I come from. He is most specific. He pauses aggressively for my reply. He throws a lump of wood at the cats and taps a long white finger on the wall while they scatter into the ditches.

Most of what we know about Horace, he begins again, comes from the poet's tribute to his father, the good-hearted, hard-working, sometime enslaved businessman from Venusia. Eduard Fraenkel used to say the same, more severely, with the threat that any student who could not be bothered to read Horace's sixth satire (shame on the distracted children of the 1960s) should not bother with Horace at all.

Much of our knowledge of Statius comes in the same way, an obituary poem to the man who had taught him all the Greek tricks he knew, whom he begged to come back to him in his dreams. Was my own father dead? When was he born? What was his religion? What did his obituaries say? The thirsty questioner senses another imminent pause and snaps, as though taking hurried confessions in a disaster zone, that I will be happier when I have answered.

So I do. W. M. Stothard was born in 1925 in the flat lands where Nottinghamshire, Lincolnshire and Yorkshire meet. When he died of cancer in 1997 there was no obituary in the newspapers. He was not quite good enough at cricket or cards, although he played both well when he was young. He was baptised as a Methodist and named after the Yorkshire cricketing hero Wilfred Rhodes; but he quickly lost both the Christianity and the name. For seventy years, from his mining-village birthplace to the bars of Royal Marines and ministries of defence, he answered to the name Max. A man of his age might reasonably have booked his space on the obituaries page during the war. My father set out for war when he was supposed to have been setting out as a student. He joined the Royal Navy despite all his family's efforts to keep him at home. But he sailed away to West Africa on a ship called HMS *Aberdeen*. He bought red-leather knife cases and postcards of Dakar's six-domed cathedral and never fired a hostile shot except at a basking shark. He was lucky, he said.

When he was not shooting fish or trading cans for trinkets, he studied the young science of radar, watching the many curious ways that waves behave in the air above the sea, turning solid things into numbers. He was not a radar pioneer in the sense that obituary writers would require. He was one of thousands who fiddled with diodes, quartz and wire to make radar work. That was how he spent most of the rest of his life.

He returned to England when the war was won and took a place at Nottingham University. He batted and bowled and played bridge and studied physics. He had a striped blue-green-yellow blazer which he cheerfully bequeathed to me and which made it easier for my friends to recognise me at Oxford in the 1970s in the dark. He had a brain that other engineers described as Rolls-Royce. It was powerful but he did not like to test it beyond a purr. In 1950, the year before I was born, he joined the Marconi Company at its research laboratory in Great Baddow, Essex, on a salary of £340 per year. He worked on many and various half-forgotten, half-successful, mostly never needed air-defence systems that protected British skies during the Cold War. He reasoned through his problems in an armchair at home, spreading files marked 'Secret' like a fisherman's nets. He preferred to solve technical glitches in series not in parallel. He found solutions singly. He hated to stress the machinery of his mind.

Later he became a manager and a salesman whom, in my own too simple student days, I would call an arms salesman. I accused him of complicity in the death industry and he was characteristically patient about that. He travelled many roads. He came to know thousands of fellows in the science of spotting fast-moving objects in the sky. He had space in his purring life for hundreds to be his friend. But he long did not seek the advancement that an obituary demands; and latterly, when he sought it, he did not find it.

He sometimes misunderstood people. He liked to see them as electro-machinery, as fundamentally capable of simple, selfless working. He was closed to the communications of religion or art. His favourite picture, his own spectacular, was a photograph of an oil-production platform being towed through a fiord. He listened to no music. He was especially offended by the violin and the soprano voice. His passions

73

were for moving parts, moving balls, jet-streams in the skies over air shows. Other minds were not his pasture.

He was a pleasure-seeking materialist whose pleasures were not taken in excess and whose materialism was only a means of science. If his cancer pains brought him pictures of any past, he never mentioned them. I doubt that they did. He claimed that he had never had a dream until the diamorphine nights that kindly killed him. He had no fear of anything unknown.

Thirty years ago, when I was setting off for Oxford to study Latin and Greek, he gave me his own father's copy of the second half of Virgil's *Aeneid*. The name B. Stothard, in a firm, now faded, script, still sits inside the flyleaf. Max had no idea why that Virgil had been bought or why it had survived. It was one of only five books in our house on Great Baddow's Rothmans estate, a freshly concreted field where all the radar engineers lived in a Marconi community of algebra and graph-paper. My father did not much care for Latin or for my studying it. But he never tried to stop me. He never closed a gate. He could easily have stopped me being here now. Without a mind full of antiquity I would not have been in Horace Square with a frowning, olive-eyed priest who continues to ask questions, more satisfied now with some small sense of my paternity, before giving his farewell guidance for the true beginning of the Spartacus Road.

III

CAPUA to ACERRA

Via Domenico Russo, Santa Maria Capua Vetere

'Spartacus went that way,' says the older man at the wax-papered card-table, pointing from the ticket-kiosk into town, away from the ancient amphitheatre towards the unlit neon signs for church-approved lingerie, twenty-four-hour diesel and a play-site. He gesticulates in a timeless animation, as though the famed escape from Capua has only just occurred – and as if the police and a

sole reporter had only just arrived on the scene, late (what could one expect?) but not too late.

His younger colleague disagrees, waving a thin finger in the opposite direction, back through the arches of the ruined arena and up to the hill he calls Tifata. From the way that he speaks, mechanically with a passionless level tone, it seems that he always disagrees; and that these two men, whether their subject is the latest game in town or the oldest one, will always see their hands a different way.

From the rest of the card-players in Scuba Club caps and soft workmen's shirts, flipping aces beside the ticket-booth, there is no response at all to the question that has been asked by two studious Koreans, one man, one woman, the man with a large logo for his national airline on his shiny black plastic briefcase, the woman with a paper bag full of papers in her hands. How had some seventy gladiators, led by Spartacus and two others, broken away from the training school of Lentulus Batiatus?

Today this is a place of discount stores and graffiti. It has been repopulated many times since it was abandoned in the early Middle Ages. But it still feels like a temporary camp, lightly ruled by legitimate authorities, heavily controlled by the Camorra and other criminal gangs. The name of Spartacus is most commonly used – and with no affection at all – as police code for a seven-year investigation into a Capuan gang of contract killers, protection racketeers and buriers of illegal toxic waste. In 73 BC this was the second city of the super-power of the West. It takes some energetic imagination to begin the task of understanding that – more energy than the sun allows.

How had the escape happened? Laxity? Treachery? Leadership? Probably a bit of all three: tired guards, tip-seeking food-sellers, high fences with gaps of decay, not so different from the view this afternoon. The surviving bits of exposed wall from the first century BC, like all Roman walls, look strong enough to hold an army of gladiators. Little economy was used in this construction. The sections beside the card-players are thick enough to have held men and beasts and a naval lake. But there will always be human error.

The couple from Seoul, each with the same bifocal spectacles, are dissatisfied with their guides and guidebooks. The man has short brown hair, straight cut across his forehead, and a face more metallic bronze than brown. He is a doctor. While touring the site I have heard him talking about bone disease and broken toes as though he had asked to see some fallen arches and been surprised to see so much marble. This is not the kind of study he likes; it lacks certainty, even plausibility; and, to judge from his dark-eyed yawns, it lacks interest too. The woman has high cheeks and lighter hair cut close

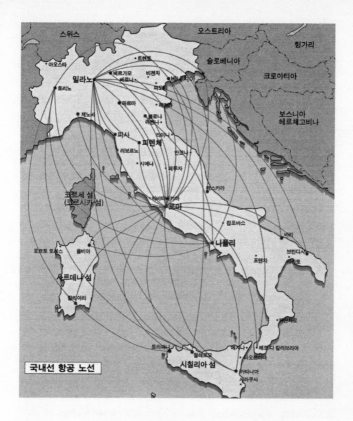

to her scalp. She is a teacher. She is the one who admits to the reasons they are here, her plans for illustrated lessons in 'great sites of history' for her students back home. Her notebook questions are as neat as the inscription on a gravestone.

Surely the gladiators would have been chained at night, locked down in the tiny cells that she could see underneath the massive circular arena? Were they allowed to sleep with their weapons? She thought not. The moment that a trained killer was given his sword, just before he set foot on the sand, would have been the most dangerous of all. A gladiator might wake at night, fighting from his sleep, screaming from his dreams. But in his dormitory cell he would have nothing with which to end a real life – either a guard's or his own.

So how had it all begun? There was no public inquiry at the time of the escape. There were private inquiries down in the underground pits, place of the rack and the whip. But no notes survive of those. All the big questions would be asked later. Among the Vespas and electric wheelchairs, parked above the place where it all is said to have happened, those questions are still occasionally asked – and unreliably answered.

The break-out began with kitchen knives and skewers. There was a plan, a betrayal, a bit of luck and, before the guards could regroup to stop the insurrection, it was too late. Some two hundred gladiators had planned to take part. About seventy succeeded in absconding beyond the gates. Outside in the narrow streets the escapers found a wagon of the very same theatrical weapons that they had been trained to use in the arena. With these they beat back the assault of the better-armed local militia. With new armour, stripped from the bodies of this Capuan Home Guard, they moved out towards the countryside. They had exchanged their butchers' blades for soldiers' swords in three rapid moves. Then they needed a decision about what was to happen next. What to do? Where to go? Who was in command?

At the first official consideration of these events, at first light next morning in the summer of 73 BC, it was merely the Capuan gladiator school which had the questions to answer. Like Symmachus' show 466 years later, it had lost some of its stars. But the questions were hardly huge. The shows would go on, and could go on. Even when the full scale of the escape was clear, the problem for the games promoter would not seem as great as that confronting his sometime pupils. The missing men were mostly new arrivals from Germany and

Gaul, prisoners traded for other prisoners, prisoners of tribes first captured far beyond the Danube, prisoners-of-war, knowing nothing of Capua, speaking a little Latin perhaps but happier in languages used hundreds of miles away. They would not get far. The incident could not have seemed a catastrophe – more a minor schedulers' issue for those planning the next weeks' entertainments.

If any of the missing men had been promised to the great games shows of the capital the predicament would have been more pressing. The promoters of Rome sometimes paid the Capuans in advance, watching their property grow fit and oiled like absentee racehorse owners until their time was ripe. If they had noticed Spartacus, they might object that he was no longer there. More probably they had not.

Lentulus Batiatus' remaining fighters would just have to be spread more thinly through the running order and the order book. There was always a market for something a bit different; it was a matter of imaginative showmanship. Some men might have to fight twice, switching costumes and weapons, short shields for long, round for rectangular, scimitars for spears, anything to make the second half of the afternoon look different from the first. That was almost routine.

Some of the plotters left behind would have been doubly unlucky. The guards needed to put a plausible number to the rack and rod. Even if the school-owner might resent the separation of good fighting arms from their sockets, the waste of flesh which might never heal, he needed to explain himself to the public officials.

What did the escapers do next? The torturers would have asked that same question. What was the plan? Who was in charge? Where did the rats intend to go? However cruelly the questions were posed, Lentulus Batiatus is unlikely to have put much store by the answers. The Romans were neither credulous nor subtle appliers of pain. They believed in the power of fear and example. They did not believe that the tortured told the truth.

This 'where next?' question is the same one that the scholastic Koreans are asking of the Capuan gamblers now. In which direction did the killers go? Which direction does the Spartacus Road take? Most travellers to the Capua Vetere amphitheatre are easier for the locals to satisfy. Most are like those in Rome, Carlo's customers, the ones who come with Kirk Douglas and Russell Crowe in their minds – or even a faint image of Louis-Philippe's Foyatier from the Louvre. The books and postcards on sale in the ticket booth suggest a regular clientele keen to pay brief homage to film stars forced to kill each other for fat emperors.

The entry-ticket for the Capua stadium allows entry also to a grunting 'Silenzio! Silenzio!' son-et-lumiere in the fifty-year-old Museo dei Gladiatori. A waxwork lion stands before a sturdy netman. The sand is scattered with simulations of blood and weaponry. After the scratchy pleas for silence come roars from beasts and crowd, the most decorous whimpers of death and a pervasive appeal for sympathy to all concerned. Only a few visitors see even this display, mostly while they make mobile-phone calls in the shade.

For the Korean couple, arguing softly now into their individual copies of the *Guida della Città*, the appeal of this fairground fodder seems particularly low. Would I like to join them, asks the woman, thin lipped as she moulds the words, sharply dressed in coral red, exuding a manic energy that these sands can hardly have felt since the games ended. Are we even sure that this is Spartacus' school? Might all the guides be wrong? The husband, dampening down the fringe over his forehead, looks on with a cooler welcome. He is wondering perhaps whether an English addition to their day might allow them to concentrate on something else, gauze-eyed lizards, sub-tropical insects, insanitary housing, water closets ancient and modern, all subjects on which there is ample evidence all around.

Examination of the gladiators' options is what his wife most wants. This is the only site here that looks like a school for the arena. This has to be the right place. So where were the escape routes? Where were the battles waged? She has already been to the sites of 218–216 BC where Hannibal fought. She is fresh from the killing fields of Cannae, contesting the precise numbers of Roman dead as though their bodies were still warm. She is single-minded, carefully carving the letters on to her pages, and not easily to be stopped.

The stones are hot. A scent of crushed mint rises from every footstep. The bushes bulge with tiny birds taking shelter from the sun. Shiny pigeons, brown moths and ragged butterflies are the only creatures brave enough to be visible. All that, if nothing else, is little different, we agree, from what it looked and sounded like 2,000 years before.

The amphitheatre is like a broken bowl. It is not Batiatus' but five circles of walls built by the Emperors Augustus and Hadrian on the same site and pillaged for bricks by everyone who lived after the fall of Rome. Just two of its eighty arches are upright. The water tanks can no longer turn the sands into a lake. There are no more lifts to haul men, animals and mountain scenery from the underground store, only the holes where Mussolini's men found bones of antelope, elephant and tiger. Even when this Colosseum was first opened for business (with or without a triumphant poem by a Spaniard or a Greek) its jagged evening shadows would have looked like a ruin. Inside it now, we can try, as far as we can, to mix present and past, see what slips away and what stays, find what we might know.

There is an age of time this afternoon. There is always an age of time among the card-players by the amphitheatre kiosk. Carlo in Rome had been anxious I might find the wrong place, the newer Capua of designer wine-bars, big business and Catholic churches, the other Capua in the river bend that was the safer refuge from the Saracens in the early Middle Ages. But this is absolutely the place he called home, the town which lost its glory well before its people, a place from which an ambitious guide, even an ambitious Spartacus guide, might reasonably flee. This is like a seaside resort where even the sea has fled. It is hard to count the passing of the hours at all.

Corso Aldo Moro, Santa Maria Capua Vetere

We all three of us have maps by which to walk. Theirs are Korean atlases of Italy – with lines of oriental letters cross-

hatching an already complex web of paths. Mine, less useful except for exercises in imagination, is the appropriate page of the *Barrington Classical Atlas* – an American work which shows only what its editors know was there in ancient times. Their maps from Seoul are palimpsests of motorway upon battle site, spidery nets, perfect for tour planning. My map is a mass of pink-and-green open space.

We can decide to use their folded encyclopaedias of facts, interlocked, webbed and linked and perfect snares for capturing any preferred part of the past, modernising, motivating, masking. Or we can prefer the teeming emptiness of ancient Campania and the emptiness of what is known, absolutely known according to lofty *Barrington* standards, about what happened here 2,000 years ago.

We take my map first. How does it work? Korea does not feature on classical atlases. I cannot be polite by starting with the shapes most familiar. So I start as a British traveller, pointing out the British islands. We begin high in Orkney, which the ancients barely knew except through the reports of a certain Pytheas, a man from Marseilles whom not everyone believed. Then a quick slip down the east coast of Britannia, noting that the Wash seems to have been broader and that a large chunk of Kent was accessible only by sea. By now we have missed York, Roman Eburacum, which, if I were not trying to think like Symmachus, would be the site of the most important event ever to happen on British soil, the acclamation of Constantine as emperor of Rome and the man who would put Christianity at the heart of his state.

Geography seems much the most reliable friend on a road trip back in time like this one. What has always been there? What is new? Leap to where Paris is today and we find a place called Lutetia, no big, bold-lettered capital city at the time when Caesar was dividing Gaul into three parts or when it was favourite home for the Emperor Julian (that 'good' emperor for pagans such as Symmachus) who tried briefly to undo what Constantine had done. Turn a page and fly over to Bohemia (were the ancient Bohemians 'bohemian'? There is a mildly obscene passage by the playwright Plautus, writing well before the time of the Capuan escape, which suggests that they might have been) or, if we want to get immediately to the Spartacus Road, rather than zig-zag as the atlas sequence encourages, go southwards to Rome, then further south to where we are now.

The range of these luxurious, pale-pink-and-green pages covers the full extent of the classical world: my trip that begins above the Scottish Highlands can end in Spanish Bilbilis where Martial was born or on the plains of the Upper Nile. After Samosata, home of Lucian, our second swordfight reporter at the beginning of this journey, we can leave Roman Syria for Sardis and follow the Persian wanderings of Xenophon's 'Ten Thousand' until they sight their first familiar waters and shout, 'Thalatta, Thalatta, the Sea, the Sea'; and we can make the whole trip without disturbance from what has grown up along the way since the death of Symmachus and his world.

We can leave Rome by the Appian Way, as Spartacus did when he was first sold to Capua, and follow the poet Horace's route to Brindisi, the diplomatic mission that he describes in his fifth satire. The maps do not show the noisy frogs, lazy boatmen and fraudulent innkeepers, but at least we can see the way clear from the clutter of succeeding centuries. We can follow Spartacus through victories and defeats without the hopes of Voltaire, Marx, Garibaldi and Hollywood. These are magic maps.

Yes, the Koreans agree. But their modern maps, with the political and archaeological scribbles, are more useful. A few minutes away, in the middle of the first century BC so their scribbles show, was a small businessman's home. In 1995, while excavating new foundations, workmen found much older ones, the domed rooms and mosaic floors of a house beside the Appian Way belonging to Publius Confuleius Sabbio, a cloak-maker. That is 'more useful' to us. That much is agreed.

After more than an hour of sipping cold waters and gritted coffees we decide that Spartacus must have considered an exit from Capua along the pavement where we are sitting, the Corso Aldo Moro, formerly Corso Umberto I, formerly Corso Adriano, formerly Via Appia. It was, and is, the

best road out of town. It had shops like Sabbio's, not heavily protected like those of the rich, not worthless like those of the poor, the perfect place for plunder. And yet, did he choose that way or another way? North, south, east, west. The air is filled with the hot salt smell of old men shelling mussels for their restaurant. The discussion ebbs and flows, pleasurably, methodically, endlessly, like the sea that is not even here.

Both of the Koreans are staring down through their lenses. They look like a pair of choristers pretending to pray but they are concentrating hard. This part of the Via Appia is a central section of the Spartacus Road. It was built almost two hundred years before the gladiators' escape, at a time when Rome's grip on the lands to its south was still insecure, when some of the local towns were reliable allies and some were not, and its role was to ensure that no revolt against Rome could ever take place again. It was the symbol of Roman power over its backyard – the whole peninsula newly known as Italy – as well as a very solid fact, a metaphor as well as mile after marching mile of square-cut stones and squat bridges like those by the lakes of Ariccia and at Foro Appio where the marshes and malaria began.

The Appia was straight where it could be, sinuous where it had to be, wide enough for a cart of wine jars going one way to pass a senator's carriage going the other, a wonder of the world in its day. This was the road that the gladiators saw as they arrived at the amphitheatre wherever they were arriving from. For most free Capuans in Spartacus' time it meant trade and money. The ornate floors of the cloak-maker's house, with its flower-and-leaf designs and florid descriptions of ownership, are vivid reminders of that. This was where Publius Confuleius Sabbio presided over his business in heavy woollen uniforms for soldiers and slaves. This would have been a house of hope and pride in dangerous times.

For a few older Capuan families the Via Appia was still a sharp reminder of lost independence, the catastrophe that came upon their forefathers who had supported Hannibal in the Carthaginian's bid to destroy Rome more than a century before. The history of Capua had long been one of alternating alliance and enmity with its rival on the Tiber. In 308 BC the two cities had fought side by side against the Samnites. Even then Livy sniffed at how the Capuans had celebrated the joint victory with gladiators fighting in enemy armour beside their dinner tables. Other writers added details of blood and wine stains mixed amid the rich Capuan food.

Capua had disgraced itself in Roman eyes by backing Carthage. The Second Punic War, the conflict which began with Hannibal's elephants crossing the Alps, had threatened the Republic for more than a decade. Capua's only gift to Rome was that it had also smothered Hannibal's warlike instincts. This had been such a beautiful and luxurious city in those days that it became the Carthaginian general's 'second fatherland'. The man who killed 50,000 Roman soldiers in a single day at Cannae suffered his own 'Cannae of the spirit', his military mind softened by the idle amusements for which Capua was famed. The teacher from Seoul loves the horrors of Cannae: 'and the Carthaginians invented crucifixion', she adds, pushing her pen into her book.

For the gladiators of Capua in 73 BC, objects of both money-making and amusement for the politically neutered local popu-lace, the Via Appia meant much less, almost nothing. Once they were out of the school, the road was merely a means to a possible end – escape, escape to anywhere. Escape to who knows where? Perhaps they took it for their first few miles after they broke for freedom. They needed to get away fast.

The gladiators had little hope of support close by. There were many landowners and businessmen in Capua who might have liked life to be different, with lighter city taxes, less mili-tary service, more influence over Roman politics and over their own. Sabbio himself was a former slave. He and his architect, Safinius, were rising members of a new business class. Safinius is still recognised by name in white mosaic on the floor he decorated in designs of ivy and grapes. But this cloak-maker and his factory-designer were not the type to support a slave rebellion. They and their kind did not want life to be so different that gladiators no longer fought in the arena or so different that all slaves would be free. The escapers could expect no help on the Via Appia here from anyone. Not even the most traditional anti-Roman conservatives, those whose families were the most nearly expunged in the wake of Hannibal's defeat, would want an anti-Roman slave band on the loose. Ending nonsense like that was just what Rome was supposed to do, meant to do, asked to do.

Capuans had much to make them content. Their city was a Las Vegas of its age and they had prospered mightily from their lack of political power. Hucksters and traders like Batiatus could be respectable burghers here. There were theatres and temples, an amphitheatre and all the businesses which went with the luxury tourist trade. Capua had long been famed for scents and carpets, bronzes, elegant black-figured pottery. It was now rich from that fame. Safinius' house and shop, with its signed and decorated floors, built by him (as he boasts) 'from foundation to roof', was just one example.

For the previous twenty years he and his fellow citizens had finally had the vote in Rome too, the Romans deciding that their neighbours' discontents had a degree of just cause. Rome's senators had acquired a new taste for profitable empire overseas, wanted no old troubles at home, and had settled their 'Social War' against the Italian towns on terms that, while not risking any real shift in power, gave citizenship and votes and hastened the creation of a whole country, the first united Italy.

At the time of the escape from the gladiator school, Rome had no need to fear Capua. Its control was total, and totally justified to all concerned. There had been only 'just wars' to that end – a fact which Roman historians had carefully defined and of which they were fiercely proud. Capuans had no need to fear Rome either. The road had done its job. It ran now only like a great black pipe through the countryside to the capital, pulling travellers and traders down, pushing art, wine, fruit, wheat and money back.

One temptation of the Via Appia for Spartacus and the escapers was its familiarity. It was the closest route to where they first stood outside their former cells. Capua's gladiatorial amphitheatre had been built unusually close to where the Appia's black stones forced their way into the city – on the north-west of the central block, near to all the most popular places to live and work, the doctor's surgeries and the philosophers' schools. It was a road designed to be seen – to be seen and understood.

Some cities had their entertainment centres at their obscurer edges, at safer and smarter sites for wild men and beasts to be enjoyed. But Capua kept to the spirit of Rome itself. Gladiator contests had begun in the middle of the Roman Forum, central to the religion, politics and geography of the early citizens. So it was too in Capua, whose highest men talked where its lowest men fought. The proud Campanian poet Naevius, one of those 'other people' whom the Romans relied upon to tell their history, had once described the verbal closeness of *lingua*, the tongue, and *lingula*, the short sword. But there is no need of poetry to prove his point here, only the sites of the amphitheatre and the Capuan forum, in clear brick and marble, side by side.

An escape route north-west along the Via Appia would be the quickest way out of town. This road to Rome also occupied a gap in what was by 73 BC an extraordinary encirclement of amphitheatres and gladiator schools around a city which, while Italy's second in size, was indisputably first for blood and amusements. This was the area where the very idea of gladiator contests began. One of Batiatus' fighters might recognise any part of the local terrain by the places around here where he had fought – at Teanum, at Cales, at Telesia, Abellinum, Abella, Suessa Arunca, Pompeii, Nola, Puteoli, Cumae, Liternum. Each of these towns, in a circle barely thirty-five miles wide, had an arena which vied with its fellows for business. In all of the rest of Italy there were only two.

The massive amphitheatre at Pompeii, built while Spartacus was in training and now the oldest survivor of its kind, held 20,000 spectators. The Koreans have already seen it. There were separate entrances for those buying the best seats and, if they had to wait for admission, a fascinating zoo of animals that were about to die. Audiences could inspect some of the theatrical stars in advance. On an especially auspicious day, there might be free gifts and free food and scented waters sprayed over the crowd.

Competition in advertising was fierce. How many lions? Watch a fight between flocks of birds. See man on man, bull on woman, bear on bull; watch pantomimes and crucifixions and a mixture of the two; enjoy painted mountains, dead men walking, the wounded dying. Watch the spectators who

were watching the shows, their political leaders and each other. Were some of these entertainments the inventions of poets? The gladiators came to know which were and which were not.

They also knew that, for all the variety in the shows on offer, there was a uniformity of harshness in the measures to assure public safety. Some towns might offer a more refined menu of entertainments, more theatre, less killing, more artistry, less butchery, more admiring of the body beautiful, fewer bodies to be carried out at the end of the afternoon. But in every place of gladiators there were the same militias trained to hunt any that might escape. The Via Appia offered a brief opportunity to break away, to avoid the professional prison warders and private armies. But the fugitives would not be able to follow it for long before turning off to safer terrain, to the emptier pink-and-green spaces on the *Barrington* maps.

The Korean doctor has a pointer with a sharp light at its end. If he needed to, he could mark dots and lines on a distant blackboard. It seems as though he might prefer to be doing that. He would rather be lecturing about feet to anatomy students than listening to his wife and her new friend. He is not, however, going to lose the plot, despite the story not being the one he would have chosen. Taped to his briefcase beside the red-and-yellow sign for KAL is a photocopied chart, with the simplest map of southern Italy on one side and a time-line of writers, heroes and rulers on the other. 'Everyone should have one of these,' says his wife, in a voice suggesting that she, at least, has no need of the crib. He pulls two more copies from his zipped jacket pocket. So now each one of us has it.

He pushes his pointer from Capua towards the sea, returning us to our rehearsal of the gladiators' best routes. There

93

was high ground where the Appia hit the coast – at Mount Massicus above Sinuessa. But this was already core Roman territory. The Capuans had been forced to cede Massicus to Rome even before they heard the news from Cannae, flirted with Hannibal and ceded themselves. If the gladiators wanted high ground here, they would have to fight for it. There had been a particularly unpleasant crucifixion of slaves at Sinuessa at the end of one of those earlier escapes and uprisings in Sicily. Support here among their fellows might not be strong.

Slaves knew best the parts of the Via Appia much further north where the road-surface most often needed repair, the parts near those many bridges in the Pomptine Marshes, the parts where the layers were eroded away even in ancient times by seawater, trundling carts and tramping feet. In the marshes a band of slaves might even hide if they had helpers, guides and food. There were few wolves in the swamps but skin-sores and fevers were more deadly than animals. Circling kites, visible every day over Campania, were there to clear away what the flux had killed. Legions were less of a threat here than locusts but, without local help, the marsh was still no place to be. The surrounding farms were small, kept by slaves who were tamed, trusted or closely confined. The Greeks who tended the most treasured grapes, in the fields full of the owners' ancestral tombs, were more likely to betray the escapers than to join them.

How detailed were the plans the gladiators had made before their break-out? Two thousand years later the British who escaped from Fascist camps talked afterwards about how no amount of planning, no obsession with the right ink for documents or the locally available maps and permits, was a real preparation for the fact of being free. The Capua escape, like so many, had to take place earlier than planned in order to prevent discovery. It is not hard to imagine this soon-to-be-famous band of trained killers, men trained to kill each other, men who would have had to kill each other or die a different death, confused now in freedom, weighing options, wondering whether their leader or leaders could be trusted.

No one anywhere but in central Capua yet knew of the events at the Batiatus school. No one beyond the school guards might ever have known. This might still have been a non-event, like the loss of Symmachus' Saxons, an occurrence of no future account. Before the slaves could consolidate their freedom, counter their owners and encourage others, they had to stay free. If any of them had ambitions beyond the next hour or day, hopes of freedom for their own age or any later age, they had to stay free. If the Romans had a legionary detachment near by and decided to put the gladiators immediately back in their places, the Via Appia was the road on which the soldiers would come. Even to make the fastest possible exit from Capua, for the slaves to use it was a risk too far.

Their second option was to the north-east. The highest of the city's five eastern streets would take them out past the settlements of Mount Tifata, through the narrow valleys which spread from the peak like drawstrings for a sack. They could see these on every clear day from the arena. Here was the mountain temple of the huntress Diana, the tourist attraction of Capua that outranked even the amphitheatre. It was not as wild as her temple of the Golden Bough in Ariccia. The Tifata priest did not have to live alone in daily fear of death by single combat. This was a sunny destination whose exhibits included a massive drinking cup and other tourist relics from the war at Troy: Capys, the founder of the city, had been a Trojan. There was an elephant skull from the war with Hannibal. Many visitors to the gladiator shows came also to worship the goddess of the hunt. They spent money on both spectacles. They loved seeing the goddess whose sword and shield inspired their sense of being Roman, just as they loved seeing the arena fighters whose swords and shields did something of the same.

Would it be wise for foreign gladiators to approach the huntress? Italian shrines welcomed worshippers of any god, eastern or otherwise, and many slaves worshipped Roman gods. That was the freedom which Symmachus would struggle vainly to preserve. But this Diana of Tifata was a goddess more suited to the cause of those who volunteered to kill animals than those condemned to do so. Before his escape Spartacus' likeliest meeting with a lion would not have been an act of hunter's courage, of his human free will which a Roman deity was there to make iron. It would have followed some infringement of his school's disciplinary code and consequent consignment from star of the show to beast-fodder.

To the south-east the Via Appia continued its way to the Adriatic coast. There they might find a ship, to Greece, to Thrace or, for those who wanted to go to other homes, to Germany and Gaul. The climb was steep. That much was clear from the lowest slopes. The ground rolled over cliffs and gorges, rolling like the sea itself until it reached the highest plains, places of wandering herds where it was said that armed slaves ran free while remaining the property of their owners. These men had to be armed in order to protect their master's cattle from other masters' slaves. They had to run free because cattle, in this landscape of spiny succulents, waterless grass and pricking birds, must find food wherever they can. Those plains were certainly places where a slave army might be made. But they were far away and high, favoured home of falcons, harriers, the eagle owl of death, and, like its brother road north-west back to Rome, this Via Appia was still the greatest of military highways.

The road southwards was another way they might choose, the way to Naples, the Greek 'new city' of Italy, founded when the Forum of Rome was still a swamp. Field slaves knew the most about the vineyards along this route, the rows of vines trained to produce grapes as close as possible to the ground, the place of youth and light, chosen by slaves who knew the thickness of leaves, the sharpness of stems and what fruit produced the wine their masters desired. The soil was like sand. The farms were like beaches long before they touched the sea. From Naples there might be boats to Sicily, where slaves had risen against their masters before and where, under leaders better trained in war, they might more successfully rise again.

These roadside fields were a temptation to any traveller, narrow passages lined by figs, wild olive and thyme, oily nuts and pink fruits imported from the east. When the thyme and olive flowered together, the ground seemed on fire with flaming, scented pillars of violet and red. Once this show was over, the ground was a carpet of crisp leaves and vines filled with the tiniest grapes, too small to harvest, left ripening into raisins for scavenging men and birds.

There were many people between Capua and Naples, men and women from everywhere, not devotedly Roman perhaps though many of the greatest Romans had country homes along this way. Places for rape and robbery? Yes, opportunities beyond dreams. Places to plan, to think, to deploy? Few opportunities at all unless they went for the final possibility, the last available answer to the 'what next?' question, just a little off the beaten tracks, the most directly south of Capua, the country paths to Mount Vesuvius. The land was flat. There were broad fields, small houses, lichen-covered rocks and gravestones. There were caves where strange airs hissed from the walls, where wolves and cattle, even men, might fall, cease to breathe and come back to life when brought outside. Many had seen this happen. There were statues of frowning mothers enthroned with their swaddled children, goddesses who might as well be dead since no one stopped by them any more. Or so it was said.

Some of the living here had made openings to paradise. On one of their walls stood painted trees and birds, a female dancer, a flute-player, a single red-wreathed man with straight-cut hair. My new friends have already seen it in the museum. From places like these someone was thinking that there was something else beyond what they had, beyond what they had lost, a new spiritual world for everyone by way of a Greek garden. The Romans who believed in Diana did not believe in that. Diana's offer of paradise was for gods alone, or for half-gods like Hercules or those rare and occasional men who might aim to be gods.

There were vast farms that stretched from horizon to horizon, land-holdings assembled by the rich from the profits of early empire, the target of recent Roman reformers but still unreformed. Here slaves saw little of their masters and worked to their deaths under the lash of other slaves. These might be recruiting grounds. The escapers might make others free and find support from them. And if they did not, they would still not be lost. Only twenty miles away lay Mount Vesuvius, the giant tilted table top that commanded the land for many more miles around. No one lived on its summit, or so it was said. Why would anyone live there unless they were fugitives, wanting to rest, to regroup and to wonder what they would do next?

Via Domenico Russo, Santa Maria Capua Vetere

Vesuvius. Teanum. Sinuessa. Beneventum. The doctor taps out the points on his chart, prodding them as though they were the dangerous red rash of meningitis on the skin of a child, hoping that under pressure they might disappear. The Koreans are back outside the amphitheatre, looking disapprovingly at its tattered Italian flag, and carefully considering all these options for Spartacus. Their other maps and pamphlets are spread about them. Their method is as strict and austere as it would be if they were themselves escaping, as if they were pinpointing the minefields of their homeland's demilitarised zones. 'Vesuvio, Teano, Sinuessa,' the doctor intones to his wife. They have no table. The gamblers lend them a box with a stiff waxy cloth.

'Teano,' she responds, sharply but after a thoughtful pause as though she has been weighing exactly what to say. No one else stirs. The card-players understand little of anything she says – and I not all of it. She sees only the slightest change in our expression, not enough for a speaker who has an important point she wants to make. Sometimes at a press conference there is a somnolent peace until the sound of a single word which alerts every reporter to a possible story. Sometimes, in an interview with an old and distinguished subject, there is a single reporter's word which drags argument and memory from a clouded mind. This seems to be that sort of moment.

'Toyby in Teano,' she insists, the words tripping out over the motor-scooters like the tinkling of a bell but still not making the difference she is hoping for. The name of Teanum, the biggest of the amphitheatre towns in Capua's ring of stadia, has struck a string of notes for the teacher – but not yet any chord for her hearers. Teanum, she says firmly, is a place to which 'Mr Arnold Toynbee, a thinker not much appreciated now except in the east', travelled back in time to see the past. 'Teano' is like a password to her classroom memory of a man who experienced history like a child.

Toynbee, she says, was one of her father's heroes, 'an historian of everywhere and everything'. From more than a dozen volumes of *A Study of History* covering thousands of years and the whole known world, 'he could have chosen so many places for his time travel'. But he chose to go back to an event which happened near here a few years before Spartacus' escape, a story originally from a missing book of Livy, one of those many which Symmachus could read but which we cannot.

Its two characters are a husband and wife from Teanum, Mutilus and Bastia, he an enemy of Rome, muffled in disguise and on the run for his life in the Social War, she safe in her house making the best of Roman supremacy. After a long flight and many betrayals, Mutilus reaches his home, makes a soft cry at his wife's window but, hearing that he is no longer welcome inside, kills himself and spatters his walls with his own blood. For most students of Roman history this was just another story surviving in a summary of a lost history book. For writers of Italian opera it must have been an occasional temptation: a dramatic end for any libretto. But for Toynbee this was 'one of those moments, as memorable as they are rare, in which temporal and spatial barriers fall and psychic distance is annihilated; and in such moments of inspiration the historian finds himself transformed in a flash from a remote spectator into an immediate participant, as the dry bones take flesh and quicken into life'. The Korean woman has written these words into her guidebook. She reads them aloud and smiles in remembered admiration.

I am smiling too. Thoughts like that – 'the experience of a communion on the mundane plane with persons and events from which, in his usual state of consciousness, he is sundered by a great gulf of Time and Space' – were one of the reasons that my own generation of classical students was never encouraged to read much Toynbee. He was an eccentric joke. In 'a quickening sight of some historic monument or land-scape' he thought himself back there, back here, out of Oxford in 1911 and into Italy in 80 BC. This was absurd – and had been so for me for as long as I had been out of school. Our proper student task was quite the opposite, continuing what the great man described as his own academic day-job, the 'tenuous long-distance commerce exclusively on the intellec-tual plane which is an historian's normal relation to the objects of his study'.

Toynbee came from a family with recurring intellectuals, as the Bachs had musicians and the Statius clan had poets. All things recurred. Modern paleaeontologists could reconstruct a lost dinosaur from a backbone or a tooth; so too, from no less mysterious relics, a historian's awe-inspired imagination could

bring a great army to life, 'through something of the same miracle performed on the intellectual plane'. The author of *A Study of History* was a twentieth-century British intellectual who took the long view of life in southern Italy. Power and poverty came around and around. He could almost see such truths for himself, bringing the old to the new in his own mind's eye.

The Korean woman is right about our modern attitude to Toynbee – and persuasive, here and now at least, in her gently implied criticism of his neglect. Arguments for all of history circling back on itself – in art, wealth, technology – have long been out of fashion in the west. In the east, the idea that civilisations rise and fall like the sun and stars, driven up by their elites, driven to destruction by their elites' mistakes, remains more palatable, certainly so to this elegant educator from the Seoul academy. 'Toyby, Toyby'. Her father had told her about him while she was still at school herself.

'Teano, Teano'. The oldest of the scooter men, his shirt worn to a shine on his back, has a different idea of that word. To an Italian patriot this tiny town has nothing to do with Spartacus or Toynbee, everything to do with the 'handshake' in October 1860 when Garibaldi, freedom-fighter against the foreign monarchs, self-proclaimed follower in Spartacus' footsteps, gave up his full republican revolution and accepted the monarchy of Victor Emmanuel II. 'Saluto il Re d'Italia,' the card-player whispers with a mocking sigh. There is a memorial monument, he adds, as though thinking I don't believe him. No one ever visits. I will have to climb over the railings. He will show me if I take him there.

Garibaldi was a poorer general than Spartacus, or so Karl Marx said. But he was a more successful political insurgent and he used his predecessor aggressively to promote his own image, writing a foreword to the first best-selling novel on the slave revolt. Garibaldi's legacy remains also as dominated as that of Spartacus by arguments of strategy and tactics, by questions still posed long after the events, about 'what if he had done differently or more?'

The teacher in red, it transpires, has triumphed on her own trip to Teano – and not just because she has reasserted her relationship with her father's favourite British historian. Her guidebook says that no trace of the ancient amphitheatre survives. But she asked and asked – and found the traces of a circular brick bowl among the scrubby trees of an apiary whose bee-hives kept the less committed away. She could hardly have been more pleased if she had met Spartacus himself.

Our Korean–British joint inquiry, along with the sunlight, is reaching its end for the day. To the east of us, as we sit among waking dogs and whining Vespas by the amphitheatre, is the cloak-maker's house and the sites, no doubt, of other businesses either unexcavated or unpreserved. To the south there are the grocery stores, the racks of recycling bins, a launderette. There would have been just the same services in Sabbio's and Spartacus' time. Slave societies recycled everything, from old socks to old stories from history.

Where my studious tourist friends thought the 'killers' would go depended finally on what they thought the 'killers' wanted to do. They argued between themselves about that. Rape and pillage until they were caught? For that they would have gone straight to the Appian Way, the Corso Aldo Moro, named now after the Prime Minister who became modern Italy's most prominent victim of terrorism. Pillage first and rape later? Find lonelier houses further away. Freedom? The defeat of Rome? Which of these and how? Surely the escapers headed quickly down what is now the Via Arco Felice towards Mount Vesuvius? Most writers have thought so. At this time the mountain was only a former and future volcano.

Via della Civiltà: Contadina, San Tammaro

On a pink wall only a hundred yards from the amphitheatre is a red-painted 'Bush e Sharon = criminali' slogan. The signature, dripping with paint as though it were blood, is in bigger letters than even the abuse of the Israeli–American alliance: 'SPARTAKO'. This is the local students' homage, displayed between their philosophy schools and the red-pepper sellers, ornamented with exclamation marks, hammers and sickles, queries about revolutionary purity and the signature of Spartacus.

For the next twenty miles there is simpler travel than in the town, with geography and nature as guides, less vivid than poetry, prose, modern politics or buried mosaic, less precise than Koreans but reliable in different ways. Scholars argue about whether the background tells more than the fore-

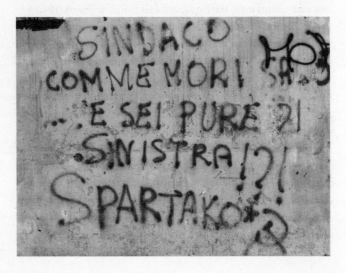

ground, the place more than the people, the unchanging more than the changing. There are those who look always to find change – and those who look always to find what stays the same. What they seek is normally what they find. After so many years working for newspapers and accentuating daily novelties in the world, if I veer now to either of their extremes, it is to the side of things staying the same.

Over the empty earth and grasses, the terrain and temperatures are close enough to how they were 2,000 years ago. The Roman town of Calatia, where the Appian Way turned east into the mountains, is gone, represented, it is said now, only by a church. But the land where the escapers walked keeps its old contours. Somehow, the sense of the escapers is also easier to grasp in this countryside, the exhilaration of being out and away, the pleasure, for however long it lasted, of having soft-edged satisfactions rather than hard prison choices.

In the summer of 73 BC the gladiators left behind the last houses of Capua as quickly as they could. Soon they were out in open country, on narrow tracks or none, in fields of shorn grain turning fast to forests. Some of the trees that had escaped the ship-fitting factories of the Naples bay were as tall as two men, others as high as two houses. None, except those faint, few and far away, were the size of those in Thrace, in Gaul or on the slopes beyond the Danube.

The sight of these roughly armed fighters, for those that saw them, was no great alarm. The countryside was always full of oddities, aliens, good reasons for locals to keep themselves to themselves. There were ever more frequently desert-lions on the hills, beasts suddenly free from their packing cases, the price of living among cities of animal shows. The only serious consequence was a clawed human face or two, some blood-matted hair and maybe a broken-necked body by the side of a road which the beasts would quickly abandon.

The chance of any ringmaster seeing his expensive charges again was slim.

Some sort of pursuit of the men, however, was a certainty. How determined would the local slave-catchers be against gladiators whose training was more specialised even than their own? The escapers could not yet know. There was hope in protection from the parched soil where camouflage patches of pale colours spread on all sides around them. Full shade fell from leaves as small as a woman's hand. Dappled ground of light and dark might hide their escape for miles as they headed away towards an end that was no less camouflaged in their minds.

Black wings swung up and downwards in the white sky – the birds that still swing in the same sky, the birds the fighters knew from the small world above the arena, the creatures that everyone, whatever their language, knew as 'crow', or something very like a crow. The screams of these birds were crrrr-sounds suggesting to the superstitious that they too knew they were crows. How long was the life of these birds? Country legend claimed twenty-seven years, the magic number three twice multiplied by itself, about as long as a lucky gladiator.

Higher through the clouds soared the slowly flapping sails that every Greek knew as Gyps, the vulture. 'The man's worth nothing, no more than a vulture's shadow' was a common saying, commonly heard. These birds would be there if their escape failed. Every size and colour of crow would be there too. Vultures preferred to feed on the ground but the black wings would take eyes from corpses anywhere, on trees, on crosses. Everyone had seen them.

There were raw seeds to eat and ground-running game birds, less familiar to the fighters, squawking 'attagat, attagat' in every dusty direction. To the slaves these were food. To the slave-owners these Attagats were the name for any runaway skulking in the grass. There were wagtails in their best summer yellow, determinedly picking insects from the noses of the cattle. Grasshoppers doubled the size of the thistle heads. The best food and the best protection were on the paths through the highest of the grasses.

The route to the gently rising mountain could be found easily from the sun and stars. There were distractions: slaves, chained ankle to ankle in lines the full length of a field, hoeing out weeds from wheat; trodden paths to villas where wine and meat would be found. The escapers had to find for themselves some little food and support. But a little food was enough and reinforcement with new men was not their first priority. They knew that to be a runaway, even a successful runaway, was not to join the free and easy. They knew that other slaves knew that too.

The very lowest place in a Roman household could be better for some (safer for most) than a place in no household. There was no free food in old age for the free. Even the gladiator school gave a perverse kind of security, a recognition of strength and skill, a chance to make some mark, to watch others make their marks, to be seen, to watch the watchers. No sight lasted for long. But then, as was clear all about, no life lasted for long, inside or outside the arena, either on the hot sand or on the shaded seats.

The paths of escape, the paths of not being seen, were peculiar in their eyes, much stranger to them than those of the arenas they had left behind. The heat-breathing rocks beneath their feet were familiar enough. The open expanses of fragile corn and firm-leaved carob trees were not. In the deep parts of the woods there came suddenly – just as it comes now – the sour-sweet smell of the sea. Vesuvius, its broken head wreathed in the seeming safety of clouds, loomed larger with every hour that passed.

When came the idea of Spartacus as bright eyed, clear skinned, outward looking, resolutely royal like a movie star on a mission? What was he like before Kirk Douglas discovered him? Why is he not a long-faced, lugubrious killer, eyes deep set, thoughtful like a gangland enforcer or Apache executioner? Has anyone any idea what Spartacus was like, even what he looked like?

A writer called Publius Annius Florus might have an answer. Imagine the past as a newspaper office (a device – or perhaps just a vice – into which I sometimes fall) and he is possibly the best popular journalist for this Spartacus Road. He is a reminder that not every Roman historian writes in long winding sentences with the whiff of library and dust. Florus is snappy. He is not a man of doubt. He knows whose side he is on and why.

This is Acerra, ten miles from Vesuvius, an ancient town even in Italy though not one recommended to modern tourists. Hannibal destroyed it first. The River Clanius, now the tamest of canals, destroyed it again and again. Its fields today, near to a once great temple to Hercules, are famed as dump sites for industrial poison buried by crime gangs. Rusting barrels from northern refineries leak their contents into land owned by Mafia friends who need a warning, Mafia enemies who need a lesson and any innocent mozzarella farmer who crosses a gang-leader's path. This is the twenty-first century's 'triangle of death', the scene of the crimes in the trials to which the police have given Spartacus' name. The statue of the Virgin Mary here is said to emit a pink light from time to time, a compensation to some, or just a nasty sign of radiation. Other local attractions include a faded mural over a bar beside the Corso Garibaldi, a familiar wartime portrait of mistrust and betrayal. There is little temptation to do anything here but sip wine (from somewhere else) and read.

The *Epitome*, as it is known, is packed with tightly compressed stories like a newspaper. In his first few pages Florus has already dramatised the first spectacular of this trip, that three-on-three fight, the Horatii vs Curatii affair commemorated back in Ariccia. His vivid version ends with three wounded Curatii for the Alban side against one surviving unwounded Horatius for the Romans. Horatius retreats, drawing his weakened opponents to him one by one in the order that each is strong enough to reach him. One by one he kills his enemies, including the one who is in love with his sister. Then he runs his sword through this sister when he sees her crying for her dead lover. Florus adds a short approving comment on the legal aftermath: 'The law pursued the crime, but his courage removed the curse of family murder; guilt was judged less than glory: *Citavere leges nefas, sed abstulit virtus parricidium, et facinus infra gloriam fuit.*'

Florus tells the story of Rome from its first kings to its first emperor, concentrating on every hero and villain he can find. He seems just the sort of phrase-maker to have given us a good description of Spartacus. Easy history is his métier. Entertainment is a big part of his aim. Whenever there is a bit of 'colour', he finds it. Like Statius, his fellow literary sufferer in the reign of Domitian, Florus is derided today as something of a hack. He certainly fitted the facts to his stories, guessed what he did not know and ignored what he did not like. But Livy himself was only a little better. A good hack can be a good friend on any road.

This one was born in the African part of the Roman Empire, not then the source of many slaves, and he lived much of his

life in Spain, the province whose silver mines were probably the worst place that any slave from anywhere could be sent. Here was the ancient economic system at its most profitable and its potentially most explosive, half-flooded tunnels below ground, choking air above and gangs of men chained leg to leg gouging out the galena ore whose lead and silver made the water pipes and wealth of the capital. Many gladiators spent time in the mines, and Florus must have known what that meant for a man and his mind.

He knows about rebellion too. He writes with delighted detail about Spanish rebels against Rome, the self-styled prophet Olyndicus with his silver spear, the cunning Viriatus with his mountain lair full of trophy togas and his ambitions to be the 'Romulus of Spain'. The pirate boys of Majorca, he explains, learnt their ship-wrecking catapult skills by getting nothing to eat at home but the birds they brought down with their stones. Florus' Thracians are much worse than Majorcans. They smoke their victims to death as though they are meat or fish. They drink blood and wine from human skulls. The only way to deal with such wild country Greeks was to cut off their hands and let them live. Execution by fire and sword was much too good for them.

Florus came to Rome as a boy and took part, like Statius, in some of Domitian's dangerous literary spectaculars. Unlike Statius, he never won – despite choosing one of the Emperor's favourite wars as his theme. It was a 'fix', he said. He sought shelter from future rebuffs in the southern Spanish coastal town of Tarraco, which had an amphitheatre, a tomb of the Scipios and much else to make comfortable a writer who would rather have been in Rome. When Hadrian became emperor, Florus was back at the centre of affairs.

Hadrian was as confident as Domitian was paranoid. He liked to see himself as a man of culture too, and later admirers more than indulged that wish. He became Florus' patron. Florus, like Statius, was close to his emperor, close enough in the new and more relaxed times to write a poem saying how awful it must be to have the top job in the world, and how he could not think of anything worse than tramping around Britain and other bits of the frozen north as Hadrian needed to do. He even got a poem back from the palace – a vivid retort of how terrible it must be to be a tabloid hack like Florus, tramping around crowded bars and flea-infested pie-shops.

Florus was not a man who shied from a sharp judgement if he had one. He had his own convenient version of the cyclic-al theory of history: Rome had been weak in its beginnings, strong in its heyday, enfeebled in a premature old age under Domitian, and reborn again under Trajan and Hadrian. He enjoyed a joust. He was part of an early school of professional pundits, 'concert speakers', as they later came to be known, whose audiences loved displays of rhetorical fireworks, espe-cially if they could repeat some of the tricks for themselves back home. While Statius declaimed his poems for prize-money in lakeside stadia, Florus read aloud his dramatic yarns.

He studied previous accounts of the wars that had made the city great, and 'gutted' them, as later exponents of the same editing art would say, for his own *Epitome* of Roman history, a compression of everything the busy reader of his time needed to know. He took most of his ideas from Livy, editing out the dull bits. He revels in place-names like Mad Mountain and River of Oblivion. He makes his readers feel even now the pain of defeated war elephants. He makes us mock with him those foolish foreign kings who were so frightened of losing their money that they threw it into the sea. He is a writer who would never have been out of work in any age.

Until about three hundred years ago Florus' efforts were well known to European schoolboys; they loved his stories of mountain Greek captives so wild that they bit their neck-bonds with their teeth and offered their throats to each other for strangulation. Who could forget King Orgiacon's wife? Raped by a Roman centurion, she escaped from prison, cut off the rapist's head and took it proudly home to her husband. A popular heroine for any day.

Florus' favourite sentence is the rhetorical question. If he had known about punctuation marks, he would have sprayed his pages with dots and hooks. He writes headlines in almost every line. He sums up his subjects in a single word. But he got a few too many names and dates wrong and gradually, as the study of Roman history was taken over by the scientific and precise, Florus slipped away out of style and is hardly noticed today at all.

Like Symmachus later and so many others, his obsession was the story of rise and fall, success and decline. But he wrote in his own popular way. His contemporary Tacitus had the subtler mind for the dangerous days of Domitian, the greater originality, the darker, conservative scepticism, the yawn of the old *Times* leader-writer over the excesses, and yet the sad necessity, of imperial rule – every quality to which we have given the name Tacitean. Florus is the proud red-top man, randomly sceptical, intensely patriotic, sometimes a bit slapdash, keen on a good argument, and possessing a welcome, not at all Tacitean, preference for short sentences and a few simple words, especially if they are violent, exaggerated and applied to foreigners who threatened Italy.

The mighty Tacitus never, as far as we know, expressed a view on little Florus. The author of the *Annals* generally praised his professional colleagues. He did not approve of much that he saw in Roman life, but his fellow historians, virtuous men in their shared struggle to describe the horrors of political life, normally received a warm word. While Tacitus distrusted most fellow senators, feared all emperors, utterly despised their freedmen and slaves, he never found a historian that he did not like: they were brave tellers of truth to power. But he did not find Florus at all. The younger man probably did not much mind.

The events following the escape of the gladiators from Capua are described at the beginning of Florus' *Epitome* Part Two, when the good politics of the early Republic were turning to the bad. There was not much space between white and black in this historian's mind. Spartacus occupies a rare patch of grey.

Florus' story moves towards its climax with a description of previous leaders of slave revolts. One blackguard ripe for colourful condemnation commanded the first slave rebellion in Sicily, sixty years before that of Spartacus. He was a Syrian called Eunus ('the very seriousness of our defeats caused his name to be remembered: *magnitudo cladium fuit ut meminerimus*'). Eunus had enhanced his credentials by pretending to be both eastern royalty and priest, dressing in kingly clothes and breathing fire from a nut full of sulphur which he kept hidden in his mouth. He was a one-man spectacular, a fascinating theatrical fraud.

Another was Athenion, leader of the second Sicilian rebellion thirty years later, a shepherd in royal purple robes with silver sceptre who killed his master, opened the prisons and defeated two Roman armies with a force that Florus puts at 60,000 men. Both these enemies are exotic aliens. Athenion's final appearance in the book is to be torn apart like an animal, limb from limb, by the local mob.

Spartacus, however, is no sort of pantomime villain in these stories. He is a former mercenary, a soldier, a deserter, a highwayman and, thanks to his strength, a gladiator. He may be a 'monster', a man well suited to the wilds of Mount Vesuvius where he begins his campaign: but he is a peculiarly grey monster.

Why? Perhaps Spartacus was genuinely the quieter type. Or, more likely, Florus is being careful in not dismissing so serious a Roman enemy too much. In one respect, a gladiator was a most disgusting enemy, worse than any mere slave. In another he is almost Roman, horribly Roman. With each succeeding slave revolt in his history, the leaders get less alien and more substantial. Eunus, the first of the line, is like some mad Mahdi leading dervishes against the might of civilisation. Athenion, the second, is more ruthlessly organised, treating slaves who refuse to join him as traitors, forging a force that commits suicide when its cause fails rather than returning to a fate of crosses and chains. Spartacus is from the next stage of what Florus sees as a piece of perplexing progress, a period that cannot so confidently be mocked.

The author of the *Epitome* apologises to his readers that his cut-down account of Rome's military triumphs has to include any victories against slaves, especially victories which came only after serious defeats. Each successive enemy in his story has to be made more worthy of the military and literary attention it received. This Spartacus ends like a minor Roman general, deliberately rather dull.

There is no sense here of how he looked, what he wore, how he spoke. Perhaps Florus did not know. Perhaps none of his many predecessors knew, or perhaps they just failed to write it in their books. Ancient authors regularly fail this modern test but it still seems a colourless effort by so colourful a hack. He writes despairingly: 'I don't know even what name I can give for the war stirred up by Spartacus: *Bellum Spartaco duce concitatum quo nomine appellem nescio.*' Finding Spartacus has been a difficult task for everyone – from the moment he left his barracks for the mountain of monsters that Florus thought so suitable to be his home.

IV

VESUVIUS to POMPEII

Vesuvio, Parco Nazionale del Vesuvio

The ground beneath the gladiators' feet became greyer and drier as they climbed. The lower slopes were thickly grassed, with rustlings of wild boar, of future food perhaps if the beasts ever ventured higher. After an hour among well-watered chestnut trees came a few minutes in sharp brush. Then suddenly the colours collapsed. Grey rock turned to black. A pockmarked path slipped like a shadow through high rock walls. Suddenly, down below was a wide, flat bowl, the size of fifty amphitheatres, with steep sides stitched about with broken fences of brown wire, the brittle stems of dried bindweed and wild moisture-seeking vines.

This was a place of fire with nothing left to burn. Weightless stones flew before every careless kick. There were bleached animal bones, and ditches which opened like clams in a cooking pan. There were cooler places too, and the protecting walls which mattered here most, the remains of a mountain which had many times lost its peak to the clouds. Vesuvius had not erupted for seven centuries, not since the earliest arrivals of the Greeks in Italy, hardly since the age of myth. But no gladiator knew that. To the Thracians and Germans of Capua, suddenly free from one alien Italian place, this must have been shockingly like another.

They made their camp. Military discipline does not leave the disciplined merely because their masters have been left behind. They chose the best site beneath the walls, distributing the food and water stolen from farmers below. Spartacus, Florus says, had served briefly as a soldier before his slaveries began. He may not have been the only one. He now had a circle of defensible space, natural towers to watch for pursuers from the highest ground for miles, time to wake and sleep. The gladiators could shout at the clouds from a path at the same level as the clouds. They could throw down rocks at the lower mists that rolled in from the sea. With a siege catapult of the kind that some of them had seen, they could dream of controlling the sea.

A chance to pause was also a chance to look at each other and to see who they were. Prisoners look different to each other when they are free. 'On the outside' means more than merely where they are. Prisoners see their fellow prison inmates from the inside in every sense: what is eating them up, what is wrong with their minds, their bodies or their luck. A fellow escaper is a different person and is to be treated in a different way. He has his weapons with him – not just for the hours of training and entertainment. He has his short sword and stabbing dagger by his side all the time. He may be calm and quiet and vigilant, as though he were back in his army unit in Germany, Gaul or Greece. He may be vicious and violent, randomly, as the farmers, wives and daughters of the lower slopes found when they disturbed the escapers' hunt for food and wine.

He is a Gaul, a German or an Illyrian as well as a gladiator. In the arena he had an assigned role, Thracian fighter with horsehair griffin helmet or net-and-trident man. But his real origins need not have owed anything to these stage identities. Tombstones tell us of these professional roles, the Thracian whose gladiatorial persona was as a Samnite. In the schools a gladiator could be characterised by the colour of his hair, the place where he was captured, the port where he was sold or, most defining of all, the demands of the programme and the crowd. On the mountain he could instead think back

– or try to think back – to what he had been before. In Gaul a healthy male slave and an amphora of average wine cost about the same. In Gaul he might have been a slave of other Gauls, or as free to drink his fill as he is now on the heights of Vesuvius.

He may find the thinking hard. He may be one of those who had survived his fights with fellow men and animals in the arena but not the feelings that followed afterwards. Psychological trauma is not a discovery of modern analysts alone. The Romans knew about it too. Anyone selling a slave who had fought a lion or bear had to declare that contest in the contract. Attempted suicides had to be declared, even escapes. Tattoos told his criminal record to anyone who cared to look. The fighter may know what is inscribed on his forehead only when he is fully away and free. Then he begins to see a wider range of futures, beyond the next meal or the next fight. He may begin slowly, but new openings in his skies do appear.

The gladiators had to make decisions about how they would live and who would command. The need to think such thoughts came sharp and suddenly to those with a long experience only of mines, chain-gangs and the arena. An acceptance of others' leadership emerged, that of Spartacus and two men called Crixus and Oenomaus, a Thracian, a German and maybe a Gaul. There was still no sign of pursuit from Capua or Rome.

Osservatorio, Parco Nazionale del Vesuvio

Down below at the foot of the mountain by the sea was some of the finest paradise known to Roman minds. There were fields – as there still are fields – of clipped and carefully nurtured grapes, distant cousins of the wild vines at the summit.

There were gardens of medicinal herbs gathered from Asia and Africa and the shores and hillsides of all Italy. On the walls of the finest houses were paintings of these plants and flowers. Ever since that night, 150 years after the rebellion, when mountain rocks became towers of glowing gas, some of those images have survived, set hard in ash.

Today Vesuvius is an elegant cone. Two thousand years ago it looked like a castle, derelict or half built. Many of the places from which Spartacus watched out to sea and land have now to be imagined high up in the air where there no longer is a mountain. Stones on which Spartacus stood are pebbles around Pompeii or dust particles a hundred thousand miles away. Geography fails as a guide in this still explosive place, where the steam pours out after rain and the scientists of the Observatory are on constant watch from halfway up the slope. After each eruption – from that of 79, when Roman gods were the cause, to that of 1631 when sinful Christians brought the fate of Sodom upon themselves, to that of 1944, when the victims blamed the Germans – the simultaneous process of replanting and forgetting begins again.

The homes on which Spartacus looked down had never been burnt by molten rock. Their owners knew fires from a mile below the earth as legends alone. There were myrtle berries and strawberry trees, poppies, pomegranates and what we now call French roses. Absinthe in tiny quantities kept away the pain from any excesses of vermouth. Basil was good to flavour olives, as long as it was watered only at midday. Bee-balm plants brought honey bees. Camomile soothed stings. Dill delighted the eyes. The alphabet of the herb garden has remained much the same here for 2,000 years, while at the top of the mountain, every year in hidden ways, in some years openly, and in a few with the wildest explosive force, Vesuvius has moved back and forth in size and myth.

The men and women who knew most about Roman science and medicine were from the east. The painters of gardens, their weeders and grafters, the people who applied the potions and ointments were almost always slaves or former slaves. They were candidates to join the mountain rebels but not likely ones. Greek doctors could kill Romans more safely by staying at home: the Romans had for centuries turned to Athens and Epidaurus for the cures of pains and the banishment of plagues. Greek cooks too could poison as easily as they could please. As for the better classes of 'speaking tools', those who could speak the language of great Greek poets, suggesting quotations to make their masters look good at parties and quips for their mistresses: why should they choose cold nights on a hot mountain?

There were slaves working on these lower slopes who looked forward confidently to promised freedom. There were freed slaves whose job was to punish other slaves. Around the port of Puteoli, not many miles along the coast, there was a torture industry. Selected employees – none of them lame, blind, crippled or tattooed (that was the traditional rule) – would whip, crucify, rack and gibbet for agreed fees. The owner of the torture house had to provide at no extra charge the rope, nails, pitch and wax that the slave's sentence, decided by his or her master, might require.

Not so very far from these houses with their menus of pain were the most sophisticated theatres and schools. The torturers were kept separate from society. They had to wear coloured caps like the medieval unclean or to live outside the city. But nothing in the pleasure places between Vesuvius and the sea, between Vesuvius and Capua, was very far from anything else. This was a tiny part of Italy, a few square miles of extraordinarily concentrated cruelty, luxury and Greek thought.

The thinkers of the area are the ones with whom we share many a modern anxiety. They thought in many and various ways about dying. Distinguished followers of Aristotle argued about how long was a man's natural life. The philosopher Staseas of Naples, plying his peripatetic trade here in the first century BC, said that it was eighty-four, a figure twice that at which the poet Statius in the following century thought that he was old. Plato's disciples preferred eighty-one, the number three multiplied by itself three times. Others thought carefully about dying because their aim was to stop thinking about it. The slopes of Mount Vesuvius were home to sellers of all sorts of ideas.

Among the most controversial were philosophers who argued that if you could just be free of the fear of death you would be free of every other sort of care too. Romans came to Campania to relax, to be rid of the business stress of Roman life. If you were looking for *otium* (that verbal opposite of the rich man's unavoidable *negotium*), a philosophy course which offered a mental detox was an attractive prospect. Epicurus of Athens had founded a philosophy school more than two hundred years before – for slaves and women as well as for free men. Like all the best gurus, he had liked to attract his followers rather than seek them, and had himself claimed a fearless death, crushing the pain of kidney stones with memories of enjoyable conversations in his past.

The Epicureans of Naples followed the same precepts. They taught the science of life, death and sight. What made an object visible? What part was played by the eye and what part by the object? Every spectacular, anything that could be seen at all, was made of 'spectres', subtle emanations that survived in the mind as dreams. The poet Lucretius, beginning his career in Rome at the time of the break-out from Capua, had learnt to put Greek thoughts into pioneering Latin. His studies for *On the Nature of the World: De rerum natura* were the perfect accompaniment for the civilised man at his bath, at the dinner table and at the games. Cicero put the theories of Epicurus into Latin too, partly to explain their power, frequently and aggressively to challenge them.

Do not fear death, said Epicurus. The dead man is nothing. The dead cannot perceive harm; so the dead can have no harm. We have no fear of what happened before our own existence. Why worry what happens afterwards? Why fear that we are about to die? If death does not come in the morning contests of our days, it will come in the afternoon. At either time it is not to be feared. The Epicureans combined the modern skills of logician, psychoanalyst and colonic irrigator. They were the first pleasure-seeking materialists. In 73 BC, with Athens a provincial backwater, Campania was their natural home.

Nowhere in the world were there so many rich and anxious men, and so many amphitheatres. What better place was there than a gladiatorial arena to see those whose whole training was to show no fear of death, to die so well, to be remembered, albeit briefly, for their exit from life's stage (in Act One or Act Three: why care?) rather than for their eager entrances or pointless running about upon it? The reward for a good gladiator was either a good end or the chance for an even better end in games to come. What a pity that so many of Lentulus Batiatus' troop – once coming on so well, the experts said – would now end up in a miserable tortured death after defeat by the Roman legions now approaching Vesuvius.

Vesuvio, Parco Nazionale del Vesuvio

It was the same need for peace that, in the following century, brought Statius to the farms beneath Vesuvius, back to his home, back to his own Greek calm. He too needed *otium*. He had not wanted to leave Rome. But leaving Domitian's Rome, however briefly, had been the right thing to do. He could not sleep in the capital for fear of his enemies. He could not write for fear of his critics. He was a man of literary business; he wrote for money, for his family, not for fun; and his business had suddenly turned bad.

Domitian's moods were not mellowing with age. Any writer who seemed subversive might be strangled; a slave who copied out his master's errors could be crucified. The virginity of a Vestal virgin was suddenly no longer a technical and antiquarian matter; live burial was restored as the rightful punishment for the woman, crucifixion accompanied by the smashing of arms and legs for the man.

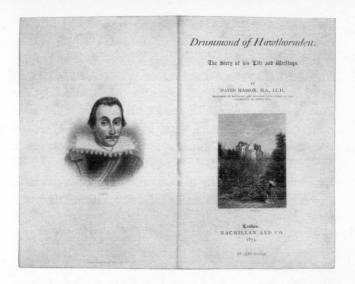

The emperor's passion for religious detail had been learnt in long lessons with Statius' father. But that was not a connection upon which an anxious poet could rely. Suddenly his most obsequious subtlety was not enough. Even his most mannered excess and expressive skills could not buy security. The critics were hostile. Who could tell who was encouraging them? It seemed safer not to find out. He took the same road south as had both Spartacus the slave and those pursuing Spartacus the free man.

Statius' wife Claudia was with him – even more reluctantly. In a rare poem about his own life he writes to her glowing words about Naples, its theatres and steaming beaches. It is not, he says, as though he were taking her off to some home town in the wild lands of Thrace. He describes their long marriage with gratitude and joy. She was always the first to hear his poems, to judge his rehearsals. She had nursed him through a near-fatal illness. They had shared the joy of his Alban prize and the frustration when the prizes stopped.

Claudia, even more than he, was unhappy to go south for ever. She was worried for the future in Rome of her unmarried daughter, a beautiful and gifted musician. The capital was the only place for the ambitious, but success did not come easily there to a young woman on her own. At the end of that journey Statius wrote what became his most famous poem, much translated over succeeding centuries, and its subject is insomnia.

This is a plea to the god of sleep, the young and gentle god who, while allowing peace to all of nature, denies his blessings to Statius. '*Crimine quo merui?*' the poet begins. 'By what crime have I deserved to lack what is given to herds and birds and wild beasts?' No reason is given by the poet for this wakefulness. There is quiet all around. He is not composing, not kept sleepless by inner noise. He is not in love or in mourning. He seems both bold and terrified. He does not request the deepest sleep: only the happier multitude can pray for that. A tiny touch from the airborne spirit will suffice: '*extremo me tange cacumine virgae*'.

This is the only thought from Statius that I knew when I first knew of Spartacus. A version of the poem was in one of the books my father had at home, a leather-like album with mostly blank pages that was used for scoring cricket. The translator was the seventeenth-century Scottish Royalist William Drummond, who had taken the Latin words and made a popular sonnet of his own, 'Sleep, Silence' child, sweet father of soft rest'. This became the version of the Victorian teachers, the anthology poem in which modern readers have found Statius if they have found him at all. It ends: 'Or if, deaf god, thou do deny that grace, Come as thou wilt and what thou wilt bequeath, I long to kiss the image of my death'.

What was this 'image of my death', nestling there for a young boy between the run-outs and the catches? Death's closest earthly image is sleep. Death is the half-brother of sleep. Greek painters often showed the two together in their mother's arms. Homer had them work together, clearing the battlefield at Troy. The popular Victorian painter, John William Waterhouse, showed them in bed together. Sleep is the closest equivalent of death in life. A kiss from this image, the lightest embrace, is an act of exquisite thrill.

Drummond, like Statius, wrote of absolute monarchs and ubiquitous mortality. His models were in Latin and Italian. He plundered them all with pleasure and abandon and, for the most part, without attribution. He wrote sometimes in Latin himself. He judiciously supported his master, Charles I, a king who, while no Domitian, was one before whom cautious criticism, wreathed in the most courtierly excess, could still be a perilous course. The two poets would have understood each other. Drummond opposed all rebellion against the established orders, watching miserably the approach of civil wars in England, Ireland and his Scottish home.

Death was his great cause. He wanted to show the folly of fearing it. His first published work was in 1613 on the death of Charles's elder brother, Henry Prince of Wales. In the same year he published *Mausoleum*, an anthology of epitaphs. In 1615 he lost the woman he was about to marry on the day before he was to marry her. His work was 'amorous' and 'funerall' and its most lasting expression was a philosophical essay called *The Cypresse Grove*. His conclusion? That humanity was hurt by excessive sense of its own importance. 'This globe of the earth,' he writes, 'seemeth huge to us in respect of the universe and compared with that wide pavilion of heaven, is less than little, of no sensible quantity, and but as a point.' Death should be nothing to us. 'For while wee are, it commeth not, and it being come, wee are no more.' There was no need or reason to fear death. 'Feare maketh us to meete with that which wee should shunne, and banishing the Comfortes of present Contentmentes bringeth death more neare unto us.' Drummond is summarising the best-known doctrines of Epicurus, as fashionable in his own day as when Spartacus was fighting in the arena.

Drummond's phrase 'the image of my death' is itself a quotation, but not from Statius. It was recycled through Italian, from an earlier writer, Cicero, the most famous collector of Greek thoughts. The Scotsman takes Statius' poem reeking of morbid terror and caps it with a motto from Spartacus' time. Mortality merits no worry: the ending of our lives is like sleep; and sleep is like the ending of our lives. 'If, deaf god, thou do deny that grace, Come as thou wilt and what thou wilt bequeath, I long to kiss the image of my death.'

Osservatorio, Parco Nazionale del Vesuvio

In the late summer of 73 BC pursuit and punishment of the gladiators were finally on their way. The Senate had given its orders. Three thousand men led by Gaius Claudius Glaber, one of the senior magistrates for the year, had the task of removing the escapers from their mountain. The rebellion would soon be over. Everyone said so.

The soldiers were not the finest that Rome had ever put into the field. The Roman citizen army was no longer the sole and necessary path to respectability it once had been. Some of the numbers had to be made up from retired men who lived along the road south. There were part-timers taken from their farms, shops and bath-houses, some playboy intellectuals in the team, men who, for small sums (since there would be neither pillage nor glory in putting down a riff-raff rebellion), could be pressed into a short bit of extra service.

Anyone with military experience might be asked to make himself briefly available for the sake of honour, old comrade-ship and some stories of his own valour that could grow in the telling.

Seen from Vesuvius, this first Roman force must have looked a little scrappier than the normal legions. But the gladiators would not have placed too much reliance on that. Roman military dress was rarely of a uniform kind. If a soldier wished to exchange a bit of enemy silver for a better cloak in Capua, the cloak-maker in his designer house would have been only too pleased to oblige him. Glaber's soldiers will have displayed tunics, belts and brooches from many market places.

Their leader was not the most tested of generals. He would have been happy with the quickest bit of action here before resuming his more comfortable city life. A few days in his mailed jacket on the Appian Way, a road he associated more with prostitutes and perfume prices, would have been fine. To be the man of the hour, a single hour, would have been enough. It was not clear at the beginning, not obvious at all, that he would become one of those one-shot figures of history, a man of whom we know very little and whom we would not know at all if he had not been the wrong man in the wrong place at the wrong hour.

Perhaps there had been frustration at Rome that the Capuans had failed to deal with the problem themselves. The Senate had considerably bigger concerns than the campers of Mount Vesuvius. They faced the remnants of a civil war in Spain, with slaves reputedly in the rebel army. They had forces fighting Rome's most serious foe of the time, King Mithridates of Pontus, ambitious ruler of the Black Sea coasts and increasingly far beyond. They also had their own ambitious generals to fear.

Yet, for all their distractions, the Romans would have had no doubt about the result. Glaber's responsibilities as praetor ranked only just below those of consul. He marched with the silver standards and axes that symbolised Roman power on the move. Three thousand fully equipped legionaries, whatever their age, costumery or terms of conscription, would be more than enough to overcome a hundred or so gladiators and hangers-on. Everyone knew what happened at gladiatorial games, the stares on the dying faces, the blood on the sand, the deaths that happened to the losers. The Romans did not lose battles, not now that Hannibal was gone. Gladiators always lost. It was just a matter of waiting. There was nothing to be done but to blockade the mountain and wait for hunger and thirst to do the rest.

Vesuvio, Parco Nazionale del Vesuvio

In their camp in the crater the gladiators knew too that gladiators always lost, that in the end there was only one outcome. Sporting prowess, it was said, might buy a man his freedom. Beautiful women might buy him for their beds. But evidence of this was as scarce for the fighters then as it is for those studying them now. Death was the end of their game. Life beyond the arena was only for their dreams, and for their admirers' dreams.

As a result of their escape they were no longer gladiators for the next days' shows. They were on a mountain surrounded by arenas, places they could see rather than be seen in. They were high when they had been low. They were watchers when they had so long been watched. They were about to cross the line between sport and war. In war, perhaps, they need not always lose.

Their training was in entertainment, education and inspiration. The approaching battle was something different, a fight in which they needed to kill the men who liked to watch them kill each other. The minds of the slaves on Vesuvius are a mystery to us. There is no way of knowing how they saw the change, whether they fired each other's spirits with stories of the arena or whether they saw the world from these heights as wholly new. Did they see themselves as more likely to die now than in their daily routine of duel and death, or less likely? Was their training an inspiration to them? Or did its truths keep them sleepless while the besieging Romans slept?

How we envisage our ends and how we envisage others doing the same are heightened by every near meeting with death – in war, in sport, in sickness, in the accidents of every moment. The Romans had more such meetings than most have today. Statius was not a military man, neither a fighter nor a showman of fighters. But while his personal spectaculars were different, he too had noted the vast varieties of dying, the every distortion of minds from fear. When he

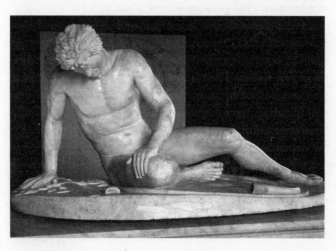

placed boxing dwarfs beside female gladiators on the Kalends of December he was marking points on the line between battles and entertainment, between killing and clapping, between war and all its baby sporting brothers. Fine distinctions are important for those who see death ahead. Everything stands on this line, from the most famous gladiator of all time to the untrained sex, ignorant of the steel, shameless in the fighting moves of men. '*Stat sexus rudis insciusque ferri: Et pugnas capit improbus viriles.*'

Statius enjoyed sharp distinctions, shadow lines between objects, ideas, geometrical planes. There are different places to draw such lines. Sometimes we like to see war as sport. Newspaper correspondents often used to do so. When Symmachus followed one of his emperors on a German campaign, he was shown a 'battle' in which the natives quickly fled, the Romans behaved like gentlemen and 'not a single dawn rapist dragged the barbarian mothers from their beds: *nec indormitantes lectulis feras matres antelucanus raptor extraxit*'. In better times in Europe writers have been able to do the opposite, to write as though sport is war.

In most sport, ancient and modern, the kind that the *viriles* citizens practised in training ground and gym, the combatants do not die. Old warriors, veterans of wars, can in sport recreate their combat pasts in comfort and safety. Young men can show off their sporting masculinity for future military use. There is pretence, illusion, a referee, a time at which the game will end. Even in Homer's *Iliad*, that ancient hymn to war and central text for Statius, there is a sporting fight that is designed only to wound, and a specialist sportsman, a boxer called Epeius, who says that he is no good at any other kind of fighting.

Epeius, Homer's sporting 'hero', is no wimp. He promises that he will 'smash his adversary's flesh and crush his bones'.

This is no idle boast: his opponent is returned to the ranks with his mouth spitting blood clots and his head lolling from side to side like that of a brain-damaged child. But the boxer is still not a warrior. When the bout is over he picks up his defeated rival just as a footballer does after a 'professional foul'. The result? No one dead, not in the sporting arena.

On the Spartacus Road, as in Homer's Troy, sport is the anomaly. Death – 'how to avoid and approach it' – is the permanent accompaniment to this journey. It was death not sport that brought Statius his critical applause. Alongside his *Silvae*, his glittering impressions, Statius wrote his own epic poem, a retelling of the Oedipus legends loaded with the most spectacular death. This was the work that he regularly read to the admiring and encouraging Claudia at night, with an impact on their shared sleeplessness and that of all its readers since. This was the poem that a thoughtful schoolmaster once read to his Essex pupils in the 1960s – to show that Roman literature was not all love and honour.

The *Thebaid* is in twelve books, took twelve years to write, and tells of the gore-strewn struggle between Oedipus' sons, Eteocles and Polynices, to claim their father's throne. They cannot share power; so they kill for it. Polynices assembles the notorious Seven against Thebes, Greek monsters from Argos against his own Greek Theban home.

Like the *Iliad*, the *Thebaid* has a boxing match among its games, one between two of the invaders, a brutish boastful animal, Capaneus – 'massive to see, massively to be feared' – against a lighter man, Alcidamas, the 'float like a butterfly, sting like a bee' style of fighter. Capaneus, contemptuous of gods and men alike, says that he would have preferred an opponent from the enemy, someone whom he could batter to death, someone who would make his bout seem more like war. But he gets one of his own side instead, a beautiful man kissed by one of Jupiter's most beautiful sons: 'whom none wants to see bloodied or beaten and all fear the spectacle: *Quem vinci haud quisquam saevo neque sanguine tingi Malit, et erecto timeat spectacula voto*'.

The sporting star, Alcidamas, though tutored by a god, is a mere sparring partner for the massive Capaneus. Statius' poetic boxing match begins as though it may go far beyond sport. It gains the best of its drama from that possibility. This was one of his show-pieces. But, because this particular match is genuinely sport, it ends with the umpire calling a halt; the giant has become too enraged for anything but death to be the outcome. The event ends at the bell. Like many a contest in the arena, like the one described by Martial in the opening matches of the Colosseum, there is no winner or loser that day.

Statius has every kind of bloody brawl in the winding length of his epic, monstrous cruelty, high-coloured horror. Capaneus collects the head of a Theban so that his dying

friend, Tydeus, winner of the wrestling match on sports day, can eat the skull, chew it, enjoy its warm, still-living blood and end his days happy. There is sharp, metallic killing, savagery without rules. Opponents rip each other's cheeks and scratch each other's eyes. The defeated will never again be spectators of this or any other spectacular.

The climax of the *Thebaid* is the duel between the sons of Oedipus themselves, the claimant Polynices and Eteocles the defender who will not concede. Capaneus, the giant boxer and despiser of everything in existence bar himself, is dead by this time. So are the champions in the chariot race, the running race, the wrestling and the discus. Only the winner of the archery prize will return to his kingdom in Argos, his survival guaranteed by an arrow which leaves his bow, flies to its target and returns safely and prophetically to his quiver. Statius would have almost sung these lines, like an operatic tenor, pouring his song over his homeland's lakes, fields and hills.

This final duel is a swordfight like a gladiatorial combat, a pair, one on one, to the death: 'Now a criminal pair begins a bout that Earth in all its miseries has never known: *Nunc par infandum miserisque incognita terris Pugna subest.*' One brother at least has to die. The Theban land on which they fight is a field for slaughter, a place drained to nothing, an emptiness over which men, temporarily, cast the shadows of giants. The squeamish turn away, just as they did in the arenas of Roman times. Even Jupiter complains that the fighters are 'raping the day' and 'staining the sun with spots'. Not even the gods should watch the climax of this show: 'The fight begins: turn away your eyes!: *Pugna subest: auferte oculos!*' This is the most vicious of spectaculars. Both brothers die before it is over. The grim grey scenes are lit and choreographed by Statius at the height of his now mostly forgotten powers. 'The wretched commoners stand high on their roofs and from every tower tears flow: *Prominet excelsis volgus miserabile tectis Cuncta madent lacrimis et ab omni plangitur arce.*'

No Latin poem has left more inspiration for writers of the end of the world. There are no heroes among the Seven. Instead there is Tydeus, psychotic killer and gnawer of skulls: many gladiators were given that name. There is the single priestly prophet among the attackers, Amphiaraus, the one who knows that the war will shatter the world but goes along anyway. There is boundless horror and grief before an outsider imposes an impossible peace.

This is a picture of the generation before the Trojan War, an image of the beginnings of civilisation that looked to Statius so very like its end. As well as brilliant bravura, the *Thebaid* showed its hearers a Greek poet grappling helplessly with the conflicts of his adopted Italian home. No Roman of the time could read it without seeing a glimpse of the Oedipal Emperor Vespasian and his bitter sons, Titus and deranged Domitian. None could read it without seeing back to almost two centuries of inner strife. No one wants war at home, fighting to the death between those who share the same streets, the same roof, the sort of horrors that happen inside one's self.

Osservatorio, Parco Nazionale, Vesuvio

The first army to face Spartacus arrived in its siege position, set down its weapons, slept and ate and waited. There was only one known path down the mountain. Glaber did not fortify his camp, the nightly duty for every Roman legionary force everywhere in the world, as defining of the military mind as parade-ground drill. Perhaps it seemed unnecessary, even ridiculous, to raise ramparts, walls and towers against a band of slaves. This was Roman Italy now, where the soldiers' hero Hercules had long ago conquered any alien giants, captured all man-eating bulls and founded his own town, Herculaneum, whose present temptations for a man like Glaber lay prominently below. This was lucky country.

The Roman armour spent the nights in clumsy piles, with copper helmets slumped on their cheek-guards, painted shields propped against walls and boulders, short swords and javelins where they ought most easily to have been found but where somehow they were not. Imagine their tents as the locker-room of a veterans' rugby team. The game was going to be fine. It was the party afterwards for which they had come.

Only the lesser weapons of the gladiators were ready for use, high above on the black rock walls, ready to be dropped down to the ground after the fighters had roped their own way down with twisted lengths of vine. Their heaviest shields, their leg-guards, the helmets with monster ornaments designed for the exotic thrill of the crowd, all these could be carefully cushioned in the grass with no more noise than that of a few wild boars awakening.

The rest was Roman slaughter – not slaughter by the Romans but of the Romans, not what the legionaries' training, education and even entertainment had prepared them for but the opposite. Hercules had been a god for gladiators too. It was said that the freed fighters had rejected their arena costumes, seeing them as symbols of past slavery. It is still hard to resist the image of a Thracian gladiator with scenes from the sack of Troy on his wide-brimmed helmet, with full plumes and smirking stage visor, smashing the eyes of a would-be spectator while he slept.

Via Pioppaino, Pompeii

How could fewer than a hundred gladiators have defeated a Roman army? This was a problem to which Sextus Julius Frontinus had at least one answer: they succeeded by tricks. Frontinus was a great man of answers. He was an engineer, a bureaucrat, a governor, a public servant, an organiser, a manager. He filled all the functions of a man whom future classicists would not take to their hearts, their minds or their armchairs.  He was something of a writer too. But like Symmachus, mourning briefly for his lost Saxons, he was much read once and is not much read now.

This sweating bar-room is a place where his modern successors have gathered for a modest conference. This is the Pompeii where Pompeians live, the place without the plaster casts of dead bodies, without the ancient brothels offering sex on short narrow shelves, without the bravado boasts of gladiators chalked on the walls. Here the streets outside are not quite so rutted and the kerbs not so thick. There are no retailers of mini-frescos or sexual-position price lists or papyrus maps.

This is Pompeii as it used to be even before the eruption, a place of common commerce, not for the hugely rich but for those with a living to make. How much to the local government, how much to the local governors, how much now to the local church which owns so many of the streets, how much to the local Boss without whom nothing happens? Whatever is left after satisfying il Commune, la Chiesa della

Maria Rosaria and 'Don Pasquale' is left to the men gathered now around the shiny-panelled bar. There are wholesalers and factory-owners whose suits match the walnut of the walls, silk inside and out with the sheen of a cruise-ship cocktail cabinet. There are agro-business representatives, trussed in grey with colour-matched ties and handkerchiefs, here to sell each other industrial measures of beer and breads, bottled-sand souvenirs by the tonne and fire-from-the-mountain plates by the truck-load. Two plain-clothed priests watch the door.

Tonight, maybe every night here, is for those Pompeiians who grow fat on the past if they can, Christian businessmen parasitic on pagan predecessors, everyone exploiting the obsession of visitors with a part of their town that they themselves dislike, a part that died 1,900 years ago. None is young. None is female. None is a tourist. The only book in view is *100 Ways to Succeed in Sales*, the sort of publication which may not add much to most people's cultural history of Pompeii but is important for ensuring that its history continues. *100 Ways to Succeed in Sales*, subtly translated to suit southern Italian rules, may be the most important book of all for understanding these constantly re-examined, reinterpreted and rebuilt streets of Pompeii. It is Frontinus' sort of book too.

Darkness has arrived early between the garages and the garden vineyards, between the vegetables under polythene and the newspaper shops. There are bulging black mountain clouds and raindrops the size of soft lead shot, each one kicking up dust by the windows as each individually falls. This is slow-motion weather. In a film we would be an organised-crime colloquium. The barman enforces discipline on the journeymen. They all look uncomfortable in their suits. They know that they are uncomfortable. But they wear what they have to wear, just as toga-wearers did.

Sextus Julius Frontinus offered answers to technical and tactical questions that other senior servants of the emperors merely asked. He wrote about water pipes, fountains, aqueducts and baths, how they fitted together, the rules of the network, who could take what from where. He wrote on land surveying, the law and practice of farmland, access, security and finance. Even the best executives, he recognised, do not learn automatically from their predecessors' mistakes. He wrote about military stratagems, a successor to a larger work, now lost, on Greek and Roman strategy. Strategy was long term. Stratagems were short term. A general could be good at one and not the other. His book set out past disasters not for the purpose of moral improvement, as historians did, but to make certain that they did not happen again.

His style was the bullet-point, a bang, bang, bang of facts that the ambitious and the prudent should bear in mind. He begins his *Stratagems* with a little light clearing of the throat: '*Cum ad instruendam rei militaris scientiam unus ex numero studiosorum eius accesserim eique destinato*: Since I alone of those versed in military science have troubled to reduce its rules to a system, and since I appear to have achieved that purpose, so far as effort on my part could do so, I feel still obliged, in order to finish the task, to sum up in a few brief words the cunning deeds of generals to which the Greeks give the single name "stratagemata".'

The looming conference of the Pompeii tradesmen looks set for a similar opening speech. Here too we have a '*unus ex numero studiosorum*', a self-styled single self-sacrificing educator of his fellow men. Throughout the world there are thousands of such management speeches made in the same manner every moment of the day. They will display pride (possibly deserved) followed by modesty (certainly false) and a promise to stress the positive (when avoiding the negative is the prime purpose). Nervousness and boredom vie for dominance in the damp air. No one today from any business anywhere can have survived a career without suffering such a 'scene-setter presentation' and probably giving one.

Frontinus has to flatter his audience: 'I ought, I think, out of regard for busy men, to show the virtue of brevity.' Only then can he flatter himself: 'others who have made selections of important deeds have overwhelmed their readers by the very mass of their research'. Our speaker here too promises to be as brief as he can, to speak 'as if in answer to questions', reassuring the red-faced-and-shirted man beside me that the small Chivas Regal he has purchased from the barman's half-gallon bottle ought to be enough.

The chairman for our Pompeii evening continues his address. The rain is hammering ever harder on the roof. The television screen still shows a Napoli football match below its display of plaster saints and silk coasters for the Madonna of the Rosary. Boom-box music bounces through the door whenever a late arrival appears. The barman calls for quiet. The words are soon lost to me in money and measurements and a mass of numbers.

Sextus Julius Frontinus was born about a hundred years after Spartacus occupied Vesuvius. His home was in southern Gaul from where many of the gladiators came. Gauls were among the worst of enemies but good with other animals if they were properly motivated and trained. During a long life in difficult times he proved himself the consummate servant of the great. If, during Domitian's reign, he ever felt Tacitean anger or the sleepless anxieties of Statius, he did not show it in his work. In the safer, more prosperous times that followed, in the good years that Statius died too soon to see, Frontinus came into his own.

Before making his mark in the national aqueduct business, he was military governor in Britain and an influential broker of power in Rome. At one point, it was said, he might even have become emperor himself. If this was ever anything more than a rumour, it was a rare folly of thought, rapidly snuffed out in the realisation of other ambitions that were safer, more rewarding and more appropriate.

Once the throat clearing is over and Frontinus has begged 'that no one will charge me with negligence if I have missed out some illustrations', the master presents his first book of 'stratagems' divided into twelve sections. 'This work, like my earlier ones, has been undertaken for the benefit of others rather than for any fame of my own,' he reminds any last doubters. The ancient flip-chart show begins.

    I. On Disguising One's Plans
   II. On Discovering the Enemy's Plans
  III. On Deciding the Nature of the War
  IV. On Leading an Army through Places Infested with the Enemy
   V. On Escapes from Difficult Places
  VI. On Ambushes on the March
 VII. How to Conceal or Substitute for Deficiencies.
VIII. On Distracting the Enemy
  IX. On Quelling Sedition
   X. How to Inhibit Demand for Battle at the Wrong Time
  XI. How to Rouse an Army's Enthusiasm for Battle
 XII. On Dissolving Fears Inspired by Bad Omens

Today's chairman has his own flip-chart and a red felt pen. If the Pompeii Rotarians are getting as good a workout as Frontinus' first readers, their commercial rivals will not stand a chance. It is a pity that the Korean doctor is not here. This is a part of the Spartacus Road where he would feel at home.

I. When concealing plans from the enemy it can be useful to dress your top spies as slaves. Do not forget to punish such men in public with your cane so that the enemy does not guess their true identity.

II. If the crushing of savage Gauls requires the presence of the Emperor Domitian himself, make sure that he appears to leave Rome for some other purpose, to make a census of the living rather than a body count of the dead. Otherwise, the enemy will make greater preparations.

III. To discover the enemy's whereabouts, always watch for flocks of birds rising startled from field or forest. If you have experienced troops against raw recruits, choose the most open ground for any battle. If the enemy is by the coast, consider using swimmers, warmed with oil and wine, to reach behind their lines: the Athenians successfully did this once against the Spartans.

References to Spartacus come under heading V. Escapes from Difficult Places:

When besieged on Vesuvius, at the point where the mountainside was most difficult and thus unguarded, Spartacus wove together ropes of pliant vegetation. Clambering down by these, he not only escaped but, by appearing from the flank, struck such terror into Claudius that whole cohorts gave way before only seventy-four gladiators.

With this one paragraph, Frontinus gives both his advice, that willow and vine ladders are a trick worth trying in extremity, and his warning, that in 'asymmetric warfare' against the weak the stronger force, which was always the Roman, had to remain on constant guard. The weak, it should be noted, could arm themselves from the terrain. Spartacus' men made shields with wicker wood and the hide of cattle. The Boii – a tribe of savages and excellent source of German slaves – had once cut through the trunks of hundreds of trees, leaving only a slim core behind, so that, at a single push, a whole forest might fall on a Roman army.

Frontinus had his own experience of quelling revolts. He knew what he was talking about, and he made sure that his readers knew. One of his greatest successes was against the miscreant Julius Civilis, self-styled Emperor of the Gauls, the one whom Rembrandt painted in his smoky rendering of romantic rebel leaders from AD 69, the year that Nero died. The artist selected the scene to portray the hopes of ancient men of Holland who wanted freedom from Rome, hoping that he might buy favour with Amsterdam burghers who equally hated any authority but their own. Rembrandt failed just as Julius Civilis had. The picture was unsold and barely survived. There was only one victor in any version of this incident, Frontinus himself, who crushed the revolt and enslaved 70,000 prisoners in reprisal – the sort of success that would sustain the spirit of Symmachus when even his own emperor dressed to impress in a German tribal uniform.

A decade or so later Frontinus became governor of Britain and an early hammer of the Welsh, leaving behind a Via Julia where hikers still walk, some massive walls and an amphitheatre near Newport. Since the Spartacus Road rarely comes anywhere near Britain, we might grab this single thought while we can: whatever the Romans did for us we did very little for them. Our ancestors offered a constant supply of dogs but only constant hopes for gold, a convenient place for a quick victory or two and a very inconvenient place to live.

Symmachus got his wolfhounds. Mamurra and Julius Caesar's men stole what was easiest to steal. Our druids were too exotic even for the arena.

'Remembrance will endure if the life shall have merited it' was one of Frontinus' phrases. His British fortifications, like most of what he achieved, live on without his name attached. The ruins at Caerleon became best known as a candidate for King Arthur's Camelot. It was easier to find the finance for the excavations that way. The moody tourist posters of the site, all green-black grass and mossy stones, are meant to remember the Round Table (the world's only gladiatorial arena with a second and more famous circular life) not the slaughter grounds of the man who wrote the *Stratagems*. When did the Roman tradition finally end here? When did the last public strangling and burning of a woman take place in a British amphitheatre? There is a record of one in 1706, and public hangings over the sands for sixty years after that. Fund-raisers found it better, wherever possible, to evoke the spirit of Queen Guinevere instead.

The author who tells us of Spartacus' first triumph is a recognisable kind of civil servant for all ages, a traditional disciplinarian, a stander of no nonsense, a planning regulator, a minister for small businesses. He is looking for obedience more than credit. And he wants that obedience to come from his listeners' reasoning. He wants everyone to know that he makes sense. He paints his pictures by numbers so that others can paint the same pictures and think they are artists too. Responsibilities for the Roman aqueducts brought worries, attention from his bosses and little glamour. But someone had to do it. In the earlier years of the Empire the water supply had been managed by smart imperial slaves. Only gradually did the grander Romans begin to realise that management was respectable, powerful, essential.

Frontinus' technical treatise about waterworks was self-consciously precise with its numbers, specifying the width and capacity of pipes, the angles of gradient, the heights of towers. The numbers did not always function as he had hoped. He did not understand how the speed of waterflow affected the amount of water. The Greeks had better mathematics. But a good flip-chart presenter can distract his hearers from little problems like that. The *De aquis urbis Romae* was highly practical at the time, essential still for anyone wanting to know how Romans filled their basins and bathtubs, how the rich filled their pools from the public pipes if they could, how the poor had a tap in the street if they were lucky.

Frontinus notoriously despised literature and art. Artists and critics have tended to repay the compliment. He was a boaster who boasted about the wrong things; while Horace wrote how his words would outlive bronze and marble, Frontinus wrote how baths and taps would outlive any poem. He was like my father. He genuinely preferred lavatory pans to painting.

Did Frontinus see art in his own writing? Very probably, even if the critics who came later did not. His chosen subjects, 'water pipes and soldiers' tricks', were themselves Roman arts. Topics and styles were available for any who sought them. If Statius, who had only just died, could make poetry from villa designs and the marbles used in swimming pools, Frontinus could see his own work on water pipes as an achievement for all time, just like the pipes themselves.

There are many like him, then and now. He chose his words with care, an important skill for entering public life in unusually perilous years – when a bad Nero was exchanged for four rulers in fourteen months, a bad Domitian for a dull but better Nerva. He was consul three times, not the job it was in Republican times but still a job. Only emperors held

the number of offices that Frontinus held, and Frontinus did not achieve such promotions by obvious or ill-placed claims on glory.

Let someone higher get the praise. Let us down here have another drink and live to see as many other days as possible. It was a reasonable policy, recognisable in this rain-battered conference room and many such rooms. Frontinus was a man behind the stage, writing for those who could read between his lines. He was a man who most likely wrote as he ruled, brutally, carefully, and saw both acts as something of the same.

Much of the business of writing is the business of imagining the lives of readers, their reactions and responses. Frontinus will have been the recipient of many an official report. He was writing for his emperor but also for people not so unlike the drinkers here – middle-managers of the municipal domains with ambitions to move up, or at least not to screw up. Civil servants can be fussier than poets about their commas. The obscurest mandarin will complain about the colon cut from his prose. Journalists rejoice, or at least pretend to take pleasure, in casting their words into an uncaring machine where nothing emerges on to the page in anything like the form that it arrived. The dullest describers of accountancy procedures cavil loudest if an adverb is displaced. Whether we call them literary artists makes little difference.

There is something silkily subtle about Frontinus. He used his obscurer facts not just to help future stewards of the emperor's water but to warn opponents of how much he knew about them, how they should stop diverting the flow if they knew what was good for them, and how they should be wary of what else he knew. He was a prototype of the later civil service aristocrat – an artist of management, tricky on tactics, reliable on facts. He had the pessimism that Symmachus and his kind would always recognise, and the success against northern barbarians that his successors could only imagine. Outspoken in praising the superiority of good water pipes over every useless glory of Greek art or Egyptian pyramid, he had no faith that technology would ever get better. His Roman water pipes – and his careful descriptions of their operation – were as good as anything was ever going to get.

In mentioning the early achievements of Spartacus, he was not making any moral point about past or future. He was not placing Spartacus in any context. He was not trying to make the facts in his writing lead on to any other facts. He thought that, just like the arts of clean water, a guide to devious military stratagems would be true and useful. Making ladders from wild vines and dropping them down the cliffsides of Vesuvius was one such trick. It had worked for Spartacus against Gaius Claudius Glaber. Perhaps other outnumbered rebels might try the same scheme. Perhaps some imaginative

Roman general might need to use the same plan on his own account. Anyone who knew as much about stratagems as he, Sextus Julius Frontinus, did was not to be ignored.

Vesuvio, Parco Nazionale del Vesuvio

A decade ago, in the hours when I was in the heaviest unexplained pain, I used sometimes to see battlefields like this one. I was never quite sure why. When a biting, bruising clash of enemies was happening below my ribs, it maybe made a certain sense to imagine other battles of blood and guts. Perhaps the free mind has its own way with a blasted body, its ways to make the time pass by, regularly some nine hours of time between the first sense that my Nero was stirring (the name was a classicist's joke at first) and his retirement from the flattened field.

Only every few months did these horrors come, but once they had begun each time they were inexorable and followed the same absolutely predictable course. Although I would later describe the pains to doctors in lurid but wholly unsuccessful detail, I never mentioned the palliative pictures. It was hard enough to get a medical answer without seeming like a late-night history channel. It took many spectaculars to discover that Nero was a large lump of cancer. During that time the pictures became the most memorable part of the experience. Looking back from this wooden table halfway up Vesuvius, the battle scenes seem certainly the only part worth remembering now.

The subjects then were never ones I deliberately chose. To attempt to reconstruct the ancient suddenness that happened on these volcanic slopes would have been absurd. Any truth about Spartacus' first battle has long lain far beyond the power of recall or reason. The facts are still far beyond even the wildest argument. There is nothing solid surviving of the battle between Glaber and the gladiators, no swords, no wine-flagons, no words.

The pain pictures were a different experience altogether, random, like a roulette ball cast into the wheeling rays of the sun. Scenes from a classical education came unwilled. During some of Nero's visits I had vivid views of this first fight in the Spartacus war, not those of a general watching high up on a nearby hill but those of a soldier seeing what was close before his eyes. It was as though I had been at the centre of this and other slaughters, hour after hour after hour.

This Vesuvius scene was one of the commonest, an assault of iron on the upholstery of my stomach, ribs grasped like ladders, alien objects left behind, broken glass, blunt knives, wave upon wave of pain, slow like an hour then blurred like a second, warfare in its unique and maddest way. After the first hot attack there came shivers and stabbing icicle shards. After the nausea of fear came the thud of the drum and the muffled horn. I might face a baton-wielding field officer. I was suddenly one of 'the wretched wounded', begging to be hit on the jaw by a drunken field-surgeon or any decent man administering the battlefield anaesthetic of his age. The aggression was grotesque. What was it all about? Such violent pain had to have some progression. It had to be saying something. It could not be without some cause or purpose.

As the dust and confusion cleared, a more organised picture show was presented on the surface of my skin. My body pumped up tight, as though with poisoned liquids and gases, the fluid components of pain. Then, on the tight surface of this slowly expanding balloon, as though from some image-projector above, appeared all the peculiarly recognisable scenes, the ladders clinging to the rocks, the climbers, the killers, the escapers, the men who killed themselves to avoid torture by the unknown. I was not hallucinating. These were more like memories than fantasies or dreams. As my stomach seemed to grow, so the pictures on it grew too and spread further apart. Then smaller images became visible, things I could not see before, people beyond the battle site on the mountain, watchers on other slopes, in the skies, in distant cities. Then the balloon subsided, briefly restoring proper proportions before shrinking into a jumbled mess.

There were no ill effects next morning. My mind was often quicker and clearer after the chaos had passed. Poets have often claimed that opium sharpens their thoughts. Perhaps pain too releases its sharpeners into the bloodstream. Perhaps the poetic drive comes not from the drug at all but from the pain which the drug is supposed to dispel? Are drug and disease in that respect the same? These questions and the shows continued until one of my long line of doctors identified both the cancerous cause and the impossibility – after so long – of doing anything to remove it. At that point the days of imagination were over. My days of argument and forensic medicine began, none of that of any relevance now on the Spartacus Road.

The task here of battlefield reconstruction is back with the historians and the poets. It is Statius again who comes closest to the terror of rebels routing sleepers – in his epic *Thebaid*, his description of Polynices' night-time attack on Thebes, a time at first of no sound, no thunder from the sky, no movement, a time, he writes, when the clouds clung together in silence, the breath of the earth stunted the grass and the sleepers' cloaks exhaled cold. Within minutes there is mayhem. 'Blood formed black sodden lawns, tents tottered over bloody streams: *stagnant nigrantia tabo Gramina, sanguineis nutant tentoria rivis*.' Then comes the fire. 'The earth smoked as the breath of sleep rolled into the gasps of death; and not one of those who slumbered lifted up his face: *Fumat humus, somnique et mortis anhelitus una Volvitur; haud quisquam visus aut ora iacentum Erexit.*'

There was no honour of the ancients in this kind of assault. In Statius' account, the god-defying boxer Capaneus thinks a night attack the cheapest stratagem and refuses to take part. The rest of the Seven assaulters of Thebes find their prey stretched out on the ground, as though already run through by swords: '*ceu iam exanimes multoque peracti Ense*'. The attackers stab randomly at backs and chests. They leave the cries of the slaughtered locked and stifled in their helmets: '*galeis inclusa relinquit Murmura*'. A final cloud of darkness falls over those who a few hours before have fallen in drunken sleep on their couches.

In the imagination of the sleepless writer in Domitian's Rome, even the attackers' dead return to watch the show, armed and mounted anew, freed from the earth exactly as in life. Only their horses retain the shadows of the underworld. Here on the still dormant volcano, in the summer of 73 BC, the exalted escapers from Capua occupied Glaber's camp, watched his surviving soldiers scatter and run, rested from their killing, resupplied themselves and, as a tiny new army, marched next in uneven formations towards the richer cities further south.

V

POMPEII to NUCERIA

Porta Marina, Pompeii

Back now in Pompeii, this is a different town, the one to which the tourists come though few have come here yet this morning. There is so far only the darkest daylight in the line of bars that skirt the ruins. Last night's rain is still smashing down on the roads outside, deluging the Spartacus campsite, sliding over the new municipal tarmac, running in rivers along the high kerbstones in the lucrative ancient streets. Old Pompeii was built on a hillside, its thoroughfares designed to become rushing waterfalls when the weather was like it is today. But that is not protection enough for those who seek the sunny side of antiquity.

This is a café that should be packed with perspiring Pompeii-seekers. But there are only five thin, shaven-headed boys fighting in front of a TV and the same number of seated men and women, Romanians, possibly responsible for the children, passing the time next to books that they would normally be selling to tourists outside. The barman looks on benignly. The little fighters, somehow both too young and too old for adult control, shout in too many different accents for them all, or any of them, to be his own family. But he treats them as though they were some part of his responsibility, not speaking harshly but trying to help by example, not taking away their wooden swords and plastic shields, as a parent might, but, in a grandfatherly way, showing how the toy weapons might be more safely held.

His advice is briefly taken and quickly ignored. The old man wants the young to block and parry like duellists, feeling the weight of each other's blows, seeking the cuts that their weapons would make if their edges were sharp. What the children want to do is to poke punches into each other's stomachs.

I still have in my book bag the two brief accounts of ancient gladiatorial combat, the Syrian's and the Spaniard's. The barman urges more of the spirit of Lucian's day out at the stadium, the subtle interplay of flashing blade. The boys want more of Martial's version, a bruising fest of endurance. They are strong and determined. They are playing their own fictional parts. They hit as though they would break each other's jaws. They look sideways occasionally to where we are sitting by the polished glasses, but not expectantly at us, only with

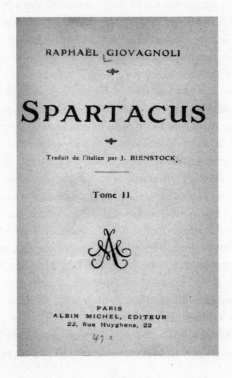

RAPHAËL GIOVAGNOLI

SPARTACUS

Traduit de l'italien par J. BIENSTOCK

Tome II

PARIS
ALBIN MICHEL, ÉDITEUR
22, Rue Huyghens, 22

the fear that their bouts might be ended by a beer-pourer's decree. Maybe this is a regular event. The frustrated souvenir-sellers make no move at all, as though they have nothing to do with the young swordsmen, which may be the truth.

The boys use their shields with as much aggression as their swords, not defending against blows but pushing as though the wood-and-plastic disc were an offensive tool in itself. One of them crouches and springs forward. One is unbalanced, gasps and falls. Two attack the faller on the ground, then stop, with their swords pointing to his neck.

This is the only theatrical moment in this game, the only part that might be recognised in the Syrian school of duelling. None of it, I suppose, would have been alien to the Spartacus school. Swordfighting has long been refined to a mere sporting art. The new swordsman has rules; he has skills like a conjuror; he draws an arm away with his eye; he nips, he cuts, he grazes; he comes from one side while seeming to come from the other. The old swordsman wants to kill as quickly as he can.

Gladiators had to learn the earliest tricks of the theatre. They were in at their creation. The promoter of their shows, the owner of their schools, could make a fight more artful by altering the length and shape of weapons, the size and scope of armour. A man with a curved sword has no choice but to slash like a pantomime pirate. Arming the upper body and leaving the legs bare will encourage spectacular sweeps against the thighs and hamstrings. But a gladiator storming into a camp of somnolent soldiers punches his target with his shield and stabs him with a straight sword in his face, his neck or his heart.

The face gives the greatest reward for anger. Enemy eyeballs crushed into blood are great recompense, the greatest revenge. A punch to the heart, from a sword held straight ahead, from a position slightly crouched, against none of the bones that stand in the way of the slasher or cutter: that is the way of massive rage, of the few against the many, until the many are few and fled or gone, and the victors, like the forces of Spartacus, are picking up their enemies' swords from the ground.

After failing once more to inculcate some chivalry into the fighting boys, the barman retires into his newspaper. It falls to his assistant to throw the brawlers out into the flooded streets, having ascertained that their parents, if any of the adults were indeed their parents, have already resumed their tourism or their trade. The rain is falling even harder now on the roof. It does not even feel like daytime any more. Soon the afternoon will never have happened and the evening will have already begun. The air is like fat cheese. Even one of Italy's eternal football matches would be a relief but the TV screen too is silk-covered, slightly damp and dark.

There are still some neglected books in the bag. Out from the bottom comes a pile of four novels, one of them with the text and title only in Italian, more histories, the Koreans' map of amphitheatre sites. The problem of what happens next on the Spartacus Road is becoming complex. The original sources disagree, the fictional reconstructors even more so.

Another look at the Kirk Douglas movie would be one good idea. At least this would show what I once thought happened next. Perhaps the barman has a copy on his shelf of DVDs. We could all watch how Hollywood gladiators fought in the arena and in battle. Was Frontinus' vine-ropes-down-the-mountain trick included somewhere? It surely must have been, although I cannot recall it right now. It would have been sensible to watch *Spartacus* again before beginning the road: forty years after the flickerings on the chemistry-lab wall it could all come back to life.

The Vesuvius scene must have been the purest Hollywood joy – epic Rome with a touch of Tarzan. I do not recall it. Was it not there? Was it too expensive to put on film? Did the producers not believe Frontinus? Would that have really mattered? Surely no one would have wasted a second on the credibility of the old water-inspector, if they had even heard of him.

Raphael Giovagnoli's blue, hard-backed, two-volumed nineteenth-century novel has a dramatic version of the descent down the sheer rocks and the brief but bloody combat which followed. This is the book whose author was thanked by Garibaldi for sculpting the 'Christ figure of Spartacus with the chisel of Michelangelo', an endorsement which helped both writer and politician achieve huge success.

Arthur Koestler did not succeed so well with his own novel, *The Gladiators*. Kirk Douglas made his movie from an American version instead. The Hungarian polymath never claimed to be much of a novelist. He preferred his opinions to his story. But, judging from his Vesuvius scene, he did enjoy the journey of his flawed heroes down the wild-vine ladders (strengthened by torn linen for fictional verisimilitude). There was the 'evenly distributed moonshine', the butchery which left the killers unsatisfied, the strident yells 'not human, but demons let loose'.

The television screen finally brightens into life. Juventus kick off against Napoli, a match from a season gone by. The day has become evening without much change in the light.

Osservatorio, Parco Vesuvio

There were new arrivals after the gladiators' victory over Gaius Claudius Glaber. There were household and agricultural chattels who had not escaped en masse like the fighters from Capua but had simply slipped away into the woods. The countryside kept alive many from the margins of Roman society, the abandoned, the adventurous, the landless poor, children forgotten by their owners, the hungry, the curious and the desperate.

Most, however, were slaves. There were old men with plain iron collars around their necks, young men in collars marked with the import tax their buyers had unwillingly paid, others wearing metal tags marking their owners' names. Some men – and even a few women – wore letters on their foreheads urging that they be sent home. In Thrace the ink marks of black and blue on a man's skin were an ornament, a chosen way of identification, like the butterfly and swastika tattoos of today. In Italy the stigmata were stamps made upon an object by its owner. Spartacus and his colleagues watched, wondered, welcomed and waited to see how many more would come.

Some men heading towards Vesuvius had no tongues. 'Speaking tool' was the name given to slaves when the farmers were conducting their inventories. But recalcitrant runaways, mutilated for one offence or many, could work on without needing to be able to speak. A silent slave, able only to grunt what he had seen in cellar or bedroom, had much to recommend him.

There were those who had been 'slaves of two masters', slaves part owned and part free, objects of dispute. There were slaves who had been told they might become free and did not believe it, those who had been too often cheated or denied, objects of deceit. And for every slave that joined there were far more who did not. For every one that joined the forces of Spartacus and the gladiators, the not-quite-yet-an-army readying itself to move south, there were countless more who stayed behind.

Quintus Aurelius Symmachus, spitting out his anger at the loss of his Saxons, had, at least, used Spartacus' name. Gaius Cassius Longinus did not.

Cassius had good rea-
sons for his reticence as he
gave what became his
notorious opinion in the
case of the murdered city
prefect. He was a revered
Roman lawyer speaking

publicly in the Senate, not a disappointed pagan-rights campaigner grumbling privately to his brother. He was speaking a mere hundred years or so after the escape from the Capua training camp, not almost five hundred years afterwards as Symmachus had been. A century was not nearly enough to sanitise the name of Spartacus in respectable Roman society. When Gaius Cassius Longinus wanted to give legal advice to his colleagues in the case of so unusually horrific a killing, he preferred the word 'cesspool'.

The incident is part of Tacitus' account of the year AD 61. Nero was Rome's emperor, the last of Julius Caesar's line, a theatrical young man who began his reign benignly and ended it as a murderer driven to suicide, a man who loved the arena as both performer and spectator, one of many failings which lowered his reputation in the eyes of the high-minded. In this same year Nero had his mother murdered in a beach house not far from here; his generals were planning an equally nasty fate for Boadicea in faraway Britain. The murder victim in Cassius' mind, however, was not an imperial parent or rebel queen, more a man like himself, like Tacitus too, a pillar of Roman society.

Pedanius Secundus, holder of the same city prefect title that Symmachus would later prize, wielder of wide powers granted to venerable men for the general welfare, had been killed by one of his four hundred household slaves. This was a rare event for which ancient Roman law dictated a rare reprisal. Every one of the four hundred had to be executed. How could it be otherwise, argued Cassius to his Senate colleagues, in a city which had long ago taken upon itself to have 'whole nations as slaves within its houses, men and women of different faiths and no faith'? What means apart from 'fear' could ensure that slaves who heard of plots against their masters betrayed those plots rather than, through silence, joining them?

The slaves of Rome, as he saw them, were a 'cesspool' which could be controlled only by the ways which had been set down in the past. It did not matter precisely why Pedanius had been killed or whether there had been one of those 'just causes' so dear to disputing Greek philosophers. Perhaps the murderer and his victim had come to blows over an agreement to sell the slave his freedom. Perhaps the City Prefect was demanding sex from a slave boy whom the murderer wanted for himself alone. Neither justification, if justification it be, was relevant in any way. What mattered was the method of preventing mass uprising by the slaves upon whom Rome had come to rely for its very existence.

Not all of Cassius' colleagues in the Senate that day agreed. Some argued for a greater mercy. The slaves of Pedanius' family, like the slaves of their own families, were their cooks and their maids, their children's teachers as well as the cleaners of their latrines, their letter-writers as well as the carriers of their litters, the men who understood their vines, the women who understood their wives, the objects of sexual passions, past and present, temporary and long-standing, experienced in different ways by all the family. Those whom Cassius wanted to condemn to strangulation outside the city walls included not only the young and innocent but the necessary and the expensive, the workers whose skills were often the only investment, apart from land, which a rich Roman ever made. Yet, according to Roman law, as explained by one of Rome's most respected lawyers, all the slaves had to die. This was economically as well as morally a wrong.

If the senators needed any further encouragement to mercy beyond their account books, there was the roar of support for the condemned from the city mob. The crowds of Rome were not always on the side of slaves. Many had lost livelihoods to the foreigners who filled Italy after every Roman conquest. On this occasion the mood beyond the Senate's high bronze doors was unambiguous. Rocks and torches sailed through the air and crashed on the pavement stones, reminders of Republican times.

The elders in their pressed white togas were not required to take any notice of the noise outside. Under the rule of Caesar's heirs the Emperor's judgement outweighed all others. But a mob was still a mob. It still meant danger. Any show of noisy opinion was also a reminder to the senators of how objectionable were the common people and how very useful were the slaves who accompanied them whenever they had to leave their homes. Well-trained attendants were the buffer between any great man and the ubiquitous mass of the urban poor, protecting his carriage, passing up the occasional note from a petitioner, pushing away many more, simultaneously connecting and separating.

The concept of the 'household', more than any concrete, brick or marble, was the building-block of Rome. The household, by law and custom, included its slaves as much as it included any other part. When homes were small, a master, his wife and a few human chattels at most, there was maybe some crude purpose in the rule that Cassius now invoked. But in Nero's Rome it made no sense, ran the argument both inside and outside the Senate. How did it deter another Spartacus to strangle those pretty little *pedisequae* who attended the wife of Pedanius when she visited the theatre? What a waste of the fortune it had cost to train that accountant!

Mercy towards the innocent was the smallest part of the argument for sparing the slaves of Pedanius. Although land investments made the debaters respectable and rich, their investments in human capital made them much the richer. A slave who understood book-keeping or banking was a multiple advantage to his owner: he did the owner's work, he saved the owner from too much of the taint of that work (a gentleman should avoid trade) and he could not set up in competition with the owner. There was no point in training a free man to be quick with figures; he might take your investment and use it to help himself or someone else. A slave was much safer. That was why the system worked, and had, for everyone's sake, to be kept working.

Inside the Senate in AD 61 Cassius prevailed over his critics. He pointed out that the 'exemplary principle' applied to their fellow Romans as well as to the 'cesspool' of foreigners. When even a magnificent legion was disgraced in defeat, every tenth man was executed, bludgeoned by his own comrades. Were the brave and the faultless then spared? No. Every great 'example' had its innocent victims, but the individual harm was repaid by the public good.

Individually these slaves were the people whom the family of Pedanius Secundus trusted most; collectively they and their fellows were the group that the state most feared. So collectively they had to go the place of execution. Cassius criticised himself for having been too tolerant when past decrees had been proposed 'in place of the laws of our ancestors'. He had done so because he wanted to keep his authority intact for when it was truly needed. This was 'that time'.

Outside in the Forum, it needed an edict from Nero to stem the unrest. The soldiers from the city garrison, like Glaber's before, were not the finest in the Empire. But they were fierce enough, lined in sufficient quantity along the execution route, to ensure that the traditional verdict would be taken to its end.

The scene must have resembled some grisly house sale after bailiffs have swept through the rooms. No one in the crowd could have known exactly the value of each slave, their place in the Pedanius family, their role, if any, in the master's murder. From the colour of their faces the children skilled in grafting fruit-trees might be distinguished from those who carried the silver cups from bedroom to bedroom. The careful blonde *pedisequa* or burly disperser of crowds might walk with greater confidence outdoors than did the kitchen staff. The trusty barber might look lost without the knives of his trade.

To modern eyes the whole long line would have seemed a youthful group: a thirty-year-old man or woman, slave or free, was entering the old age of ancient Rome. That was another good reason for keeping talent alive: enough investment was failing and dying without this. There were those in the line who would soon have regained their freedom, men and women who had kept profits from their business activities on behalf of their master and had agreed a price. There were those, like the killer, it was said, who believed that they should already be free. Informal contracts between owner and slave were a source of constant misunderstandings and deceits. Some of the condemned column, identifiable by crippled shoulders and useless legs, seemed to have been questioned about the crime. Others, no less stumbling, were survivors of previous interrogations upon lesser matters.

Some murmured Greek words and words from other parts of the Empire that few onlookers understood. Populations of whole cities, if not quite whole nations as Cassius had claimed, were now Rome's slaves. There were Gauls in the gardens and farms, Persians by the dining couches, Thracians, Africans and Spaniards in flooded mines and choking factories which a civilised Roman preferred not to think about too much. Some may have been teachers of Greek, or even teachers of the Greek philosophers that Gaius Cassius so despised. In the most sophisticated households a course of lessons that began with schoolroom debates (is there ever a just cause for a son to kill his father or a maid her mistress?) could end with no less subversive thoughts on whether it was rational to have a public life or to fear death, or to fear only premature death, or only the pain of dying. The Emperor Nero loved all things Greek.

Left behind in Pedanius' household were only slaves who had already been freed. Another Senator had argued that they too should be removed, not executed but deported from Italy. Nero had countermanded this proposal, as Tacitus tells us at the end of his account, 'lest ancient custom, which pity had not relaxed, should turn into cruelty'.

Traversa Mercato, Ercolano

This is Ercolano's business district, the new investment zone of the second city which Vesuvius destroyed in AD 79. The hustling businessmen of old Pompeii had the hot rocks and ash. The wealthy holidaymakers of old Herculaneum got the

superheated steam and mud. Both events are celebrated now in an electronic version in this market square.

There are few foreign tourists here at virtual Herculaneum in the late-

morning sunshine. There were only a few more Leica-bearers and waterbottle-carriers a quarter of a mile away, clicking and gurgling through the original ancient shops. Ercolano has long been the also-ran of the race to volcanic fame. Technology has made little difference. It is a municipal election season. A melon-man with a loudhailer is selling fruit with a passion that makes sense only if he is also buying votes. And, in this least promising part of the Spartacus Road, where the European Union is the benefactor, the relics of saints the true reality and the ancient ruins more profitable in holograms and on screens, there is my first sight of a Spartacus as he was drawn in his own lifetime.

The picture sits on a table in the first hall of gadgetry. Tourists are about to be invited to see Ercolano as it used to be, to put their feet in the fish ponds and hear the splash of the water, to wander though the rooms of rich men's houses, to cower before the fires of Vesuvius, to thrill to the opportunities of digital power. This Spartacus is, by contrast, the simplest of images, mere reddish ink on paper, two gladiators fighting each other from horseback to the musical accompaniment of a masked trumpeter. The names of both men are written backwards; this was the local style, only slowly replaced by Latin order here. The first is FEL POMP, Felix the Pompeian, the lucky man from Pompeii. The second reads SPARTAKS. The caption on the printed page claims that the lettering and the language suggest a date just before 70 BC.

Nothing in my tour of Pompeii was as useful as this, certainly not the Frontinus night in the bar or the next morning of swordsmanship for boys. The lashing rain had left the guides amazed that any tourist, even an English one, would be mad enough to walk their streets. The gladiators' quarters, where skeletons, chains and helmets were once found? Closed. The amphitheatre? Open. It provided a little shelter from the pounding storm. But nothing like that in Pompeii was ever used for anything except the gentler spectaculars, pantomimes and poetry improvisations. So said my self-appointed companion, the friend of the boy whose job was to protect parked cars.

The vineyards? Those were much more interesting. Look, I could see how the stakes were placed by the roots – and how the volcanic preservatives from the mountain saved the secrets of Pompeii's gardeners. The ancients grew their plants much closer together than we do now and here was the concrete proof. Time, surely, now for everyone to take shelter and try some of the produce. There was wine from these vines on sale, made in the ancient way and sold at imperial prices. And there was good wine too.

Ercolano has been a better experience – not just for the sense of things preserved closer to their ancient life here (there are ropes and fabrics and wooden beams among the ruins) but because I had missed SPARTAKS till now. The fresco cartoon is itself Pompeian. It was found in the doorway of a house identified by archaeologists there as that of a priest, Sacerdos Amandus. But it has its due prominence today in the library of the Herculaneum Experience, a temporary promotion in this place where the earth moves every day, whenever a new visitor arrives.

Precise dating is difficult. But the words and pictures of SPARTAKS and FEL POMP are agreed to be some of the earliest from either town. No one knows who the picture's original owner was, but the idea of a prosperous householder in the mid-70s BC with a collection of 'big fight' memorabilia has a certain appeal. The picture may not refer directly to the Spartacus who escaped from Capua. Spartacus could have been a stage name of many gladiators, the living nominees daily replacing the dead. Yet from now onwards it is at least an image upon which to hang the story. It is only the roughest outline, a piece of graffiti flattered by the designation 'fresco'. It has lines of the human form and a name but does not exclude many possibilities of the truth. As in a children's book, the spaces for head, helmet, reins and shield can be tentatively, or maybe boldly, coloured in.

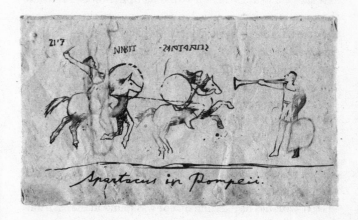

Spartacus in Pompeii.

After defeating Glaber, what did Spartacus do next? That is a harder question than the one asked by the Koreans at Capua. Somewhere around here in 73 BC, the victor of Vesuvius must have stood much emboldened after the Roman retreat. There was not just his success in arms but the growing numbers who began to join the gladiator force. The escapers could suddenly imagine the anger that would be felt in Rome, imagine it with pleasure before they had to imagine it in fear. But what then? The government of Rome did not take humiliation well. New legions would rapidly return.

Before winning the luxury of escape routes from Italy by land or by sea – or making any other choices – they had to win new victories in the place where they stood now. Military preparation was the priority. Military preparation was what a gladiator corps with new recruits was most able to do. Gladiators were well trained themselves. The men whom the Romans had once taught to fight – in their armies, their amphitheatres, on horseback or on foot – now taught fellow slaves, whose skills were in the kitchen or cattle pen, to fight against Romans too.

Exactly how and where and what did they fight? Even on this sunny day in Ercolano, with the inspiration of an ancient outline and the perpetual palest-blue view over the rooftops to the sea, the task of finding out is not a pleasant one. The evidence is confused. Assessing it requires patience better deployed in a library than in a market square – even a place so expensively and electronically equipped by so beautiful a bay.

Via Mare, Ercolano

In suburban Essex in 1962, a tweed-jacketed primary school teacher, known to us only as Mr Cook, decided that an eleven-year-old boy setting off for competitive examinations elsewhere should know a little local history. He had looked out from the low school gates, around the Great Baddow streets of boxes where the children of the radar-designers lived, and failed to find very much to his taste. He himself bicycled to Rothmans School each day from rural Danbury, several miles away, a village which owed its name and greater respectability to King Canute and his Danes.

The one man of Baddow whom Mr Cook deemed a model for an educable schoolboy was a writer called Alexander Barclay, a sixteenth-century priest, poet and vicar of the village church. Barclay, whose books included a satire in verse, *The Ship of Fools*, and translations from the Roman historian Sallust, had been awarded the Baddow vicarage during the short, extremist Protestant reign of Henry VIII's son, Edward VI, a success for a former Benedictine monk which, in Mr Cook's view, showed exemplary flexibility. Barclay's satire had been sharp, unusually pointed for its time, and directed precisely against corrupt courts, fake intellectuals, romantic dreamers and other undesirables who flourish in every age. His translations had 'improved the English language', a task to which any of Mr Cook's more literate pupils might cautiously aspire. There was certainly no better Baddow man with whom an ambitious examinee from the Rothmans Estate might usefully display acquaintance.

I took his advice, not to any obsessive extent (*The Ship of Fools* is still little more to me than a name) but sufficiently to be able to write, here in Ercolano, that Sallust, historian of the Roman Republic's greatest wars, was the first Latin author that I knew any little thing about at all. After the retirement of Mr Cook, as I later learnt, the school began a slide into a more progressive era. It changed its name, to Larkrise, after Rothmans was deemed to have unacceptable associations with cigarettes. The Duke of Edinburgh had paid a nearby visit and made some smoking-behind-the-bike-sheds joke which upset the headmistress. Vicar Barclay would have been grateful for the comic possibilities of that – and I am grateful to him for my first encounter with the writer I have been reading here over the past few hours.

Sallust was a man who could have given the very best directions on the Spartacus Road. He lived at the same time as the events he describes and was not wholly hostile to Spartacus. Sallust was thirteen when Glaber's men were routed at the foot of Mount Vesuvius. He was in his forties when he retired to his luxurious library and gardens in Rome. As a politician, he supported Julius Caesar and hated Pompey. His successes and failures, glories and disgrace, all happened in the shadow of the Spartacus rebellion. His retirement to record the history of his age was at just the right time for some perspective on it all. He had a short, sharp way with words, a host of enemies on which to deploy these weapons and a brain that, unlike many of his kind, was not soaked solely in moral precepts. He ought to be the finest source for learning how Spartacus created his army and what he did with it next among the richest towns of southern Italy.

A manuscript of Sallust's account survived for centuries in a French monastery and is now split between libraries in the Vatican, Orleans and Berlin. Some of it was saved, like so much classical learning, because its reverse side was used for commenting on parts of the Bible, in this case the thoughts of the acerbic St Jerome on the book of Isaiah. Once this was noticed at the end of the nineteenth century, the texts were subjected to some of the finest minds of the age, and every part compared and cross-referenced with quotations made by other writers and editors, those, like Symmachus in the last years of the Roman Empire, who had Sallust's full text in their libraries.

The result is a quilt of tiny patches. Symmachus' own speeches survived much better from this same process of chance, rescued in 1815 from the Latin translation of the 'Canons of Chalcedon', re-emerging from injunctions of the early Church against theft from dead bishops and appointments of deaconesses under forty. Sallust's account of Spartacus survived in shreds through the wielding of an unknown bookbinder's knife. All that we have are a few powerful paragraphs and an intermittent stream of passing facts.

Here on this pitted table of Herculaneum rock, alongside canine excrement and broken glass, are the photocopied pages, fresh from the book bag, of what happened when two new Roman praetors, Varinius and Cossinius, were sent to clear up the mess left by the first: 'they had lit fires to frighten the soldiers of Varinius into flight. . . . a journey . . . to turn aside from . . . but Varinius, noticing in the daylight the absence of abuse . . .'.

Write each fragment on a piece of card. There is soon a small pack: sick and deserting Roman soldiers, corpses propped up on the walls of the gladiators' camp, Varinius terrified of ambush, Varinius rashly leading his new and inexperienced soldiers. Dissent seems to be growing in the slave army's leadership, with Crixus and his Gauls and Germans wanting to fight while Spartacus remains more cautious. There are notes of rage and rape, assaults on married women and young girls which Spartacus cannot stop.

Sit in a library and there are various versions of how these words – with others from other chance places – might stick together to make a narrative. Sallust had strong views and the prose style to tell a good story. Like every Roman historian, he wrote to make a point, about the failings of Rome, their most reprehensible causes and characters. He also had a cold honesty which comes through even the most 'lacunose' pages.

Lacunose? Full of holes. A miserable-sounding word for a miserable state of affairs if you are trying to read a history as it was never meant to be read – in tiny pieces.

Many of Sallust's characters were very like himself. His first book, which has survived with barely a lacuna at all, was a tirade against political corruption during Rome's war against King Jugurtha of Numidia. From that came his most famous phrase for later quotation dictionaries, put into Jugurtha's mouth, that Rome was 'a city for sale and would perish if it could only find a buyer: *urbem venalem et mature perituram, si emptorem invenerit*'. Sallust's own notorious and massive wealth came from Numidia too, a province which he had governed on behalf of Julius Caesar. He was a preacher of morality possessing all the power of the reformed sinner.

In his later years he sat in one of Rome's finest private homes, a retreat built from the proceeds of extortion and corruption by a man whose retirement message was how extortion and corruption had sapped the Roman character. Self-knowledge was not his greatest strength. But applying modern objections to hypocrisy would not leave many ancients standing.

Philosophical consistency was not his strength either. Sallust saw slavish greed and barbarian avarice everywhere, in civilised Romans and uncivilised foreigners. Were greed and corruption then the natural states of man? He seems to suggest so. Yet his fellow Romans had once been honest men and true before the foreign flood of slaves and money. So were they somehow born different, a chosen race before the rot set in?

His answer was that public virtue in Rome, by public discipline, had become more highly concentrated than in Asia and Africa. Romans had made themselves special. They had their land, their religion, their piety: the combination was absolutely special. But if that was Rome's glory it was not a glory that made Rome more secure. Corruption could always come from sudden changes in culture, sudden opportunities and interactions. Not even Rome was immune. As the Vicar of Great Baddow would later translate, 'A noble and famous cytie' might easily be 'corrupt and accloyed with infect cytesyns'. Its very success endangered it most. Pernicious individuality and restlessness for change were forever and everywhere threats to hard-won public virtues.

Sallust enjoyed his anxiety and arguments but, most of all, the historian wanted to tell his tales. Grumpy rich ex-politicians, turning to history in their later years, have a long-proven record of rhetoric over reason and conviction over consistency. Yet Sallust was a good source on what he knew. Later writers recognised that. Domitian's palace tutor, Quintilian, a subtle judge, quotes him constantly, much more than he uses Livy's moral guidance.

The idea that Sallust's history of the events here in 73 BC might be read later only in fragments would not have pleased its author. Broken words on pieces of card would have been a rejection of everything he stood for. Modern writers on warfare have grown used to the notion that the closer the stance to the action the less clear the truth of the whole; that the individual soldier, and often the individual general, has little idea from his place in the lines whether the battle is being won or lost; that the best the participants can hope for is a few facts passing by like cloud. The author of these frag-ments would not have recognised such doubts.

Sallust belonged to an age where big men were confident of what they did and what they saw. A survival in some five hundred shards – scattered observation and severed sentences – is what he would have wanted least. He was a big beast, a politician whom a Frontinus or a Symmachus would have recognised as an equal. He was no mere artist like Statius – although he wrote his own romances on Trojans and Amazons. He was no hack like Florus – for all that he had some fine headline-writer's skills. He was not cowed as so many later writers were. He was no genius, not the Roman Thucydides, not the scientific and analytical master of history that his later admirers wanted him to have been. But he had a real sense of what a Roman Thucydides would have needed to be. If anyone were to find the complete text of his *Histories*, a clear narrative of this part of Rome's slave wars would surely be there.

A peculiar frustration on this stop on the Spartacus Road is that, if such a text were ever to be found, this is also one of the most likely places. Beneath the earth in this section of Herculaneum, beyond the perimeter of the tourist site, lies the immense villa once owned by Julius Caesar's father-in-law, the infamously yellow-toothed and sallow-skinned bohemian Lucius Calpurnius Piso. Fifteen years before the defeat on Vesuvius, Piso had planned a peculiarly ruthless campaign against a friendly tribe in Thrace, one of many attacks that brought gladiators to Rome. When the mountain erupted in AD 79 and buried this town in its mud, it buried his library, his military history, his collections of musical theories, poetry and plays – and those added by his heirs. When these rooms with pigeonholes for scrolls were entered again by tunnel 1,800 years later, hundreds of works were recovered, hundreds more destroyed and thousands left behind.

The villa once contained a substantial sculpture collection too, with one of the liveliest busts of Homer, old and blind, with his ear cocked as though listening to divine instructions or the latest teller of a war story. Among the marbles and bronzes were also busts of philosophers, Epicurus and his successors, men of self-contained calm who had nothing to do with war or politics, who denied that the gods had anything to do with humanity, whose mantra was that, if gods existed, they had nothing to do with us, did not care about us, and we should not care about them. To think otherwise, ran the message from these portraits, was the way of avoidable madness and misery.

Most of the written works found beneath this soil were by Epicureans too, detailed formulae for banishing the fear of death, arguments that so influenced the upper echelons of the amphitheatre audience in these pleasure towns. The writer with most words in the library of the Villa dei Papiri was Philodemus of Gadara, a friend and client of Piso who probably taught Horace too. This Syrian disciple of Epicurus

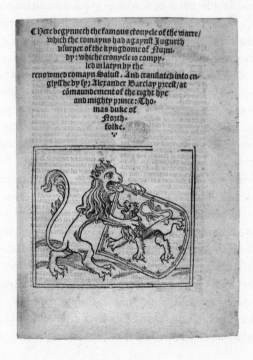

argued not only the logical case for despising death but the psychological case too. He wrote a book called *On Death* and selected from his master's metaphors well. All humanity lived in 'an unwalled city'. There was no defence against mortality. Romans could defend themselves against many attacks, more successfully than any predecessors anywhere. But there was no wall against the obliteration of a body and mind.

He wrote on other subjects which scholars have reconstructed from the first discoveries at this palatial seaside villa. Much effort has been devoted to explaining his charred thoughts on sound and meaning in language, most of it proving Philodemus's mediocrity more than his magic. But there might yet be much more still in this library, if it were to be excavated fully from above – with appropriate compensation, of course, to the tomato-growers and dog-breeders, the carnation-sellers and car-washers, the fortunate apartment dwellers who enjoy the view enjoyed once by Caesar and Horace.

There could be the lost Spartacus books of Livy, of Sallust, of Caecilius from Calacte, whose history of slave wars was known in antiquity but is not known even in fragments to us. There could be lost history plays by Naevius about the myth of Rome's foundation; or tragi-comedies by Andronicus, a Greek who took the Roman name Livius and wrote so many of the city's dramatic spectacles, not ones respectable enough to survive, in which riotous sex and nudity were forever at the service of carefully selected plots.

There might be unknown works by Nero's 'arbiter of taste', Petronius, who set near here his *Trimalchio's Feast*, a literary masterpiece of exotic sexuality, cookery and cemetery architecture. This is a place of many philosophies, many philosophers and much teaching. Petronius wrote that it was human fear which created the gods: '*Primos in orbe deos fecit timor.*' Statius of Naples borrowed the same line and gave it to his giant boxer of the *Thebaid*, Capaneus. Giambattista Vico of Naples, summarising human knowledge 1,700 years later, borrowed it again. In the pigeonholes of the Villa dei Papiri there could be thousands of clues to lost corners of antiquity, from stratagems for invading Thrace to the prettiest pantomimes of subversion.

There might even be more Statius. The poet of Naples was thirty-four years old when 'Vesuvius rolled out its fires'. Sixteen years on, back home beneath the 'broken anger' of the mountain, he pondered whether future generations would ever believe that whole cities, an ancestral landscape, lay dead beneath its recovered fields. He was expressing, with all the particular power of this place, that most common fear of those obsessed by decline and fall, the fear of being obliterated even in others' minds.

In the library there could be more examples of the poetry that, in Statius' case, albeit from only two tattered manuscripts, disproved his prophetic gloom. There could be unknown early works by the writer who pioneered our most spectacular poetry of doomsday and the designer swimming pool. Or, as opponents of the excavation counter, there could be just more music criticism from Philodemus.

Archaeologists will not know unless they are allowed to look. The case for delay is that the techniques needed for safely reclaiming and reading the fragile rolls improve every year. The case for excavating soon is that Vesuvius is set to erupt again and that, while the businesses above may be insured against their losses, the unclaimed library of Piso would be lost without any hope of recompense.

In the meantime, to look at Sallust's *Histories* here is like sitting an impossible examination when the answers are locked away on the other side of a small door. Or it is like recreating the likeness of an ancient rebel from a few chestnut-red chalked lines, of a philosopher from a word or two and some pieces of marble, of a faceless general whose whole statue is undamaged behind a screen. It is an irritant, a peculiarly persistent one.

Piazza Guerritore, Nocera Inferiore

After defeating Glaber, the free slaves struck two nearby towns, robbed, raped, burnt and moved on again. The citizens of Nola were the first to face the new enemy. They were army veterans. Their houses and gardens were their prize for fighting. They had fortifications and the knowledge of how to use them. None of that kept Nola's narrow streets from the rage of the slaves who took their first tastes of freedom and power in a place of plenty.

For the victims this was a shock beyond anything they had imagined before. They knew of their own violent exploits. They had heard the tales of Homer. They understood the epic savagery of human seas that hammered and bludgeoned in huge waves. But the defeat of freemen by slaves was no part of any epic story or any experience in their lives. This was the unthought, the unthinkable. The survivors of civil war who had settled in Nola had plundered and pillaged cities themselves, as their commanders had ordered. But this was destruction without precedent or order, with no time for anyone to wonder, if even they could, whether mass destruction always looked like this to the objects of hungry, angry, thirsty men determined to rape and kill.

Their daughters and wives were stamped on and stabbed like the Trojan women of the poems that everyone best knew. That is how the Greeks and Romans saw their wars, how they connected their present with their past, how they made sense of life and death. In Nola every horror was here and gone in a few hours. Those that the slaves could not rape themselves they raped with spears and spikes, leaving body parts for the dogs of the streets. Only a few women were stolen away to new slave lives as the Greeks stole the women of Troy. The men from Capua and Vesuvius were not yet organised enough for that. Their leaders were not yet generals of an army. They did not yet take slaves of their own.

Had Spartacus and his colleagues commanded the carnage, compelled it, taken part in it, tried to stop it or, as is common enough, held all these positions at different times? Nothing was clear. The only true clarity was the result, a terror beyond the terrors of which anyone and everyone knew.

Here and in the coming months began the myth of Spartacus and a peculiar kind of fear. Slave wars brought the horrors of which Homer had written but from a different place, from their own homes. Family slaves might suddenly not only look like rootless foreigners but act like them, viciously, vainly, with an anarchic sense of their independent worth. There was exaggeration of these fears. There was denial. There were questions. How different was a Gaul from a Roman? How different was a slave? Did anything new need to be done beyond defeating and punishing the insurgents with all possible speed?

Hundreds of thousands of Gauls were slaves in Italy. Most had arrived in the past decade. Some had been free men and women at home. Some had not. All Gauls were notorious for nasty practices. Nailing their enemies' heads to doorways was one of them, a delight that was beloved, it seems, both by the savages themselves and by those, like Florus, who made their living by writing about them. Gauls wore the tightest trousers and carried the longest swords, aliens to be feared in every way. What did such things mean? Backwardness? Stunted development? Development in different directions?

Subtler men than Florus, historians of the time like Pompey's friend Posidonius, came to see the moral and cultural significance of customs such as the nailing of heads. Posidonius, a tutor to Cicero, had been born in the same Syrian town as Eunus, the leader of the first Sicilian slave war. He had travelled to Gaul, spoken to Gauls and tried to understand what they did and why. He is only a minor character on this road but the first whose surviving portrait in stone catches something of his mind. His bust in the Naples museum is a copy of an original carved in the years of the Spartacus war, a sorrowful image of a thinker, his head twisted to one side, his eyes deep set and his mouth in an eternal act of admonition. He seems to have been a most unusual man of his time, believing in the equality of fellow human beings, attacking cruelty to provincials and slaves, arguing that Romans should live up in public to their private ideals of austerity. But pioneers of difficulty are easily forgotten. Unlike Florus' horror comics, Posidonius' work has survived in only a few scraps.

Most Romans never quite understood why Gauls and Thracians might be different, and never wanted to. When slaves revolted it was as though some ordinary stuff of life,

bread, flower, olive oil, were suddenly discovered to be, in certain fixed but unknown proportions, the most inflammatory explosive. Later slave-owners transported their possessions from Africa to the West Indies, from one faraway place to another. The Romans brought their slaves home. In every house was the common kindling of the hottest forest fire.

The achievement of overwhelming Nola was terrifying to all around who heard of it. Ancient cities would normally fall to a siege when one political party inside the walls did a deal with those outside. There was no slave party in Nola. There was no slave party anywhere, certainly none here in neighbouring Nuceria, now a place of pink houses and erotic fountains, then the leading ally of Rome south of Vesuvius, a tempting target which suffered in the same devastating way.

By the time that the second Roman force arrived to succeed where Glaber had failed, the slaves were more formidable still. They were better armed, with looted iron weapons and fire-hardened spear-tips. They were more numerous. The broad farms and pastures south of Nuceria, towards the bitter lakes of Volcei and the rich villas of Vittimose, were recruiting fields for an army that could now both threaten and inspire.

Cossinius discovered for himself the new threat to the established order. Feeling sufficiently relaxed to take a bath in a spring, he was forced into ignominious retreat when some of Spartacus' men swept down in his direction. The praetor escaped with his life, if not his dignity, intact – though not for long. His death was the first senior casualty of the rebellion. His camp was captured. His supplies were lost to the slaves. His legate Furius, whose leadership skills seem to have been stronger in the courtroom than on the battlefield, led his force of 2,000 men to an even greater defeat. There were defections to the slaves from those who survived, a devastating disciplinary failure for the Romans. A junior legate, Toranius, had the unenviable job of travelling back up the Via Appia to explain to the Senate what had been going on.

Varinius , the surviving praetor, still had 4,000 legionaries, some of them feverish from the cold of fighting at the end of the season, many of them the unenthusiastic survivors of the earlier debacles. He fought on none the less. That was his task. He was a man who played by the rule book. The message that he gave to Toranius is lost.

He then chose a camp site near to the slaves' own encampment, curbing their freedom to hunt for food. He built walls, a moat and protective towers in the approved way which Glaber had so disastrously abandoned. Spartacus countered with a night-time escape. He impaled corpses on stakes outside his gates and dressed them as sentries. He lit campfires as though for an evening of watchful eating. He set heads of the dead as guards above his palisades. His army retreated and regrouped a few miles away, where they could forage for supplies without immediate threat of attack.

In guerrilla warfare the slaves had a better chance for longer. That was why Frontinus wrote his *Stratagems* with a star role for the staking up of dead bodies to look like watchmen. Book One: section V: On Escapes from Difficult Places. The slaves seemed to the Romans as devious as Odysseus and the Greeks at Troy, slipping off the beaches at night in order to come back later with deadly force. Which side was the besieger and which the besieged? Probably, neither had so fixed a position. It was watch and wait for both. When Varinius noticed that he was facing an empty enemy camp, with none of the usual dawn chorus of rock throwing and abuse, he sent cavalry to the nearest high hill to see where his enemy had gone. Fear of ambush brought the riders back. Thus the dance went on.

Varinius sought reinforcements on the coast at Cumae, just south of Vesuvius. He must have realised by now, and hoped that the Senate did, that he needed much bigger forces to be sure of success in these strange times. With his new legionaries, still far from the best men that Rome could offer, he grew more confident. There were still more hit-and-run successes for the slaves. When the decisive encounter with Varinius came it was a devastating defeat for Rome. The conflict began to have an impact even on towns that escaped the slave army. Farmers left behind the autumn wheat that was ripe in their fields and headed for the hills, the beginning of a life-before-food policy that was another risk to the safety of the Republic.

It was now possible, indeed unavoidable, to speak of a 'victory' by the sometime Thracian gladiator. He may have been in dispute with his original colleagues, with Oenomaus whose name disappears from the story and with Crixus who would play a much bigger part in it. But Spartacus had a collection now of fasces, the symbolic bundled axe and rods which accompanied a Roman magistrate wherever he went. Varinius' lictors, who carried these fasces on their shoulders, were Spartacus' prisoners. The instruments of punishment and execution by which Romans defined their power were with rebel slaves. So was the general's horse.

Florus, as usual, gives the headlines and the outlines. The Greek biographer Plutarch adds details of his own. If there remained more at this point than some bookbinder's fragments of Sallust's *Histories*, there might be more of what Toranius was told to tell the Senate. What Varinius wrote for him will have been a careful selection of relevant facts that would best protect the writer's back from the knives of Rome. What Sallust wrote was his own selection from that, designed to show the dire morale of the legions when generals took more care for their own futures than for the city's.

What readers have now is a vivid reminder not to trust any account too much.

The terror campaign grew fiercer before the final battle against Varinius. Spartacus led a vicious recruiting expedition southwards to Forum Annii, a bid for support which, for the women and girls who came their way, became a repetition of the rape of Nola. Lacerated bodies lay dying slowly in the streets. Local slaves joined the rebellion and gave up their masters and mistresses, the family treasure, whatever they could bring; in Sallust's words, there was nothing, no matter its moral or religious meaning, which was inviolate 'to the enraged, enslaved minds of the foreigners'.

Individually and in small groups, slaves from the fields and towns of Campania swelled the triumphing forces. The need to discipline the newcomers even to the level of the first arrivals was immense. There were more disagreements about tactics. Early problems of food supply were solved from the stores of the ravaged towns. Early problems of organisation were not. Sallust tells us that Spartacus himself tried to stop the mutilation and abuse. He begged his men repeatedly to recruit rather than avenge. They should speed up the process of levying new forces and stop the sex and slaughter. He was 'wholly powerless' to make a difference.

There are surviving fragments of Sallust's *Histories* which have no certain place in the narrative, which could apply to countless battles against Spartacus in which Roman soldiers faced their deaths. There are moments in any war which little change, hour to hour, day to day, millennium to millennium. The statement that 'each man recalled the one most dear to him . . . the final duties of a soldier' is one of these flexible lines of words which fits all the many places that textual critics have put it. But the idea of its original home being in the fears of the army of Varinius before the last battle of 73 BC is an especially attractive one here, a moment on the Spartacus Road when we are aware of facts we have long lost and can recall others recalling what they too were soon about to lose.

The final duties of a soldier? He might write his will, sign over his goods to his wife or children or comrades, arrange the witnessing of his will, or all of these. There were many spectacular deaths in ancient warfare, lauded and recorded, but many that happened hidden under airless heaps of other corpses. If no one sees a man's death or notices how he dies, his written will becomes the last testament to his character.

VI

EGNAZIA to BOTROMAGNO

Via Traiana, Egnazia

After their victory, the army that had begun as seventy escaped gladiators and had now defeated four Roman commanders went south for the winter. Without the immediate threat of reprisal, the Thracians, Germans and Gauls, with camp-followers now and animals, a total fighting force of perhaps 40,000, could consider what they had won so far and what they might aim to win.

Egnathia was a town at the beginning of a long arc of south-eastern ports from which boats could be bought, hired or hijacked for Greece. It was the last stop on the road to Brundisium, the most tempting target for a Thracian slave-leader whose ambition was to get home. Some of Egnathia's merchants and manufacturers spoke the Messapic languages from Troy and Thrace. Their words are known from inscriptions written in characters that are like Greek but are not Greek. Their pottery is still found for miles around, shaped simply, painted solid black, with tiny yellow and purple birds, white eyes, white impressions of looms and feathers.

Today Egnathia is a dead city by the sea, so close to the sea and so low beside the sea that it seems extraordinary that any of it has survived, a brushland of limestone and marble, with stunted columns spread over field after field. There is an amphitheatre, for actors not gladiators, shaped like a small pear. There are shopping arcades, streets and theatres stretching along more than a mile of dunes that would otherwise be bunkers for the golfers of Brindisi. Some of the old homes are small, square rock-pools now, with niches in the walls where lobsters live like forgotten gods and tiny fish swim in and out like parlourmaids. Egnathia has stood with its windows open to the Adriatic for 2,500 years, defying its frailty. Today even the clouds look more permanent than the stones, great piles of superimposed black on white, stamp-albums in the sky.

The road from Capua arrives here like the bed of a dried river. The limestone blocks of the imperial age, the ones that Statius or Frontinus would have seen, lie on top of a layer of earlier stones from the age of Spartacus and Horace, and beaten mudtracks from centuries before that. The Via Trajana runs directly above the Via Minucia that the slave army followed, above earlier paths with names long lost, square-cut stones above ancient sediment, with the current surface strewn with rocks from later antiquity when the travelling stopped and Egnathia was buried by shingle and sand. There was no single dramatic action of the earth here, merely tides and floods, no volcano, merely the abandonment that Symmachus feared when the north of Europe came to dominate the south.

This town of the mysterious Messapics has been an exotic antiquity for most of its life. It became a Greek city and then a Roman one. Like Capua it suffered by backing Hannibal, the wrong enemy of Rome at the wrong time. Horace came here on his Journey to Brundisium: the poem that began in Ariccia and Foro Appio ended a few miles further to the south. His last flurry of the trip is to mock the Jewish magicians of Egnathia who make incense burst spontaneously into flame and bewitch the unwary with their powers. Horace has no problem with other peoples' religions. There could be any number of foreign gods. Probably there are. But they have nothing to do with him, his welfare, his future, or with the foreigners either.

That was what Epicurus taught, and Philodemus on the slopes of Vesuvius too. The fundamental obstacle to man's happiness was his fear of anything like Hercules, Diana or fire spirits. It was proper to fear pain, including the pain of dying. But any last pains were hardly important and had to be separated absolutely from irrational fears or ridiculous hopes of life after death. In that way all pain could be better borne. Students could grasp this vital truth by emulating their master's life and studying all his works. The nonsense of a divinity with the time and inclination to entertain tourists was one of the clearer nonsenses – easy even for a semi-detached Epicurean like Horace to expose.

A staring head of one of Egnathia's eastern deities was found here at the point where the main road meets the main town square. He is Attis the castrated boy, blank as a drug addict, stern as a dominatrix, with hair in ringlets under a pointed cap, an object of much devotion in Thrace, in Troy, in all the lands between the Mediterranean and the Black Sea. Next to him was his altar, carved with flutes and tambourines, and the offerings of the priestess Flavia, devotee of the Magna Mater, great goddess from the hinterland of Troy.

It is an oppressive afternoon in the almost empty town. The sky squats like a crushing metal bowl, oiled to an iridescent sheen, fringed with frayed wisps of ribbon. There are

dozens of magpies, as still as in a taxidermy museum, enough for a prophets' convention. Two for mirth, three for a death, four for a birth, six for hell, seven for a secret, as children used to sing. Only three pairs of tourists are peering down into the sea pools and subterranean stores. Distant black rainclouds bulge in the shape of giant zeroes, threatening to break the calm with a roll from the sea towards the hills.

Imagine here the woman whom Spartacus is said to have taken on his travels, the wife who saw him sleeping in the Roman slave market with serpents coiled around his head, those portents of good fortune or ill depending on how we read the letters. She was said to be a devotee of Dionysus, the god whose cult was celebrated enthusiastically in this part of Italy once called Great Greece. It would be charming to think of Spartacus and his family among the Egnathians for a little tourism, some worship of home gods, lessons in Epicurean thought, water therapy or retail relaxation. But it is safest to say that they never were here.

Leaders of a slave army cannot take trips into the scenic destinations on their way. They either sack a city or they pass it by. They are either the ones who strew the road with temple rubble, who knock the heads off the Great Mother's statues; or they camp outside Egnathia, maybe thinking about what it would be like to be an ordinary enemy force, to have potential allies inside, but knowing that they cannot have them. Slaves cannot take ancient towns in the normal way of their time; for slaves to take a town is to subvert all the normal ways of any town.

It is easy, however, to imagine Horace meeting his Jewish trickster here. There is a large rock, the size of a card-table, in the right place where the Via Minucia meets Oriental Religion Square. Horace has travelled cheerfully from Rome on his sensitive diplomatic mission, the one he does not want

HORACE'S JOURNEY to BRUNDISIUM
Continued...

... To Beneventum next we steer;
Where our good host by over care
In roasting thrushes lean as mice
Had almost fall'n a sacrifice.
The kitchen soon was all on fire,
And to the roof the flames aspire;
There might you see each man and master
Striving, amidst this sad disaster,
To save the supper...

Know it you may by many a sign,
Water is dearer far from wine;
There bread is deem'd such dainty fare,
That every prudent traveller
His wallet loads with many a crust;
For at Canusium you might just
As well attempt to gnaw a stone,
As think to get a morsel down;
That too with scanty streams is fed;
Its founder was brave Diomed...

The 'Egnations next, who by the rules
of common sense are knaves or fools,
Made all our sides with laughter heave,
Since we, with them, must needs believe
That incense in their temples burns,
And without fire to ashes turns.
To circumcision's bigots tell
Such tales! For me, I know full well
That in high heaven, unmoved by care,
The Gods eternal quiet share
Nor can I deem their spleen the cause,
Why fickle nature breaks her laws.
Brundusium last we reach; and there
Stop short the Muse and Traveller.

to tell us about. He has made his whooping *egressum* from the big city, enjoyed his *modesto* inn at Ariccia, survived the frogs and mosquitoes of the Foro Appio canal, suffered a burnt-thrush supper at Benevento, stomach ache at Capua, a wet dream after a woman stood him up in a mountain village, and is now almost at his journey's end. The light is dim. The priestesses and their tambourines are close by.

Horace has eaten and drunk variably. Some decent wine has survived the years when Spartacus and his army scoured the countryside. The local bread is full of stones. He cannot be bothered to tell us much about Brundisium, 'the mere finish of his narrative'. It is 'The Egnatians', as the Englishman William Cowper renders them 2,000 years later, who get his full, final attention.

The idea 'that incense in their Temples burns, And without Fire to Ashes turns' is fine for 'Circumcision's bigots' but no good for Horace or any other pupil of Philodemus. Epicureans are happy to concede 'that in high Heaven, unmoved by Care, the Gods eternal Quiet share'. But they must never blame those Gods for human disasters. They cannot 'deem their Spleen the Cause why fickle Nature breaks her Laws'. The reason why the wrath of slaves eliminates a bustling town must be found elsewhere.

Thracians, Germans and Gauls pillage the fertile countryside inland of Egnathia. Soon they have bigger prizes on their minds. They are heading south and west to Metapontum, another Greek city, equally alien to Rome, even closer to the worship of Dionysus, fortunate for four centuries but since Hannibal's war not so lucky and in this winter between 73 BC, when the slave war began, and 72 BC when it exploded, not lucky at all.

Viale Orazio Flacco, Metaponto

The best spectacular is a battle between two sides, two groups each with a strongly fashioned identity, Gauls vs Thracians, Greeks vs Amazons, Tanais vs Phasis, bears vs dogs, Athenians vs Spartans, Roman heroes vs Hannibal's villains, Seven from Argos vs Seven from Thebes. Every part of the battle idea can be manufactured if necessary. A gladiator can switch from Thracian to German with the speed of a theatrical extra or a transferred footballer. The supporters do not care if half of their team was last week playing for the opposition; they care only if their team loses or they do not have a team.

In the arc of Greek colonies on Italy's southern coast the game of Greeks vs Trojans was the best and oldest. A place in mythology was essential for civilised life. This was a rivalry that did not need any longer to be vicious or violent. The stories of Troy were remembered to everyone's benefit, long enough ago for all wounds to have healed, powerful enough in the mind to produce a sense of belonging to more than just the local countryside.

Metapontum was not the first of these Great Greece towns. Within little more than a century of the events that inspired the *Iliad* and *Odyssey*, there were renewed Greek expeditions in search of land more fertile and less crowded than at home. After the battles at Troy around 1270 BC there was a slow exodus westward. Old rivalries came west too. Metapontum was founded here between the Basentus and Bradanus rivers as an act of seventh-century pre-emption, to prevent neighbouring Tarentum, most prosperous of the early colonies, from growing too strong.

All the new arrivals brought with them the memories of their past in pictures as well as poems. So visitors can still see today the painted images on which they thrived. From the ground at Metapontum have come vivid battle scenes of Greeks vs Amazons, with fighting women trampled under horses' hooves, a queen with an axe above her head, a man carrying a naked maiden with blood spurting from her breasts and thigh. This is what Statius' Greek ancestors in Italy would have known, before the different realisations of the stories in the spectaculars of Domitian's Rome.

There are pots depicting the Theban civil wars and the wars of gods and giants. But much the most popular subjects come from Troy, the great patriotic war depicted in seventh-century images of soldiers scrabbling for dead bodies, the Greek Patroclus, the Trojan Hector (not always clear now which one, possibly not always clear then), the heroes of their shared history book, more significant for those away from Greece than those at home.

What did the ancient colonists look like themselves? Who built this town that Spartacus and the slave army were approaching? Archaeologists here have a surprisingly clear answer to that, better than we have for anywhere without an industry of portrait sculpture, better, in fact, than for many places where the local great do get memorials in marble.

This Metaponto way of reconstructing the past is through the modelling of skulls from its first graveyards, using clay and plaster, coloured match-heads and mathematical calculation. Each face of these ancient dead comes with the best assessment of its muscles – the temporalis, masseter, buccinator and occipito-frontals, the definers of appearance, it seems, throughout any century.

Like most sporting supporters, these men and women of ancient Italy do not have too much in common with their heroes. A dour matron with thick nose and thin mouth and centre-parted hair stares out from the guidebook. More than twice as many women as men were buried in the graveyard excavated by the Basento river, the female ages averaging somewhat younger than the male, both numbers different from normal expectations and neither easily explained. There is a young boy, with huge eyes, frothing curly hair and a mouth half open as though he is about to speak. There are men with sharper noses, fuller mouths, swept-back balding hair, dimpled chins, none of them modelled on peerless Achilles.

These are the forensic scientists' contribution to this journey. There are necks and skulls here of animal-eaters and eaten animals. Travellers who seek pictures of the past have now the work of 'archaeozoologists' and 'zooarchaeologists' as well as poets and sculptors. This is another war zone of scholars. Whenever the dust is sifted from a newly discovered tomb, there are 'splitters' who doubt that anything is connected to anything else and 'lumpers' who make massive claims from the most tiny fragments. Occasionally the two can agree.

Some reconstructors see racial differences as evidence of freedom and slavery. Most are heads that were simply short and wide or narrow and long, many poisoned by lead since not even Frontinus, six hundred years later, knew of killer water pipes. There are heads from colonies of dwarfs, nicely fit for the Colosseum trade. Many of the skulls here have patched and pocked walls, with parts as soft as sponge proving the presence of malaria. The dead in this cemetery also suffered syphilis, 2,000 years before any European met those American natives who have traditionally borne the blame for Venus' disease.

International science now sits alongside poetry here. Arnold Toynbee, who likened his writer's imagination to that of a palaeontologist, would doubtless have approved. On a timeless road like this one the new is no impediment. It need not displace the old baggage. It just adds its weight. The skull is not the brain. The sack of Troy, which happened centuries before these men and women drank lead or exchanged syphilis, was remembered in their great epic songs. The Metapontans' identity with that mythic history is still as certain as any identification through diseases borne by sex, pipes and mosquitoes.

Greeks vs Trojans? That game was the constant reminder of how the wanderings of their distant forefathers matched their own. Both Agamemnon's and King Priam's heroes had left Troy when the great fight was over, the winners to come home, the losers because they no longer had a home. Any city in this area with any claim to top-division status had to have a founder who had fought in that war in some way or other. This was not the Seven against Thebes. Troy had been a good war.

Which side they had been on was quickly not of great importance. What mattered more was how famous they had been. When the big players had all been allocated, any member of the Greek or Trojan squadrons would do. Wealthy Capua had the Trojan Capys. Aristotle wrote that Rome was founded by unknown Greeks who, like Odysseus, had been blown from their homeward course. At Rome itself the choice eventually fell on a Trojan prince, Aeneas, who also features on vases found here. In 73 BC the hero of the *Aeneid* was still a minor figure: his story had not yet had the benefit of Dido's suicide, prophecies of global domination from the underworld and all the other enhancements from the poet Virgil, Horace's travelling companion and the Emperor Augustus' most successful myth-maker.

At Metapontum the founding hero was Epeius, the boxer in Homer's *Iliad*, the same man who inspired Statius by preferring sport to war. Epeius was also a factotum carpenter. He mended ships' timbers and carried water buckets in and out of Agamemnon's tent until his big moment when the besiegers needed a wooden horse in a hurry. The sporting boxer, with a little divine help, made the world's first armoured personnel carrier. Odysseus and other heroic Greeks were the armoured personnel. The Trojans towed the beast inside their own walls, thinking that the Greeks had abandoned the siege. The rest, as they say, is mythology.

The people of Metapontum kept Epeius' adzes, saws and other tools in the temple of Hera in their main square. Neighbouring cities also claimed the horse-builder and his toolkit as their own but this was no cause for conflict. A carpenter might have many blades. These tools were not like the foreskins of future Christian saints. The quantity of entombed axes, brackets and nails found here suggests much more than a society of wealthy woodworkers. Epeius was claimed as founder both by Lagaria a little way along the coast and by Pisa, about as faraway in Italy as a Metapontan

could imagine. That did not matter. The Trojan toolkit stayed in the temple and all was right with the world. It told them who they were.

Sometimes there was the rekindling of the old war and the fighting of new ones. Greeks fought among themselves, often following their loyalties to their mother cities back home. In the sixth century BC, the Metapontans joined some other Greek colonies to destroy one of their neighbours, Siris, whose founders, like Rome's, came from the Trojan side. There is a clay obelisk from here inscribed in praise of Hercules from this time, and inscribed too with the plea that its maker, Nicomachus, should be known in future for his double effort in the art of poem and pottery.

Nicomachus chose his routes to immortality well. On his pale-brown tower of clay visitors can still read the words he fired on his work, the greeting to Hercules with each new line written left to right, right to left, left to right, the ploughing style. In the early years when the potters of Italy were free men, we know many of their names. When the manufacturing moved to factories of slaves, the signatures stopped.

Painted terracotta was the art of Metapontum. There was little stone for building. There was no great harbour. There was fertile land and the ingenuity and slavery to work it. Valuable houses were distinguished from the humdrum by fired panels depicting their owners' long-legged horses, their women and their workers. Over the centuries after the fall of Troy, there were intense cultural and commercial rivalries. There were spats, sometimes nasty spats, but nothing to match the Homeric battles of their founders. The presiding spirit here became the practical and the devious, the carpenter's way not the warrior's.

Metapontum had the biggest and oldest political arena in the Greek world, the biggest purpose-built talking shop, almost seventy yards across with space for 8,000 people, an amphitheatre of words, most of the rhetoric eloquently empty once Roman rule began. It had a famous stoa, a long shady colonnade open to the air on one side, the distinctive mark of a Greek town where philosophers and traders met. Its public decorations there were domestic as well as heroic: the terracotta figure of a reclining man toasts his son in his wife's arms, the 'wetting cup' of wine directly beside the struggling baby's head. Wealthy families had exquisite miniature fishbowls for their dolls' houses in the Gnathian style. The city's silver coins carried the insect-like imprint of an ear of barley. Its fields and streets were neatly marked in rectangles, befitting the boast that in one of them lay the bones of Pythagoras. The Greek mathematician's house was an Italian tourist destination. Cicero, combative student of all thought that was Greek, was one of many over the years who came.

In 72 BC it was still a civil haven in the southern countryside. Roman Metapontum had become a capital of science. Its farmers were masters of breeding and owned the biggest cattle in the world. To have the heaviest bulls was not just a benefit in beef; it gave the people of Metapontum the biggest tractors of their time, the best ploughing, the best chance of driving back the inland forests where bear, wolves and elk thrived and of extending their fields of sheep and goats and barley.

Like the Capuans the men of Metapontum had supported Hannibal against Rome. After that their freedoms and privileges were similarly reduced. Their stoa became a warehouse for the occupiers' camp. Much of their business had moved to new Roman towns encroaching from the north, like Venusia, birthplace of Horace. This street outside the town museum is now named amicably after the invading poet.

Metapontum had suffered like Capua, and it had succeeded like Capua too. Money for luxury had long been the most important requirement in a place faded from its greatest days of extravagance but still a prize. On the land between their two rivers, the Bradano, straight as a Roman road, and the Basento, bent like a corkscrew, they piled wealth on top of their memories until the forces of Spartacus brought back their earliest memory of all, the sack of Troy, and this time the people of Epeius the carpenter were on the losing side.

Tavole Palatine, Metaponto

For Arthur Koestler, writing his first novel, *The Gladiators*, in the mid-1930s, the rape of Metapontum was the night when the Spartacus revolt was doomed. Koestler's quest was to match the story of the slave war with two events of his own time, the Russian Revolution that had succeeded and the global communist revolution that had failed. He turned Roman Italy into a model of twentieth-century Europe. He examined causes, the real and the imaginary. He analysed

reaction and its absence. He showed the impact of the conquered on the conquerors and the stresses that come from importing empire into the cities of imperial states.

The economics of slavery fascinated him, the mobility of cheap labour from abroad, the opportunities and the threats to citizens at home. He had come across, by accident he said, an aristocratic Roman political system which could not meet the challenges it had brought upon itself. He saw the conditions for a Roman revolution and he sought the reasons why the Spartacus revolt, like others later, had failed to match the rebels' hopes.

The Gladiators is more about Lenin and Stalin than about Spartacus. It is gripping fiction, far more solidly constructed than the American successor on which the famous film was based. The guide at Hera's temple here has read it. So has his father. It is the only novel that he has ever read which mentions Metaponto.

Fifteen columns of the ruin still stand upright beside the motorway to Taranto, survivors known locally as the Tavoline Palatine, proudly outliving the rival shrine in the town centre where Epeius' toolkit was kept. There is not much of ancient Metapontum taller than the orange-groves and cornfields which this morning are lashed with hailstorms from a blue-black sky.

Koestler's explanation of the Third Slave War was that Spartacus was too weak. He did not eradicate dissent. The problem of his leadership was not being too rapine and ruthless, rather that, in ruthlessness if not in rape, he offered too little. In the novel the attack on Metapontum is carried out against Spartacus' orders. A breakaway group, led by his fellow gladiator, the German Crixus, leave their fictional winter home, Sun City, for a new bout of insurrection and plunder. Spartacus has constituted Sun City as a community without gold or silver or traditional orders of rank. Crixus is tired of seeing Spartacus act as statesman, signing treaties with Rome's enemies, coalition-building for the war ahead. He wants to maintain the revolutionary fire by taking more revenge and more wealth, more quickly, from the rich. Metapontum is the place chosen for his massacre. 'What will the girls be like in Metapontum?' his men ask. 'Like opened oranges,' comes the reply, 'that's what they will be like.'

Fury, death and lust were mingling in a horrible chorus which strangled the thundering of the surf . . . 'All the cities the slaves had sacked in the course of their campaign had suffered and been maimed through the wrath of the oppressed; but the town Metapontum suffered only for one night, for in the morning the town Metapontum was no more.'

What does Spartacus do? He sends troops to arrest Crixus and his faction. After heavy losses on both sides, he brings them back to Sun City, sets up thirty crosses and crucifies his colleagues, including some who escaped with him from the Capua school. The men are tied and hung and spend the night screaming and abusing the revolution. 'In steadily lengthening intervals they had been screaming. When one of them fainted with pain and exhaustion, he was torn back into consciousness by the cries of the rest, and he cried with them.'

Crixus' support grows among the men who watch these long executions. Large parts of the newly communist slave army back the insubordinate against their leader. Instead of continuing the crucifixions, instead of defying Crixus with yet greater force, instead of letting the ends justify the means, following what Koestler called 'the law of detours' from a noble revolutionary's noble aims, Spartacus does the opposite. He signals his humanity.

'The crucified men screamed again, with hope this time.' He cuts down the destroyers of Metapontum from their crosses. Only one has died. Spartacus allows Crixus and his supporters to set off north on their own in search of other wealth to redistribute. He loses his own faith in the ideals of Sun City. He fails the big revolutionary test that, in Koestler's analysis for this novel, every successful revolutionary must pass.

Like every guide on the Spartacus Road the novelist and philosopher of communism brings his own light. He had been a witness to communist revolution. He had direct knowledge of what groups of the armed and enraged will do to those who are neither. We do not know where Spartacus' army spent its first winter. Since no town could have accommodated it, either practically or politically, without ceasing to be a town, it is likely that Spartacus set up one of his own, a winter camp that would have looked like a town after a few months, just as army camps, and refugee camps, have always done. Koestler plausibly describes how his own Spartacus did a deal with the elders of Thurii, a former Athenian colony some sixty miles from Metapontum, a pact in which his army was supplied with food in return for not invading to steal it.

The pattern for criticising *The Gladiators* was set by George Orwell. Koestler's Spartacus was a mere 'modern man dressed up . . . a primitive version of a proletarian dictator'. Koestler lacked the imagination of a Flaubert who, in the crucifixions and human roastings of *Salammbô*, could 'think himself into the stony cruelty of antiquity'. Flaubert was writing his horror story of ancient Carthage in a mid-nineteenth-century time when there was 'peace of mind' and the mental space to seek cruelties in the past; Koestler and Orwell had only to look around them for political terror. More importantly in Orwell's eyes Spartacus is presented as neither power-hungry nor visionary but as the subject of 'some obscure force which he does not understand'.

Koestler has faltered between allegory and history. If Spartacus is the prototype of the modern revolutionary, and obviously he is intended as that, he should have gone astray because of the impossibility of combining power with righteousness. As it is, he is an almost passive figure, acted upon rather than acting. The serious weakness of this story is that the motives of Spartacus himself are never made clear.

Orwell is persuasive. Koestler, however, was right about the likely facts, too right for the success of his novel. The motives of Spartacus have never been clear. They are as difficult for historians to find as for novelists. There is agreement that at around this time the stoa of Metapontum took its final fall, that a thick layer of finest pottery began to be covered by broken tiles and burnt earth. The city was never a force again. Maybe Spartacus was indeed too soft to be a true revolutionary. Maybe he did prefer individual humanity to absolute power. The distinction is not likely to have meant much to those who crossed his path in that first winter of freedom.

When his army was wrecking Metapontum, Spartacus was most likely here with them. The patch of ground on this journey where Spartacus most plausibly stood is on the podium in the middle of Metapontum's amphitheatre of words, with its three Greek temples beyond the terraces in front of his eyes and the shattered Roman camp in the sweep of his left hand. He would have seen how one group of landless foreigners had built new lives in a new country centuries before, and he may have wondered how his slave army, or any part of it, might do the same.

Today it is a park for archaeologists and fighting childen, both deploying their own forms of imagination here. Except at these Tavoline on the edge of the old town, there is much imagination required in Metapontum. The main temples in the centre have gone except for foundations pitted with algae and grass. There are small column sections rolled close to their original places like wheels of harvested corn. There is just enough of the once giant theatre to weigh the conflicting arguments in a place built to hear them. Even at the Tavoline the hailstorm is a bigger attraction than the standing stones themselves, drawing the single guide and a single postcard-seeker from their shelter, all of us thrilled to watch the anxious swallows, the balls of ice pinging against the pediments and the rising steam from crushed oranges and corn.

Viale Orazio Flacco, Metaponto

The slave army began the year 72 BC in two parts. Crixus led his followers back northwards past Brundisium and Egnathia to the Garganus mountains, the bulbous boil on the Italian  east coast where he may have hoped to repeat the triumphs of Vesuvius. Spartacus led the larger part of the force northwards too, separately and behind. Whether this represented disarray or convenience is hard to say. If Spartacus was conducting a wholly different strategy from Crixus and trying to leave Italy for home, Brundisium would have been the place to take a boat, or a fleet of boats, for Thrace. Instead, both parts of the army headed north, keeping on the move, living off the land, terrorising everywhere they went, looking for opportunities to defeat Romans and to grow in strength and power.

There must surely have been voices raised for a fast departure from Italy. At least some of the slaves had fresh memories

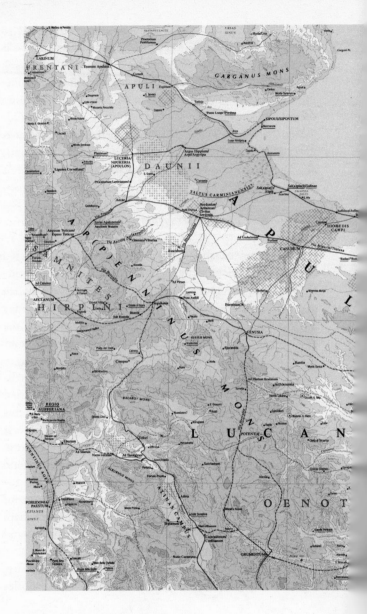

of freedom at home. In a fragment of Sallust, saved in the Vatican thanks to the book-cutter's knife, the historian describes some of the slave army wanting to leave somewhere as fast as they can: 'in the fear that wandering about disbanded as they were at that time they would be surrounded and cut down . . . at the same time . . . the worry . . . hence it was necessary to leave as quickly as possible'.

But there will also have been those with no memory of freedom anywhere but in the slave army. Many Gallic slaves in Capua would have been slaves in Gaul too. German slaves from the Vesuvius towns might have been slaves in Saxony. The same was later true of African slaves taken to the Americas. Some had been free, some had been temporary prisoners-of-war; but debt and other crimes had already made thousands slaves for life in their own home country. For the whole army of Spartacus there was no haven of freedom. For even a part of it a haven might have been hard to find.

Florus says the slaves also sacked nearby Thurii. This part of the Spartacus Road is recorded as one of exultation and display. The slaves took prisoners. They put on shows. One woman whom the slaves had raped committed suicide. The gladiators staged a mock Roman funeral for her at which four hundred male prisoners were forced to fight as though in the arenas around Capua. 'Those who had once been the spectacle were now to be the spectators,' wrote the Christian commentator Orosius. 'It was as gladiatorial entrepreneurs rather than as military commanders that they staged these games': the slave-leaders even charged admission.

Their main military aim was to do more in 72 BC of what they had done in 73 BC. The Romans had instructed their two new consuls for that year to make sure that the 72 BC result was different. Their names were Lucius Gellius Publicola and Gnaeus Cornelius Lentulus. Both were friends of Pompey, the most powerful Roman of the age, who was then away in Spain fighting other rebels. Both were military veterans and adept political survivors – Publicola, a gentlemanly intellectual in his sixties, especially so. They were not the finest generals Rome ever put into the field; the 70s were not a vintage decade for leadership. They were probably the best available.

Sallust tended to dislike all friends of Pompey. Lentulus seems to have been a Pompeian whom he disliked particularly. The new commander was irritating, one of those whom the historian could not quite define. He defied the senatorial categories of *stolidi* or *vani*, heavyweight or featherweight. It was difficult to work out whether he was anything at all. Publicola was simpler, the pontificating type. Neither was one of nature's born conquerors. They did, however, command regular Roman legions, unarguably the world's most successful fighting men.

Viale Europa, Montescaglioso, Basilicata

On the concrete blocks behind this roadside bar, a few miles north of Metaponto, a man in a tight, washable suit is sitting studiously at a metal table. In front of his face he holds a large black square of film, raising each corner in turn towards the midday sun and noting what he sees on a lined yellow pad. Struggling in his unhelpful jacket, he places a second film over the first, then a third over them both until even the most blistering sunlight is blocked and he has nothing new to write at all.

Although his struggle to keep the layers aligned is over, the perspiration does not stop. He wipes his forehead, strips down too late to his pale-brown shirt, and tries to keep the sweat from the linen map that lies beside his coffee. Maybe he is himself a map-maker or an improver of maps, a maker of cartographical novelties, with new restaurants, next to old battle sites, the kind the Koreans liked. There does not seem too pressing a need for new guides to the roads of this upland plateau. The line of antique-pink train stations, the one regular reassurance for drivers, does not suggest much past or future movement of the tracks. But there is always a market for novelty and perhaps his job today is to satisfy it.

Alternatively, he may be a fellow journalist, a photographer, an art director for some local magazine. Not so long ago, designers often used to hold up their negatives as he is now doing for the second time, checking 'colour separations', for pages long forgotten, in technologies that are in most places obsolete. My father used to do much the same thing at home, peering through giant circuit diagrams the size of a broadsheet newspaper page, taping one to another, the next to the next, until he had a finished diagram of some ingenious machine for seeing submarines or missiles far away.

Doctors still use shadowed film to show us the hidden parts of our bodies. The first time I studied carefully what was inside my own was in a display like the one now intensifying at the metal table – with a commentary from a man who was also in a slightly too tailored suit, also sweating damp on to his ghostly pictures. The objects of our attentions looked first like fishes secreted among swaying reeds, rubber tyres and ragged carrier bags: webs of veins spread like netting all around. With added images the creatures became clearer. A thumbprint pointed to a place behind the stomach, below the liver, a pike-like shape marked out by meandering intestines. Then came a show of colour pictures, no longer a dark pond scene but a bright tropical tank. The connection between these watery images and the wilder sights that a cancer can produce was a long time in coming clear.

The man at the table makes his last yellow notes, refolds the linen that he has spidered with fresh blue lines and walks quickly down to his car, letting his jacket flutter lightly on to the back seat. Map-making is all that he appears to have in his mind. There are dozens of pathways from here towards Gargano, some skirting the sites of old Roman villas, some passing directly through the farmyards and fields. The few main roads are clear. There are minor ones too. In 72 BC there were many more minor ones – and many anxious people ahead wondering which route the armies of Spartacus and Crixus might take.

Botromagno, Gravina di Puglia

There was once a high farmhouse here with a view over its furthest fields, standing in a broken line of settlements between Metapontum and the Garganus mountains. Southwards to the Mediterranean ran the thin Bradanus river; towards Naples and the Greek cities of the west were the drover paths packed hard for centuries by the feet of sheep exchanging the winter grass of the coast for summer hillsides. Immediately above was Mount Irsi, visible for miles about, and behind it miles of hills like calm waves on the sea.

In 72 BC, in the spring haze of midday, the landscape was warped and twisted, frustratingly so. On this day the farmers badly needed the surrounding earth to be level, more like the tables on which they ate, less like wooden boards left out in the yards and soaked by rain. Whatever was happening in the distance, the sight ahead was of the same shimmering patch-work of brown and yellow stains, some straight-sided fields drawn by their own hard labours, some rounded blots like spilt ink, oil or wine, some constantly changing as the clouds

cast down their shadows from the pale sky, some fixed as boundaries that for centuries had been there.

This prospect to the south was broken in many parts. A stranger might walk north towards them, emerging clearly for a while before melding back into the hills. The smoke of approaching fires, as pale as the edges of the clouds, might do the same. So too might an army of many strangers and many fires, seeming for hours to be moving away towards other farms, then suddenly to be approaching their own home in a storm of fly-eating birds and flesh-eating flies.

Such shifts in direction were not mere illusions nor even the choice of the marching slaves. The high land set its own paths, nothing so clear as a road along which so many thousands of soldiers might choose to travel, just a gentle indication of its harder and softer slopes. There were deceptive lines of dark-brown pits, then ruts of yellow earth more golden than the far distant beaches. If the army of Crixus had found the oldest paths for its vast, massed exuberance, this path to Botromagno is where it would have come.

Roman farms were sited not to be secrets but to get the best of sun and water and the trade in what they bought and sold. The high ridges were healthier than the valleys. This was a place where the east–west and north–south paths naturally crossed. Long before the building of the Via Appia a farm here was on the road to Greek Italy. Long before the Greeks came to Italy this was a settled place. In the fields grew grain and olives. Deep in the coolest parts of the riverside ground were the dolia where the wine matured, giant earthenware jars with wide collars around their rims. The farm had fine soil for growing grapes. It had rooms of looms where slave-women worked on clothes for their masters and themselves with as much left over to sell as they could make.

'Better have the selling habit than the buying habit' was the motto of Cato the Elder, guru of gurus for Roman agriculturalists. He advocated yard-sales for objects past their best, old coats, old fences, old people. Much buying went on too. The farm kitchens of Botromagno were stocked with delicate pottery, not just the thick-walled red-and-black-glazed ware which ploughing has turned up in so many seasons since but pale-grey cups like porcelain and fragile bottles for hand-cream and scents.

This was not a fashionable retreat for a rich Roman looking for leisure bloodsports, art and philosophical debate. It was a 'working farm', the term not yet needed to represent something different from 'gentleman's playground'. The owner's family lived in two storeys of the main house. There was a small colonnaded courtyard on the east towards the Adriatic and, on the western side, a walled garden with water tanks which caught the rain. To the south of the garden were three workers' rooms, single-storey, thick-walled with interlocking blocks of soft volcanic stone, close-fitted rectangles and sharp-pointed cones.

Once there had been a clear square place for vegetables and fruit, but gradually, in the years of peace, the space for slave manager and slaves had grown, connected by a corridor to the owner's quarters. There were stalls for six oxen close by, enough ancient tractor-power to plough all the fields they could see. Two hundred years ago the owners had built fortifications too, high walls within which the field-workers could flee at the first sight of trouble. But these were long gone.

Many of the workers were women, a group rarely remarked upon by visitors seeking stories of man-manacled-to-man in prison-factory chain-gangs. Roman experts recommended the calming presence of the 'pastoral Venus'. Even the strictest master of a farm like this one saw himself as the father of a family. Within the greater family were lesser ones. There was argument, at the time and since, about whether it was the most productive use of slave labour to mix cooking and child-rearing with the work of plough and spade. But communities of families were a common outcome, and in many places not just the most easy and natural but the most profitable too.

The need for thread-spinners and cloth-weavers was immense. Their output, unlike that of the potters and stonecutters, has long ago decayed to dust – though not before use and reuse in its day that would have impressed their most parsimonious successors. In the spring of 72 BC the women of this farm were producing more than future children to be future slaves. A single toga fetched a serious price in the shops of Capua or Rome. For the buyer it was a big investment. Whiteness was especially hard to achieve, by cleaning, shrinking and bleaching, the 'fuller's arts'. Thread-spinning, like childcare, was work for women alone and less recorded even than cloth-weaving, which men might sometimes do.

The woollen thread for a single weaver required around a dozen spinners. Archaeological historians have made both economic and wooden models, willing and counting themselves into the workplace here, estimating that it took more than three forty-hour weeks to spin the woollen thread for one soldier's tunic. Spinning and weaving a tunic might take a month. The shops of Sabbio in Capua, his competitors in the other Colosseum towns, his colleagues and their customers in the Roman army, all had to be supplied with cloth. Even the two approaching legions of Lentulus and Publicola, a fraction of the total Roman forces that then held territory from Syria to Spain, wore cloaks and coats that had taken 2,000 women a year to make.

The counting historians argue about what sort of machinery they should assume for their calculations. Were the looms the classic type painted on the black vases of Egnathia, with the vertical threads hung from a bar and weighted to keep them taut? Or had this farm and its neighbours acquired the newer double-wood-barred looms which did not need the stone weights? This is a frustrating question for anyone who badly wants it answered. The places where the most loom weights survive, often seen as centres of the most intensive weaving, may not have been where the most cloth was made. A weavers' room with the latest double-barred technology would have left the least traces, just as a room of microcircuits will in future leave less behind than a cash-register. Local children have long collected weavers' weights, running new threads through the holes. Sized and shaped like lollipops, these relics are recognised easily with or without their decorations punched in patterns of crosses. The wooden beams which replaced the weights have long gone.

Did customers even always want the advanced seamless cloth, woven in larger pieces, which the new looms could provide? Marble busts of those who could afford such portraits suggest that cloth from the old looms, made in small pieces and stitched together in the manner of their forefathers, carried high status, higher for formal purposes perhaps than the smooth widths made possible by the 'double-beamed' machines. 'Antique chic' was at the heart of many a Roman wardrobe.

Whatever wearers wanted, on and off the farm, and however quickly the new techniques came to Italy, the need for thread remained the same. The spinners had husbands who worked these fields. To judge from where the loom weights are found, much of the weaving took place outside too. The families had children who would work these fields and spin and weave in future. Conservatism in a Roman household meant not just keeping life as it was but stalling the natural process of decline.

Here the slaves had their half-jar of wine a day. It might have been the dregs, the watered-down brew of the third pressings, the *lora*; but it was sugar and pleasure in a place where many men and women, slave or free, had neither. There were more vegetables than meats on their tables. But there are 'faunal remains' – sheep, goat and pig with a three-foot shark and tortoise – in the latrines. Not all of that was from the masters. Lentils, the 'poor man's meat' which Roman experts highly recommended for slaves, were rich in vitamin C and calcium that helped its consumers survive.

Rural life was not that of the literary idyll, not for anyone bar the politicians and poetry lovers who sought their *otium* from the *negotia* of Rome, mostly on the western coast rather than here. But when we build a picture from this farm, and from others like it, we see small rooms where a slave family would live, hearths where they could bake their own bread and bring up families, some of whom might survive and stay with them. Although there was no certainty of that and families could be split and sold, certainty and stability were available to few of any kind of any class.

War took the free before the slave. Farms here were destroyed when Hannibal was fighting Rome. Destruction came again when the southern cities were fighting Rome. Disease took both free and slave the same. Only one set of lungs has been preserved from this time, from Rome itself, those of the so-called Grotta Rossa mummy, and their condition is that of a sixty-a-day coal-miner with a DIY asbestos-disposal habit. The air inside the farmhouse may have been as fetid as a city hovel from sheep-fat light and dung fire but outside in the fields it was sweet.

Outside in the fields, in the first spring days of 72 BC, came the first whispers that three armies were on the move, the Romans south from the city down the Appian Way, the main slave force under Spartacus somewhere northward from the Gulf of Tarentum, the second force of slaves under Crixus coming more directly north to Garganus from Metapontum, in broken lines, their numbers uncountable, their main mass heavy along the banks of the Bradanus. Master and slave stared out together into the shimmering circles of hills to see whether or where they should run.

◾   ◾   ◾

Almost fifty years later, Horace is casting his mind back to what happened next. He knows nothing of Spartacus from his own memory. He was not born until seven years after the march to Garganus. But he knows what the slave army did and what it meant.

Horace's birthplace was nearby, Venusia, the small town whose founding had been the first fixed Roman assault on the local Greeks. His father had been a slave, very likely a free man who had been enslaved during Rome's war against the

Marsi, the Latins, the Venusians and other associated allies who wanted better rights, citizenship and votes at Rome as well as the privilege of fighting its wars.

His early boyhood was spent among the military families from the legions who, in reprisal after that Social War, had taken over the Venusians' homes and schools. His own education, after his father regained the freedom to be the generous parent, was in Rome, far away from the patronising big-boned centurions' sons he so disliked. His university was at Athens where he met Brutus, Julius Caesar's assassin. Aged twenty-three, fuelled by idealism and friendship, he had risked slavery or death himself by backing Brutus and Cassius in their failed fight against Caesar's heirs.

Horace knew directly of Italy's civil wars and never wanted another. One of his earliest poems took the theme that the present age of destruction was even worse than those of the past: 'A second generation is wearing itself away in civil strife and Rome the city that neither treacherous Capua nor violent

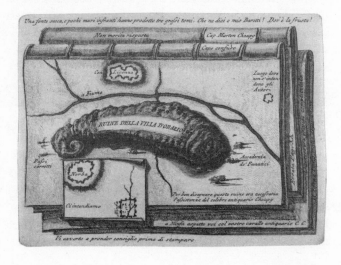

Spartacus destroyed is collapsing from its own power: *Altera iam teritur bellis civilibus aetas Suis et ipsa Roma viribus ruit. Quam neque . . . nec virtus Capuae nec Spartacus acer . . .'* If a future Spartacus and other destroyers were to be kept at bay, Rome needed an answer, a surer means of saving a civilisation which, while seeming sometimes strong, was so very fundamentally frail.

After backing the wrong answers to his problem, Horace had restored his fortunes by luck, literature and charm. He last appeared on the Spartacus Road, still as a young man, at Egnathia, near the end of his Journey to Brundisium. By then his support for Caesar's killers had been fully forgiven. He had become accepted as a junior member of the Caesarian party, aged twenty-six, travelling across Italy with a diplomatic mission to reconcile the future Emperor Augustus with his rival, Mark Antony. There was then still one last civil war in his life ahead, the one which finally brought one man to undisputed power.

Eighteen years after that, now aged forty-four, Horace is looking back in his second Spartacus poem at all the events which have shaped his life. His father, to whom he owes so much, is dead. The poet now has his own country house, modest but close to fashionable Tibur in the hills outside Rome. Augustus is in charge. Tota Italia is at peace, proudly bearing that name from the Alps to the Messina Straits – but everything depends, he thinks, on Augustus remaining in charge.

'*Herculis ritu*' is the fourteenth ode in his third book. 'People of Rome', it begins, we thought that Augustus had lost his life on campaign in Spain. But now he is back, a monster-slaying saviour like Hercules: 'let his wife go out rejoicing to greet him! And the sister of our dear leader too. And every mother here of men who've been fighting and maidens who await those men's return.' Horace declares that he will never fear death through *tumultum* and *vim* while his leader is alive and in command of the world.

The second half of the piece is very different. In it he calls his own slave boy for perfume ('*I, pete unguentum, puer*'), for fine wine that has survived those old Italian wars and a favourite mistress so that he can celebrate this homecoming in his own way. But if the girl cannot be prised from her house, too bad. He is not now as enthusiastic for a party as he once was in his youth.

This is a little-loved poem. It has been hard for readers to sympathise with grateful devotion to a 'dear leader' who has made possible a life without terror. This fourteenth ode is criticised as cold and obsequious, not just chilly formality to an autocrat but a sickening combination of public and private, of 'Hail to the Chief' and 'Horace at Home'. The two parts, taken together, have long been decried as even worse than each one alone. Readers have always preferred the poems of Horace that highlight what we like in ourselves, irony, wit, the association of human feelings with the natural world. One of the best loved is the ode immediately before this one in Book Three, '*O fons Bandusiae*, more glittering than glass . . .'

'*Herculis ritu*' merges private and public fears for a frightened age. *Vim* and *tumultum* were common Latin words for making light of the very worst of events. They were the source of terror, of the fear that comes from the inability to trust what is closest at hand. 'Slave war' was a phrase to avoid. Horace's father, his home town and countryside had known every kind of fear founded on that source of violence. Horace himself had travelled the cattle-roads here around Mount Irsi as a herdsman, doing the work that slaves, in the years after Spartacus, could no longer be trusted to do. He had known

Odes 3 XIV

People of Rome!

We feared that our Caesar was lost in Spain like Hercules, lost seeking glories that can be won only by death. But now, we hear, he is a victor on his way home.

So, let his wife go out rejoicing to greet him! And the sister of our dear leader too. And every mother here of men who've been fighting and maidens who await those men's return. Let respect be the order of the day.

And, as for me, I'm going to have my own little celebration too. None of my old fears will plague me as long as Caesar is alive and ruling the world.

Go, boy, get perfume and flower garlands and a jar of old wine, Social War vintage if any of that eluded the grasp of marauding Spartacus. Get Neara here too, quickly, with her hair up in a scented knot.

But if that's a problem, if her guard pushes you away, don't worry. Come back alone. Old age cools hot blood. Of course, I wouldn't have put up with a snub like that in my fighting youth at Philippi.

the breadth and depth of terrorised insecurity and now is established, a man with a place.

Part of his job was, in his own small way, to help Augustus stabilise the future. He could subtly rewrite the past. He could soothe, refine and calm. Augustus wanted an ordered, dignified history for his country and a foreign influence that was restricted, as far as he could make it, to the metrical subtleties of poetry. Horace has a personal stake in this comforting illusion of old and certain morality. He knows Augustus and his family. He knows Augustus' daughter, Julia, who has already welcomed home her husband Marcellus, Augustus' nephew and favoured heir. His fear for them all is real. As for his own homecoming party, he is pleased that he too, like the politics of Rome, is less erratic and irascible than he was in the year he fought for Caesar's assassins against Caesar's adopted son at Philippi.

Is there any wine that escaped the war which enslaved his father? Bring it out. Is there any of it that escaped the ravages of Spartacus? Not too much, it seems. Wine itself may not have a memory. But some wines will be forever flavoured by the events of their vintage year. How does Horace describe Spartacus? He is '*vagantem*', wandering aimlessly violent around the Italian south or, as one manuscript has the line, '*vagacem*', a word which appears nowhere else in Latin, meaning more or less the same but with a sour dismissive taste.

In the spring of 72 BC the armies of Spartacus and Crixus are still on their way north. Some tellers of this story like to place the fate of this region – the desolation of its farms, the destruction of its weaving-looms, spinners and weavers, its broken dolia of fine wine and after-wine – all under the charge sheet against Crixus, the monster of Metapontum. Botromagno is certainly in the line of march for the renegades-of-renegades who were heading for Garganus. But Spartacus was never far away: 'Go, seek perfume, my boy, and garlands and a jar recording the Marsic war, if some amphora managed to elude pillaging Spartacus: *I, pete unguentum, puer, et coronas Et cadum Marsi memorem duelli, Spartacum si qua potuit vagantem Fallere testa.*'

The archaeological evidence from these fields is that at some sharp time between 80 and 70 BC organised society ceased to exist, not just here but higher on Mount Irsi and at Bantia near where the poet was born. Cicero describes the burnt-out villas and shattered economies that followed the assault. Decades later all that had been restored here was a tiny area of habitation in the middle of a plateau whose lands all around had been worked and occupied for nine hundred years.

As the slave army approached, there was not much time for the slaves of this farm to decide whose side they were on. Archaeologists are used to surveying chaos and seeking a sense of how quickly that chaos came about. The excavators of Botromagno in 1991 found a pear-shaped pit in the southeast corner of the farm, a hole full of pottery and animal remains, the evidence of a latrine and a place piled rapidly with household wreckage.

This had been a house of hard work and low luxury, one of the earliest examples of 'the Roman villa' before those words came to stand for leisure rather than business. There is much that the connoisseur can deduce from the shape of a broken lamp (once purchased in Metapontum), the absence of amphorae shaped with spiked bases for transport (the people here drank most of the wine they produced). Glass beads, copper jewellery, dice, charms, cosmetic spoons, lead rivets and iron spikes, all had been swept into the same pit.

With them were seventeen coins, all well worn, the newest dated thirteen years before the army of Crixus passed by. This was the currency which, when barter terms and notes of credit were not enough, was precious fuel for the farm economy. Why were the coins in the pit? That was not so easy to decide. This was not a hiding place. It was the most fly-blown hole in this farmyard ground. There was no ban in these days on taking coins to the latrine: that came only when emperors objected to their image coming close to their subjects' excrement. A hundred years later a pile of cash could be seen as a miniature spectacular in itself, a polished display in silver, gold or bronze. Any image of a face held properties of the face itself. An autocrat did not want to see the shit of others let alone be seen in it. But that was not yet the way.

There was at all times, however, the habit of holding small change in the folds of toga or tunic, folds from which they might easily fall if their owner was interrupted suddenly in his after-work ablutions. There was no shortage of shocks for the ancient farmers of Botromagno and, on at least one occasion, a very sharp one. If archaeologists can speculate along such lines, so can any traveller on the Spartacus Road.

VII

GARGANO to POGNANA

Corso Matino, Mattinata, Promontorio del Gargano

Most men in the army of Crixus would never have noticed the Botromagno farm. The first to arrive found gardens of spring cabbage, a pond swirling and muddied by pigs, clear wine in the underground tanks, vineyards and wheatfields sparsely sprouting for the season to come. The last found lifeless water, rubble-strewn courtyards, trampled fields and the savaged bodies of slaves, split and splayed, those who had once woven and spun there and some new arrivals who had quarrelled over the spoils.

Some of the men and women from the household, slave and free, had escaped, seeking places where a mass of 10,000 fighters, advancing unopposed like a flood, might miss. There were maple groves and thick-packed oaks that a platoon might pass by rather than through. Some slaves willingly revealed the hide-outs of the free, some resignedly, some under threat of death. Some joined the household's destroyers with the hope of having a better life.

Crixus' first fortified camp was here on Mount Garganus. As soon as writers began to describe Italy as a boot, with its toe towards Sicily and its heel hard on Africa, this was the spur, a rough ball of rock pushing out into the Adriatic. It must have seemed a suitable place for Crixus' purpose, too broad easily to be besieged, its steep hills and valleys lessening the advantage of the legions. It was chosen perhaps, as Vesuvius had been chosen, for safety and for visibility to new arrivals. The gladiator did not have the benefit of the pink-and-green *Barrington* atlas, the spider-webbed road maps of the Koreans, the latest negatives of the cartographer in the tight suit, or any reliable maps at all.

Around the shoreline of Garganus today runs a thin metal layer of railway lines and crash barriers, holiday villages, rusting factories and the cages for reinforced concrete hotels. The passing of 2,080 years has replaced one rim of impermanence with another and done so many times over. The first Greek fishermen here described the circling of distant seabirds, like smoke rings over the waves, shearwaters maybe, white wings which they identified as the sailors of Diomedes, father of Tydeus the skull-chewer at Thebes, hero of the Trojan War who founded his cities from here. Benevento, where Horace fled the burning kitchen and where the sweating priest interrogated his Spartacus Road tourist, was just one of them.

The fisherman of the Middle Ages looked out over the sea for the return of the Archangel Michael, warrior saint and weigher of souls at the Last Judgement, who made his first western appearance here and whose return has been watched for since 493. The worried restaurant-owners of today look up from the main street's barrack-like Alba Bar, with its rusted sign of a pouting, dissatisfied sun. They see the EasyJet in the sky and wonder how many on the flight will drive their hire cars this far up the coast.

Inland, up the slopes of the mountain, much less has changed, maybe nothing. There are thick forests of oak and beech, some of the only reminders left in Europe of the landscape before the Romans came. Horace saw and heard them and used them to demonstrate to an anxious friend the precisely opposite point, that all things pass: 'Not forever do the oaks of Garganus creak, nor are alders always widowed of their leaves: *Non semper . . . Querceta Gargani laborant Et foliis viduantur orni.*'

This is not Pompeii, a soil stripped back to the era when the picture of Spartacus was painted there on a wall. It is not like Herculaneum; there are no beds and curtains, no libraries of Epicurean poetry. Only the earth itself is the earth on which the armies fought the next great battle of the Third Slave War.

Capua is at this point only one hundred miles away to the south-west. The original gladiators with Crixus must have wondered what had been achieved so far. Their road had certainly not been one of great progress in distance. They had, however, taken prodigious quantities of revenge in death and rape and drink. Most importantly, they had looked at Roman men and women as Roman men and women were used to seeing them, as objects for use. All these objects were the same. While Roman households had favoured slaves, personal favourites, slaves who were trusted, even loved, the slave army did not have favourite masters. It did not have the luxury for that. Those owners who had trained and educated the foreigners in Italy, or learnt about their cultures and beliefs, were no safer than the exploiters whose means of communication were the rack and lash.

In expanding to numbers that might defeat the legions of Rome, the insurgent army had made unprecedented progress. But there were still five slaves who stayed in slavery for every one who joined the free. It had not sought out every possible recruit. Its commanders were not sure whom or what they wanted. Thracians, Germans and Gauls, all good angry men, might reasonably disagree about what numbers were needed, what risks had to be taken to attract newcomers. Agreement on that would have required agreement on something much larger, a strategy, a common intention, a plan.

Escape by sea would be best achieved by a small group, like the seventy who had originally escaped: both mountain travel west to east and the seizure of boats were complex tasks. Escape by land, fighting northwards to the Alps, would be best achieved by forces of about the size they had now. A new government for

Italy, success where Hannibal had failed and for which slaves under rebel Roman command were fighting Pompey in Spain? That would require a mass revolt in Italy, victory upon victory and aggressive recruitment after every one.

The gladiators had trained and retrained in the use of weapons, recognising quickly that Roman war and Roman war-games were wholly different. They had trained slaves to use spears instead of spades, swords instead of sickles. The first escapers were now divided between two slave armies which, whatever the causes of that division, were separate centres of command which the Romans had to confront – both on the peninsular mountain of Garganus and on the flat-lands, canals and sea-marshes behind. The slaves' closeness to Capua, their failure to make progress in distance, hardly mattered now. Their former master, Lentulus Batiatus, was just one of many in the cities of Italy who were awaiting the result without the will or power to influence it in any way.

Via Carlo d'Angio, Monte Sant'Angelo, Gargano

The coming battle between Crixus, the gladiator, and Lucius Gellius Publicola, legionary commander of Rome, would be only a small event in the histories of Garganus. Much more influential, except on the Spartacus Road, was what happened five hundred years later when the local bishop  three times saw the Archangel Michael here and ordered that this mountain top of primeval trees become a place of worship for the mightiest protector of Christianity's power.

The cave of Sant'Angelo gained its first altar and angelic repute at the time of the third and final appearance before the bishop. Precisely a hundred years after Symmachus lost his Saxons and saw his ancient Rome absorbed by a new Rome, Garganus gave up its pagan obscurity for a stellar status under the new dispensation. Five hundred years after that it acquired its exquisite bronze and silver doors, carved in Constantinople with angelic feats of arms and an exhortation to pray for the man who paid for them.

Since then it has never ceased to draw pilgrims to its underground air, the first of all the Monts St Michel and Michael's Mounts that eventually spread as far as Cornwall. There are hundreds of the faithful here now, hoping for a chance to keep the silver polished with their sleeves, Italian nuns in black and white, priests with sweat-stained books, German fathers in green leather jackets, women in bright-red cashmere, an incomprehensible collection of children and air-stewardesses as though this were an excursion after a diverted flight to Lourdes.

St Michael, so the bishop said, led followers to his cave by diverting an arrow fired at a stray bull, not just saving the bull but sending the shaft straight back at the archer who had fired it. A magic bow was always a powerful theme. Any pagan in AD 493 seeking a smooth adjustment to the latest true faith – from prophetic Amphiaraus in the Theban wars, through the Roman war gods, to the wars of Christianity – found this a comfortable place to begin. Michael was no kind of turn-the-other-cheek saint, no feet-washing apostle. He was the field commander of the Army of God, the captain of the host of the Lord, protector of Adam and Moses: the 'saint' was a courtesy title.

Some early Christians preferred to adopt military champions from their own time, St George, St Theodore and others who had died in the torture chambers or gladiatorial arenas of Rome. But there must have been an easier comfort from an archangel, a suitably distant figure, identified by prophetic arrows like those of ancient Thebes, by mystic skills like medicine, by the healing of dreamers in womb-like caves, by the diversion of rivers by lightning blasts like those of Jupiter. When this hero for all eras was deemed to have appeared in Garganus, his first apparition outside the lands of the Bible, there began a force which endures to this day.

At the beginning of this trip, in a first flush of sympathy for Symmachus, I avoided the Quo Vadis church where a stone footprint marks Christ's last appearance before St Peter. To wait for an hour to see the landing place of St Michael does not seem right either. There is a long queue of devotees in the white-floored rectangular courtyard, some of their faces covered, others obscured by candle shadow but occasionally one lit brightly by an overhanging lamp. 'This is a place of fear,' reads the inscription in Latin over the entrance, 'house of God and doorway to the sky.'

I am looking idly over the crowd. There are black-eyed, black-hatted priests but not the man who now knows so much of my family past. The face in its borrowed veil escapes me completely, so too the little red hat which merges with those of the Virgin flight crew. Only when the Korean woman from Capua comes quickly under the lamp is it clearly her, or almost clearly. She is gone as quickly as she has seemed to come, down into the tunnel, the same determined swish of shoulder, the same look back to the doctor with the shiny black case, who must be there somewhere but whom I cannot see at all.

Why is she here? This is hardly a 'great site of history' for the edification of the children of Seoul. Garganus is a place of two stories, the Third Slave War and the appearance of an angel, both lacking much in the evidence that history teachers crave. She is not a Catholic. She never seemed or suggested so. Perhaps she changed her plans after Capua. Perhaps she has given up the itinerary that would have taken her from Cannae to the Rubicon, beyond Rome itself into the battle sites of the Empire. Perhaps she too has stayed on the Spartacus Road.

She will not have knowingly visited the exact site where Lucius Gellius Publicola lined up his 20,000 legionaries against the 30,000-man army of Crixus. Unlike the place of the archangelic visitation, we do not know where the battle site was. She may, as a knowledgeable student of the times, have queried those military numbers, arguing that the Romans liked to triumph over greater forces than their own whenever it was at all possible to claim so. She may have imagined the battle scene, a melee of slingshot and bright shields, stabbing swords, sharp on both sides, crunching through khaki-wool and leather, the unbeaten slaves against their first full legionary test. She will certainly have known the result, total defeat for the army of Crixus, the slaughter of thousands of his men, the deaths of both early converts to the cause of the gladiators and those who had joined them only a few days before around the Mount Irsi farms.

Via Guerra Giuseppe, Mattinata, Gargano

One ancient writer about Spartacus knew exactly what it was like to be pursued by ruthless and inexplicable rebels. His name was Appian and, before he came to Rome, his home was Roman Alexandria. A fragment of his lost autobiography survives which explains why.

There had been the call of a brown-necked crow in the sky over oozing black land. The sun was rising over the water and the two men who heard the bird were happy to have survived

another night of the rebel advance. They knew that their boat was close by and that within hours they could be away and safe. But the call of the crow was not a good sign. The older of the two was acting as guide. He stiffened and became con-fused. We have lost the way, he said in panic, pointing towards the place from where the cry had seemed to come. The crow screeched again, sounding even more like a human voice in the hot, flat swamp that glittered brighter with each new minute of morning. Now we have completely lost the way, he moaned.

Appian was the younger man. Later in his life he would write one of the longest accounts of the war between Rome and its 'gladiators, slaves and riff-raff'. At this time he was a refugee in another war, in the mud and grey-green flax fields of the Nile delta, where in the spring of AD 115 Jewish settlers

had suddenly, and for reasons still obscure, risen violently against their hosts.

In order to save his life, Appian had to find his boat in a shifting landscape of silt-choked inlets and short-lived lakes. There was no other human in sight. This was dawn in a war zone and he did not expect to see anyone who could help. The insurgents were not far behind. A revolt which had begun hundreds of miles away on the African coast closest to Greece had now reached almost to the Jews' lost homelands.

These rebels, who had won a terrifying reputation for rage and destruction, were commandeering ships at the delta from west to east, from Alexandria itself, which had attracted a massive population of the Jews expelled from Roman Palestine forty-five years before, to Pelusion, near modern Port Said, which he and his Arab guide were attempting to reach that morning. The Jews had torn down Greek temples at Cyrene, modern Libya, a Roman province since the year of the Spartacus horrors. Shrines of Apollo, Artemis and Hecate were now shattered wrecks, no longer an affront to the newcomers who believed that there was only one God, their God, and that Olympian variety (or any other kind) was an abomination.

The behaviour of these fighters – and their solidarity with one another – was extraordinary to Greek and Roman historians. The Jews would 'eat the flesh of their victims, make belts from their entrails, anoint themselves with their blood and clothe themselves with their skins: they sawed prisoners in two from the head; others they fed to animals; and still others they forced to fight as gladiators'. The atrocities are mentioned in a range of sources. Jews were believed to roast their captives alive. The people of Pelusium represented an especially pernicious example of religious bastardy to the Jews, favouring a deity with features of both Zeus and Baal, a multiple god served by crazy priests whose dietary laws banned onions. The Jewish rebels had destroyed bath-houses and colonnades because they were Roman, and killed to the orders, so it was said, of a man they called their Messiah. The whole of their society seemed to take part. Even if some of these charges were formulaic or false, there is no reason to think that Appian would have disbelieved them.

High in the sky the crow called again. The future historian had no reason to think that this sign was any more propitious than the previous two. But this time, as he later wrote, the screeching was not bad news but good: 'when the Arab heard the bird for the third time, he was very glad. This was a prophetic cry. We have been lucky to lose the way, he said. This is a short-cut.'

Appian had no more faith in Arab prophecy than in the Jewish kind. He was a sophisticated Greek, a proud citizen of the world's first metropolis, and saw himself as above all such superstitions. But, on this occasion, he did not have much choice but to follow the hopes of the guide who counted brown-necked crows. 'I smiled,' he wrote, 'although I thought we were still lost and feared for my life. Everything was hostile. I believed his prophecy. Right then, we unexpectedly saw another branch of the river, the part that is closest to Pelusium, and saw a galley passing. I went aboard, and this turned out to save my life: my vessel on the other branch had been captured by the Jews.'

After this escape Appian lived on to enjoy a life in Rome as well as Alexandria. He saw how after two-and-a-half years of struggle, Hadrian's legions crushed the revolt, the most dangerous Jewish uprising in Roman history, and how the Senate taxed the survivors to restore the ruined roads and temples. He became a Roman citizen and wrote a history of his new home, stressing the benefits of imperial rule, the desirability of a grateful populace and the dangers of civil strife. In Egypt the once threatening King of the Jews was turned into a theatrical effigy, an Alexandrian Guy Fawkes, and made a regular and exemplary spectacle to discourage imitators.

Appian made himself a pioneer of geography as history; he took each part of the world in turn and portrayed its progress towards a good and Roman life. He loved Rome but never stopped being Greek. He is one of those many ancient historians damned in schools with the charge of unreliability about government institutions. More important on the Spartacus Road are his claims that the slave leaders banned the use of gold and paid fair prices for their bronze and iron, his notes of how humans change under pressure of events: his words were the ones which introduced Spartacus to Karl Marx. He liked writing about Roman victories but considered, like Symmachus, that it was important to learn the lessons of failure. An occasional disaster could have a salutary effect. He read and rewrote the work of other writers, including different sources from those used by Sallust and Livy. He is also the only writer on the slave war who we know spent a morning in his youth being himself pursued by vicious foreign fighters who were suddenly and inexplicably rising up to destroy his country.

From the pages of Appian, sitting in academic comfort, some two hundred years after the defeat of Crixus on Mount Garganus, comes the sober report that 2,000 men fell before the army of the philosophical Consul, Publicola. For the slaves this was the first defeat. For one old Roman this was his finest hour. When Publicola's colleagues had spoken of his earlier political triumphs, reconciling the schools of Epicureans with their intellectual adversaries in Athens, it was with a wry smile on their faces. This victory may have been only against slaves but this was beginning to be a real war which needed real victories. Publicola was its first Roman winner.

Via Archita, Mattinata, Gargano

Beside the recycling bins for the white-cubed hotels and shops of Mattinata lies dusty newsprint left by pilgrims and

tourists from around the world, curled copies of *Ola!* and *OK!* in Portuguese, sports pages from all the publishing cities of Italy, *Il Mattino* from Naples, *Il Corriere* from Milan, *La Stampa, La Repubblica*, two sections of the *Washington Post* and a single copy of *The Times* from London, folded and refolded like paper hats. There are fading words about footballers and film stars, Obama and Berlusconi, and the Mafia refuse crisis which has left so much of southern Italy, away from the tourist streets, a dump site for black bags.

Il Corriere has also the story of Viola and Cristina Ibramovitc, two girls aged fifteen and thirteen, two Roms, as gypsy immigrants from the Balkans are known in Rome. They are said to have been working together selling trinkets on the beach at Torregavata, north of Naples, when a wave knocked them down in the shallows, dashed them against some rocks and left them '*annegate*'. That was the headline. Both were drowned. Both bodies were removed from the surf and laid out on the sand. After a while both were covered with towels, taking their place in the line of all the others stretched out for the weekend afternoon.

The life of the beach was not disturbed in any way. As the indignant reporter describes, the corpses' neighbours continued to apply their sunscreen, keep a close eye on their picnic baskets, telephone their friends, crack open the *minerale* as Neapolitans do on every Neapolitan beach.

After an hour an official vehicle arrived and a cortège of men in casual uniform identified which of the bodies were dead and carried them away. The front-page picture told that part of the story. The raised brown knee of a woman sunbather, her head lying back under a green umbrella, represented Torregavata's farewell.

The reporter had clearly enjoyed his own part in these events. It was not his job (though maybe he would like that job in future) to write leading articles or comment, to ask why this had happened in that way, why it seemed so wrong or what he and the God-fearing readers of *Il Corriere* would have done, or should have done, if they had been on the beach.

If the two girls had drowned before the writer's eyes, would he too have continued with lunch? He thinks not. If they had been Roman girls rather than Rom would that have made a difference to the beach parties? He thinks so. If the Ambre Solaire had stayed in its tube, the prosciutto in its basket, would that have been because the picnickers felt too upset or ill to continue, or because it was the right thing to do? He has no space to pursue that thought.

Presumably it was not a matter of the girls' immortal souls since that issue for Catholics – Neapolitans and Romans as well as Roms – is decided elsewhere. It would have been a matter of common respect which, if it exists for the living, is there for the corpse. Neapolitans see the gypsies as criminal trash who have no business on their beaches. For those without the protection of friends, family, fellow citizens, popularity or the law, there is no respect, no responsibility, and no need to spoil the day if they drown.

Corpses on a beach? That is the next part of this Spartacus story. Time is collapsed on our road. Two dead from the upper Danube would have meant nothing much here in 72 BC. But 2,000 dead men, perhaps three times that number, here and all across the Gargano, must surely have made some impact. There might easily have been thousands of slaves floating around here after the defeat of Crixus and his men.

There was no requirement for Publicola's legions to do anything except, if it became absolutely necessary, to get the nuisances out of the way. There would have been little looting opportunity. When slaves defeated Romans, they stripped the bodies for cloaks, weapons and armour; victories were their fuel. But the Romans had no need to reciprocate. There was no reason to do anything but leave the remains to rot, no beliefs that made them guilty in any way of ignoring all corpses altogether.

They will have left any bodies of their own men on the rocks and hillsides too. The commanders knew well the Theban legends of Greece, the sharply different fates of the two dead brothers when their war was over, the home-boy Eteocles buried, the invading Polynices unburied, their sister Antigone punished for giving them equal respect. These were mere stories to the Romans. For weeks after the defeat of Crixus there would have been flesh everywhere here, not all of it the flesh of slaves, every part decaying into the sand and soil.

Corpses on a beach? It was a surprise when I came upon this street today. It is named after the most famous corpse ever buried here. My notebook is open on a low white wall along the Via Archita, sole memorial in Mattinata to an ancient inventor, numerologist, astronomer and autocrat, the inspiration of a single mysterious poem in Latin and of mathematics and geometry in every language. Archytas of Tarentum was once, it is said, a dead body on these sands. Horace wrote about him and set his poem here.

Roman poetry did not run by the Roman military code. Most of it was Greek to the core. Poets were allowed, even encouraged, to show that death was not the end. There were other possibilities after the last breath. There was a poet's convention that on a beach, indeed especially on a beach, a dead body might even speak, might ask for its traditional Greek burial, the three handfuls of sand that were a price of entry to other worlds. Horace's thirty-six lines form one of the stranger works on this theme, and one of his own strangest, set near what is now the Via Archita where the pilgrims sunbathe after their exertions for St Michael and the hoteliers watch anxiously for anyone who might fill their empty rooms.

Archytas is not himself the speaker in the poem. This pioneering scientist and sometime ruler of Metapontum's neighbour, Tarentum, already has his burial. His gravestone is being addressed by someone else: 'You measured out the

A MESSAGE FROM A CORPSE to a GRAVE

Horace Odes 1. XXVIII

You measured out the globe and made mathematics from a million grains of sand, but none of that much helped you, Archytas. A few offerings of dust confine you now by the Mattinata shore. It makes no difference that you drew maps of the stars. You were always going to die.

Even mortals whom the gods most loved had to die, even heroes of Troy. Your own hero too, Pythagoras of Metaponto, had his place on that same path to that same universal night. **

Some men die before everyone's eyes, as spectacles of war. Others slip unseen into the sea. I was one of those whom no one saw. The South wind sent this sailor down. So you, who are a passing stranger at this grave, place some shifting sand on my corpse. *

Do that thing and you will win safety from the wind and the waves, with a guarantee from Jupiter, who rules the sky, and from Neptune, guardian of Archytas's own hometown.

Don't do it and you and your children will surely suffer. Perhaps one day a passing stranger will pass by your own dead body. The dead deed won't take long. Three scoops of sand, please, and then be on your way globe and made mathematics from a million grains of sand, but none of that much helped you' is the opening cry: '*Te maris et terrae numeroque carentis arenae Mensorem cohibent, Archyta.*' The praise for earthly achievement was well deserved, as Horace's more learned readers might have known. Archytas had been the autocratic elected ruler of what was once the greatest city on Italy's southern coast, Greek Tarentum, home too of Livius Andronicus, the popular playwright whose woman-in-chains drama *Andromeda* had once been such a draw. From Archytas' city had come many lost writers of the risqué and burlesque, the comic spectaculars on tragic themes which filled the game days before the gladiators began.

This ruler of Tarentum was an equal of Pythagoras and a friend of Plato, the promoter of philosopher kingship and the immortality of the soul. Archytas was even famed for once having saved Plato from slavery – in the hands of a less thoughtful Sicilian monarch. He had also founded the science of mechanics – and made a flying wooden dove which propelled itself on unseen strings as though by magic. He had studied the stars and invented various forms of what we now call solid geometry, the measurement of shapes which are not there and which we cannot see. This was useful: it taught priests how they could double the volume of an altar if that was what their gods required. This formula was a long-lasting truth, a rare thing on this Spartacus Road. It was also a liberator of other imaginations. However much or little his readers knew of this military sage, Horace recognised Archytas as a champion expander of the human mind.

The nameless speaker on the beach is wondering how such an extraordinary figure, a king who once measured earth, sea, skies and altars, can be confined in so tiny a space on a beach. 'A few offerings of dust confine you now by the

Mattinata shore and it makes no difference that you drew maps of the stars: '*Pulveris exigui prope litus parva Matinum Munera, nec quidquam tibi prodest Aerias tentasse . . .*' Shakespeare took the same thought when he had Prince Hal consider the corpse of Harry Hotspur in *Henry IV Part One*. 'When that this body did contain a spirit, A kingdom for it was too small a bound; But now two paces of the vilest earth Is room enough.' Shakespeare's speaker, however, is alive, and on his way to becoming King Henry V. After some twenty lines of Horace's poem it becomes clear that his unnamed speaker too, like Archytas, is already dead. The words come from an unburied body, a neglected prey to the lapping waves.

This is an angry and defiant corpse, spitting out its message that some men are *spectacula* whom the Furies give to the god of war while others end their lives in the sea. Young and old stand equally in the rush to death. The tour of the world's horizons taken by the great thinker Archytas was of no more benefit than the journeyings of any soldier or sailor. That is the message of the corpse on the beach, aimed at conceptual conquerors, pioneers of solid geometry, manipulators of curve and plane, at everyone, friend of Plato or simplest fighter, who meets the same end and needs the same burial rite, the three handfuls of sand or soil or dust.

The drama takes an unexpected last, dark turn. The corpse's final lines are spoken not to Archytas, nor to anyone else who is already dead, but to whichever living human is closest, to the reader, to whomever is alive and passing by on the beach. Fail to do your duty and eternal damnation on you and on your children.

Horace did not himself believe in the route to eternity paid for with a handful of dust. He hoped for immortality for his works, for his civilisation, but not for himself. He recognised the needs of tradition and respect but knew that those gifts were not universal. He was fascinated by the beliefs and disbeliefs of others and knew how a poet could use them, creating an everyman of this peculiar peninsular place, home to temporary tourists, pilgrims packed in one small cave, wraith-like seabirds that the ancients here saw as drowned sailors from Troy, the burial place of a defeated slave army and a philosopher king.

There may have been once a solid, stone monument to Archytas here. The ruler of Tarentum was believed to have fallen in battle on this Mattinata beach, leading his forces against the locals of Apulia. Horace may have heard the story in his childhood and seen the evidence. He may have seen it only in his mind. It is just as well that neither Horace nor the character in his poem can see the Via Archita today, twenty yards of rubbish bins and graffiti which, even 2,500 years on, seems a poor reward for such a pioneer.

There were other shifting memorials to great men by the seashore which Horace would certainly have known – including that of Pompey, builder of Rome's first permanent theatre, patron of Publicola, loser in his Roman civil war against Julius Caesar, beheaded on the Egyptian sands in 48 BC by men seeking favour with the winner. When first erected, Pompey's headstone bore the legend 'Rich was this man in temples, poor now is his tomb', an understated tribute to as ignominious a death as that of any Roman, stabbed at the water's edge, unwatched by any but slaves of foreigners, his head hacked from his body and sent in a box to his all-conquering rival. By the time the young Appian's ship was reaching Pelusium, chased by killers, guided by crows, the memorial was just another target of Jewish destruction in the mud of the Mediterranean Nile. The old Appian was later able to see its restoration by the Emperor Hadrian, a grave that became a tourist attraction, a place to watch the waves and contemplate the death of famous men for centuries to come.

Via Guerra Giuseppe, Mattinata, Gargano

Spartacus and his main army moved out from here towards the north. The coming months were those of his greatest success, the source of his inspirational repute in centuries ahead. Garganus was the exception. There were no more Roman winners that year. Lentulus and Publicola were defeated in swift succession in encounters which the Roman writers obscured. Appian suggests that even Italian towns, from their own hatred of Rome, were helping the slaves now. Roman soldiers tried to join the army of Spartacus and were rejected by the slaves.

Gaius Cassius Longinus was the next to lead the national response. He had been consul in the year the rebellion began. He too was a friend of Pompey the Great. A later bearer of his name became one of the most famous Romans of them all, the assassin of Julius Caesar, Shakespeare's man with 'the lean and hungry look', the only successful commander when the cause of the tyrant-killers, with Horace on the wrong side, collapsed near the Greek town of Philippi. Defeat by Spartacus, somewhere near the balsamic vinegar and Ferrari factories of modern Modena, did not figure high on the family curriculum vitae, then or since. His descendant was still repaying the debt, and bearing the same name as a burden perhaps, when he called for the death of every slave in the household of the murdered City Prefect more than a century later.

Spartacus was now in the high ascendant. If his war had been like Statius' boxing match, between the massive power of a

Capaneus and the quick-footed wiles of an Adrastus, between the infinitely resourced and the merely resourceful, this would have been the time for a sporting umpire to call it off.

Via Vignolese, Modena

Carlo is from Cracow. He is on the pavement outside the bicycle-repair shops and TV stores. He has his own twelve-inch screen and a suitcase of DVDs, many of them imprinted with newspaper titles, the *Telegraph*, *The Times* and the *Mail*. During the 1990s Britain became a world-leader in the wiles of selling news with free gifts. As a result there are tomato-smeared 'special copies' of *Paddington Bear*. There is a *How to Get Ahead in Advertising* that has long lost its gloss. Or would I like *An Inconvenient Truth* in French or *La Dolce Vita*, with matching mudstains and mascara, courtesy of the *Observer*? Almost anything is possible. For more than a decade many films suffered this fate. After a Hollywood release, a bank-holiday TV showing, a few weeks on a 747, a cable premiere in Kabul and a targeted campaign to make C1 under-twenty-fives see the benefits of a free press, even the best movies have ended up here in Carlo's case.

It is probably not his real name. I have been beginning to doubt whether Carlo from Capua, my tin-armed, chemo-dyed guide in Rome, was called Carlo either. It does not matter much. This man is more like a ghost than a centurion. His skin is the colour of a water glass with a few drops of coffee. His neck is threaded like a thin steel bolt. In the tiny alley behind him, hardly more than a fissure between two walls, the sort of space which a rumbling lorry on the next street, or an earthquake a thousand miles away, might close for ever, there is a leather sofa. He places the TV at one end.

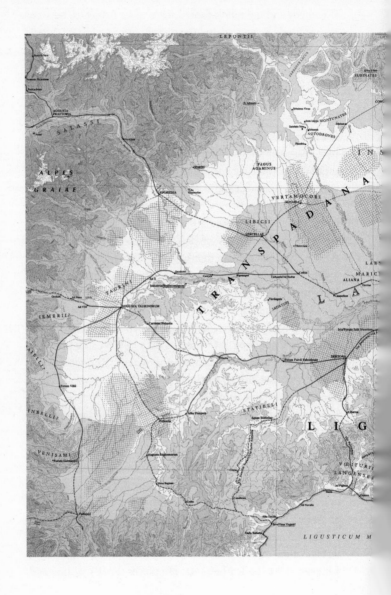

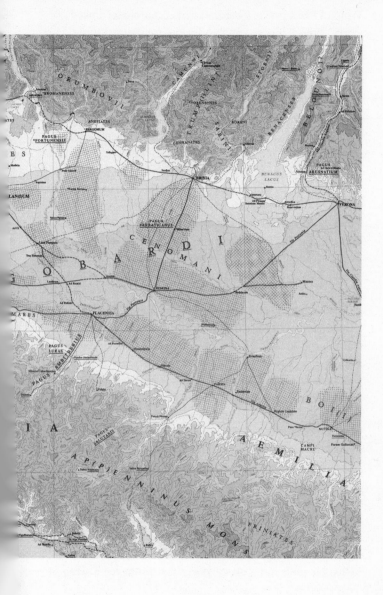

Would I like a preview before I make a purchase? I need not worry about Chinese knock-offs. His are the real thing. He has *Romeo and Juliet* and *Roget's Thesaurus, Driving for Beginners* and *Dr Johnson's Dictionary*.

Does he have the original *Spartacus*? I have wanted to watch Kirk Douglas again ever since leaving Rome. I am too far along this journey now to have only memories from school. Did we see the whole film even then, or just a part or just a trailer? I have no idea.

Carlo gives me a curious look, removing his dark glasses and revealing pin-like pupils and unevenly plucked eyebrows. He unzips a side pocket of his case and brings out a see-through DVD travel pack plastered with the words 'Bombay, Bahrain, Penang', the Spartacus gay cruising guides to the world. Nakedness, whips, cruelty and sweat have made Spartacus a gay trademark. This is now, it seems, what my subject is known for best.

It could have been worse. Carlo might have offered the collected speeches of Rosa Luxemburg. The Spartacus Road took many turnings as it left the ancient world. German communism and gay fetishism were only two of its destinations. The combination of Karl Marx and beautiful Greek bodies was irresistible. When revolutionary muscle was yoked to buggery and beating on demand, the result was a potent brand. It still survives in the criminal charges against Bush and Sharon, hammered-and-sickled on to the philosophy-school walls of Capua.

But not tonight, thank you. Surely Carlo had a copy of the Kirk Douglas epic? A digital guide to gay clubs in East Berlin is not what I need. At least one desperate newspaper, somewhere, at some time, must have given away *Spartacus* the movie. He goes to another zipped pocket, this one full of DVD specials, triple sets, Mozart operas, original collectors' items. He pulls out a plastic cover that protected a scrap of deep saffron paper, flocked and pitted, fit best to repair a stain on an Indian restaurant wall. On it was a sword-arm, torn off at the wrist, and the letters ACU. He puts the disc in his player and turns away.

Flies settle on the furthest plastic sofa arm as though it were genuinely the cow-skin it was once meant to resemble. They burrow into the horsehair as though it really were the hair from a horse. A dark-blue cloud fills the screen. For several minutes there is nothing but music, bouncy marches struggling from the base of the machine, trilling romantic hints dulled by insect-infested cushions. Even on a Chinese knock-off you get some sort of picture. So far this could be 'Favourite Tunes of the Fifties', a free gift from your friends at the *Daily Express*.

Then credits roll. The letters SPARTACUS appear in expanding angular capitals, as though written on pleated curtains blown by the wind. This is, at least, the right film. There is a swirl of blue and terracotta, like watching a land-mine slowly explode or a seaside picture postcard stretched in all directions. The lash of whip and yellow sky suggest we may have reached the desert mines of Libya which the soundtrack has prom-ised. The slave ship which brings the hero to Italy is a grey-black beetle; the gladiator school of Capua a cowpat with creeping grubs; until Carlo returns, bounces the

257

monitor on an exposed metal spring and there is a man's head in a boiling pot of soup. The story has begun.

The escape from Batiatus' kitchens is easier and clearer than the Koreans and I imagined it back in Santa Maria Vetere. Kirk Douglas's school is not in the town by the site of the later amphitheatre but safely, maybe even correctly (who knows?), in the most isolated countryside. It is so unprotected as to be abandoned after the break-out. The gladiators even return there to make a pair of captured farmers poke swords at each other while the former netmen and pikemen look on – a show which Crixus organises and Spartacus nobly brings to a halt.

The gladiators gather on Mount Vesuvius, setting up what is almost a small town there with women and children and new arrivals to be trained in the arts of war. Spartacus has his own woman, not a Thracian priestess but Varinia from Britannia. As the plot flickers on, the sense of a love story overwhelms the sense of any other kind of story. It might look different in CinemaScope but the fighting slaves do not seem to fight anything, or even do anything. They do not make the abseiling escape from the mountain top that Frontinus reports. They do not defeat Glaber's irregular army; they simply occupy the camp. By the time we reach the big battle which they are going to lose we have not seen any of the battles which the slaves actually won. More than an hour and a half has slipped by, painlessly for audience and Romans alike.

Somewhere near here in Modena there occurred one of the biggest upsets in military history, the defeats of two Roman consuls and the governor of northern Italy by a band of slaves led by a few gladiators. Anyone making an epic movie of a rebellion that 'came close to destroying Rome', as a dark voice intoned at the start, might reasonably have shown scenes of slaves fighting and winning. It is near the end now and there has not been a victory of any kind.

Carlo comes back. He blanks the picture. Do I want the DVD? I am not sure I will get another chance to play it but, for ten euros, it is worth it anyway. What was it about? he asks. He gets impatient. 'So an army of Germans, Greeks and other trash like me has a good time in Italy for a while and then gets kicked over?'

There is not even much pillage, and certainly no rape, in the film. The gladiators' treasure-chests fill up with gold without apparent violence. Kirk Douglas is a benign Pied Piper, charming childlike followers from the countryside. There are no funeral games for Crixus, none of the sacrifices of Roman prisoners that Appian describes, nothing at all of the crucifixions of Romans, the staging of spectaculars in which Roman fought Roman to the death. This is a peculiarly wimpy Spartacus, without victory, without viciousness, without violence, without anything much except the love of a good woman and an eye on a very distant future.

Varinia's eyes are very much the sharpest thing on the screen, flashing, shining, speeding from side to side like a soccer linesman in a glow-black vest. She is a spectacular in herself, looking, being looked at, as if she were nothing but an eye. She must be even better on the big screen.

Via Aldo Moro, Pognana Lario

It was now the winter of 72 BC. Spartacus had led his troops to the northernmost edge of the country, the kneebone of the Italian boot. What next? At some moments the slave army had its eyes on the Alps. At others it showed its back to them. Sometimes the whole force looked the same way, sometimes in opposite ways. There were passes through the mountains, or the local people said there were, and places of safety on the other side, or some thought that there might be. There were also roads back south that the slave soldiers knew much better, roads direct to Rome, roads bypassing Rome to the east, hundreds of towns, farms and villas where they could bring terror, take pleasure and increase their fighting strength.

Spartacus had to make a decision, sticking to a previous plan, changing it, following, leading, commanding, listening, or all or none of those things. He had momentum, the weight of a successful movement of men and machinery. He did not have a strategy but he did have some choices, two main choices, to leave Italy or to stay.

VIII

TORNO to PICENTINO

Villa Pliniana, Torno

Sometimes at night sleepers in the house awoke to the rattling of iron chains. Some of them had merely heard the noise. Some had seen the man who carried the chains, his steps crippled by the fetters on his legs. The seeing was much the worse. Once the sound had turned into vision, the image never died. Even in the daylight the horror remained, worse in the day than in the night, the memory of crushed wrists and ankles bringing more fear than the apparition itself.

This was the start of a ghost story from a first-century man of Como. A Roman senator who had two homes near to here told it to a friend from whom he was seeking advice. He described how eventually the clanking chains had made it impossible for anyone to remain in the house of the spectre. It was put up for rent or sale at the lowest price on the slim chance that some newcomer in town might move in, either foolhardy or unaware.

Eventually, a philosopher called Athenodorus saw the price, discovered the reason for it and took the challenge. He sent his servants to bed but stayed awake himself, writing in his notebooks and keeping the utmost concentration on his theories so that no imagined body should enter his mind. At first, there was nothing but the general silence of the night;

then came the clanking of iron and the dragging of chains. He did not look up or stop writing but steeled his mind to shut out the sounds.

Then the noise grew louder, came nearer, was heard in the doorway and then inside the room. The philosopher looked around, stood and recognised the ghost that had been described to him, beckoning that he should follow it outside. He told it to wait and went on with his work, bending over his pen and paper while the intruder rattled its fetters over his head.

After a while, and at his own convenience, he stopped his writing, picked up his lamp and did as the creature wished. The ghost moved off slowly as though the chains were a real weight upon it, turned off into a courtyard and disappeared. The philosopher marked the spot with a pile of dried grass and leaves and went to bed. Next morning he told the local magistrates that the place should be dug up to see what lay below. They found bones twisted with metal bonds, the remains of a body that had long ago rotted away. After their removal the apparition never recurred.

This story stuck in the mind of its teller, Gaius Plinius Secundus, known in English as Pliny the Younger, one of the greatest figures of this area where the Alps make Italy's natural northern wall. The lakeside town of Como was his birthplace and his two villas here were among his favourite homes.

This is the part of the Spartacus Road, a piece of lakeshore oppressed by cypress and sunless cliffs, where I am not a total newcomer. I heard this ghost story before I ever read it, back in 1969, here in Torno on the way to studying at the University of Perugia. I worked in a hotel at Pognana Lario a few miles back from here, rising higher than I deserved in a business whose owner deeply distrusted his fellow Italians.

Ghost-hunting seemed to be a local obsession then. Julius Caesar, the Emperor Nero, Spartacus, Hannibal, Hercules:

everyone had some sort of local connection. The favourite object of pursuit was Pontius Pilate, who appeared from time to time on a shaded part of the shore, stamping on the pebbles, it was said, where the grey grass grows down now to the waves. But there were problems with Pilate. Not only were there no buried bones but Como was not alone in claiming to host his grave. There was competition with other mountain towns for the credit, principally with Lausanne, where the condemner of Christ had once bitten a diver on the neck, with Lucerne's Mount Pilatus, where he had been seen jotting names in a notebook of his fellow damned, with Tiersee where he roared like a bull and Ehsten where he boomed like a bittern.

Pliny, by contrast, was indisputably the local man made good. My ghost-hunting guide was the sixty-year-old sales-man who brought Galbani yogurts to the hotel. It did not take us long to negotiate appropriate discounts for *naturale*, *fragola* and *frutti di bosco*. The rest of our time, which, like the man himself, was never less than ample, was spent spiriting personalities from the past. Pliny the Younger was his absolute favourite, a man of sympathy and understanding who thought and wrote about apparitions as well as, if I were watchful and acute, sometimes becoming one.

This hero had a glancing contact with many of the people and places of the Spartacus Road so far. He was a seventeen-year-old witness to the great eruption of Vesuvius in AD 79 in which his mother's brother, the Pliny known as the Elder, died a scientist's death, sailing too close to the scene in order to understand it more precisely, gassed by its incandescent dust. He knew Statius, the poet whose father had died while at work on a poem about the same eruption. He was a friend of Frontinus the water-man and took over his priestly job as augur when Frontinus died. He also shared his friend's inter-est in water sources if not in the stratagems of slave wars. The great attraction of the house known today as Villa Pliniana was – and is – a spring which overflows into a basin three times a day, some kind of natural siphon which Pliny described with a painter's care.

Pliny would be pleased that he was still being pursued and read so long after his death – but not surprised. His legacy was something to which he gave serious thought. He had reached the consulship, the acme of a political career even under the Empire. He had endowed foundations. He had collected art. He had won famous cases at law. He had written letters too which he expected to be influential long after their writer was gone.

In one of them he writes to Tacitus describing what he had witnessed twenty-five years before at the eruption of Vesuvius and how a decision to stay at home and study his Livy had saved him from the same nasty death as his uncle. He hopes that his reputation will win him his own place in Tacitus' work. Unlike his uncle, who had fought cavalry battles on the Rhine, he was never a fighter himself. Risk and danger were not his choices in life. But he had powerful friends with whom he corresponded on gossip and ghosts, warfare and water mechanics.

Pliny's letters did not survive quite as he intended. Like so many companions on the Spartacus Road, they exist now only through the thinnest thread of chance. The popularity of Symmachus' letters, four hundred years later, was key to the collection and publication of Pliny's too. Symmachus set a brief fashion and Pliny was the bigger beneficiary. But he stands firmly now at the beginning of a long line of men and women who have created careful images of themselves, not in stone but in autobiography.

These letters bring us unusually close to an individual personality. My Galbani salesman approved Pliny's interests in strength and health, subjects newly associated with yogurt in the 1960s. From this plump seller of milk products I learnt about Pliny's marriages (three), his sadness at his third wife's inability to have children, the stresses of his personal and courtroom trials – and the description of Vesuvius, remembered almost word for word, how death came like sleep to those who inhaled the gases of the mountain.

He was angry at how much less we knew about natural disasters that had happened so much more recently. There had 'never been a newspaper reporter like Plinio', he said, ignoring the quarter-century gap between the eruption and Pliny's decision to file his story. I did not appreciate Pliny the Younger then: or recognise how, by getting close to the greatest spectacular of his time but not too close, by mixing vivid bravura with judicious modesty, by staying alive and filing crisp copy to the correct address, albeit a little late, he had good claim for induction in the journalists' halls of fame.

Pliny had a strong feel for 'human interest'. He tells the story of a Roman matron who agonisingly conceals the death of her son from her dying husband until, finally, broken by grief, she stabs herself and hands the sword on to him with the words, 'It does not hurt, Paetus.' Pliny's verdict on this was: 'immortal, almost divine'. My Galbani friend liked it too. It reminded him, he ruminated, of the years after the war, of how long the pains of the conflict were repressed, of how eventually they had to emerge. There were no suicides while Mussolini was alive, only when he was dead, and long after he was dead, shot near here at Monte Tremezzo; his father's sister had seen it.

The philosophical milkman rambled along the path to the Villa Pliniana, through the world of his old friend, as though no part of it had changed. He had little interest in the new houses by the silver-striped bays of the lake. The Galbani seller was cautious about whether he had ever himself seen the ghost of his hero; he hinted he had come close. He always spoke about him as one would a newly deceased neighbour and friend.

He described how Pliny had collected statues of emperors, how he liked to look around him and see the fatherly Augustus, the troubled Tiberius, sweet Caligula (in the marble version), Claudius without his limp and Nero with his favourite musical instrument. There was Vespasian the squinter who came from nowhere, his cheeks folded like piles of cushions, the emperor who began the building of the Colosseum. There was his smug, bulging-browed, narrow-mouthed son Titus, the hammer of the Jews, the Elder Pliny's friend from German-fighting days, the emperor who completed the world's greatest stadium. After him Vespasian's second son, the lascivious, sideways-laughing Domitian. Finally, the plain and puritan Trajan, pursing his lips.

There is no contemporary portrait bust of Pliny himself. The statue that he chose to commemorate his achievements was a small Corinthian bronze, with a lengthy marble inscription of his own best deeds. This was a typically careful choice. To commission a very splendid bust of oneself might have been excessively showy (a practice best left to the emperors in his garden). To do nothing might have been perversely modest (like dear Frontinus, collector of water and stratagems, who banned any tomb for himself because his aqueducts were quite enough). A good-quality antique with some suitably deathless prose? The perfect compromise.

For the man who sold Como its yogurts there was no greater pleasure than to sit by the intermittent spring at the Villa Pliniana, reading Pliny's description of it, picnicking as Pliny had done (but as was not always possible in years of abandonment and war), placing a ring on the dry margins (as Pliny had) and waiting for the inundation. 'Is there some force of water hidden out of sight which sets the spring in motion when it has drained away but checks and cuts off the flow when it has filled up?' He did not know the answer to his hero's question. He just wanted to take himself back there to when the question was asked. In 1964 he was soon about to retire from milk-products and to smile his tubby way through Latin books instead.

By the time that I had left him and spent a year in Oxford, that kind of identification with the classical past was foolishness, fraud and fallacy. The Latin never again flowed so easily into my head; and no one could admit then to a gap-year with a ghost-hunter. Back here now, I am back in his mind and a bit closer to his hopes. It is possible to recreate parts of the ancient world, and not only with Hollywood togas. We can know and imagine. We can build upon others' knowledge and imaginations. We can select from our sources as from a guide-book or anthology. We do not need them all. An ancient source – a text of Pliny or Statius or Horace – is just what it says it is, no more so, no less. It is the spring or well, not its water. The source has always been there, sometimes hidden but unchanged in itself. The source is the same in every age. The water is not the same. We find the source. We drink the water. The water is different every day.

Even on a high blue afternoon the air is heavy. The cypresses seem capricious guards, sometimes protecting the narrow house from the mountains, at other times seeming to lever it into the lake. Not even a line of blocking, black Mercedes limousines can crush every spirit. If we were on the Pliny Road rather than that of Spartacus, it would be very much easier to bring our subject solidly and certainly from our thoughts.

Pliny never mentions Spartacus. He would have been disturbed to know that a gladiator's ghost was worth anyone's pursuit – unless, perhaps, to improve the prospects of a house sale. Like many thoughtful men of his time, he was ambivalent about the arena. He wrote proudly to a friend of not paying for public games or gladiator contests but paying for a children's home instead. He recognised that an inscription over a library or bronze masterpiece would be visible for longer than would a few hours of violence. But when the occasion was the funeral of a very dear wife there was still need for the 'most powerful spectacle of all', a gladiatorial gift to her departing spirit. No one knows now how many pairs he thought appropriate. It seems unlikely that Amazons or dwarfs were part of the show.

The Colosseum was a tool of calculation for a man of sensibility, a way of thinking about decisions even when he was not choosing the gladiators themselves. The arena was a metaphor and a means of communicating problems at law and in life, rather as we use football and cricket today. Pliny had its customs in mind even when he was presiding officer of the Senate, when he and his colleagues faced a judgement similar to that in the case of the city prefect, Pedanius Secundus, four decades before. When a senator had been killed in his own house, what should be the verdict on the freedmen of his household? The slaves had to die, but should the ex-slaves be considered guilty too? And if the freedmen were guilty what should be their punishment, exile or execution?

Pliny's problem was how to put the options to the vote. His preference was for leniency. How would that outcome best be won? Guilty vs Not Guilty was one way, a one-on-one contest that everyone could understand. Another way was taking all the options together, Not Guilty vs Exile vs Death in a simultaneous three-way fight.

In AD 61, the year of Pliny's birth, Nero had allowed the slaves of Pedanius to be executed while intervening on the side of public opinion to save the freedmen. In the summer of AD 105, in a new era of freedom after the death of Domitian, the Senate could decide on the freedmen for itself. Pliny supported the Senate group wanting a total acquittal for the freed staff of Afranius Dexter. There was reason to believe that it had been not murder but assisted suicide. Other groups in the Senate, equally matched in numbers, wanted banishment to a barren island or execution.

How the votes were taken, as later parliamentarians would better understand, would critically affect the outcome. Pliny went for the three-way simultaneous option, estimating that some of the votes for banishment would come over to those wanting acquittal. Instead, the death-penalty advocates moved en bloc behind the banishers. The freedmen were thus condemned to rot on some Mediterranean rock.

'In some of the public games,' Pliny wrote ruefully to a friend, 'one gladiator draws a lot which entitles him to stand aside and fight the victor.' He could have tried first for a not-guilty verdict before pitting the executors against the banishers if he lost. As this self-consciously decent man struggled with the birth of tactical voting, the squeeze and other developments of later democracy, the only analogy in his mind was the Colosseum.

Slave-owning was a practice that could, he thought, be modified. The worst masters might be encouraged to behave like the best. There were proper means of making the slave-owner safer. He kept slaves on his farms but he prided himself on never keeping them chained and on judging each by reputation or character not, like livestock, by their appearance.

This did not, he recognised, make him safe. He describes the murder of a man at Formiae by slaves who surrounded his bath and stabbed him in the stomach, neck and groin. This particular master had been cruel, horribly forgetful of the fact that, like Horace, his father too had been a slave. But even kindness and consideration were no protection. Reasoning capacity could not be relied upon in a slave. Brutal character could not always be spotted before purchase. An owner could never feel wholly safe.

In the Galbani man's view, if one were to have been a slave in ancient Como, Pliny's would have been the house in which to serve. He offered lettuce, eggs and beetroot at his table and mocked providers of sows' innards, sea urchins and Spanish dancing girls. He would have helped you write your will. He thought that a man's last written words were the best testament to his character. He loyally honoured his uncle's memory, compiling one of our earliest bibliographies. The listed works included a twenty-volume history of Rome's wars with Germany, a project inspired, its author said, by the ghost of a dead commander and which Symmachus, three hundred years later, would have surely had on his shelves.

Pliny wrote plays that have not survived and poetry which has survived in just enough quantity for his reputation to have been better without it. But his prose, a companion to the poems of Statius, is a portrait of a world far away and how one inhabitant of it wanted to stay in our memory. To the milk salesman he was simply '*simpatico*', a man he could understand, and there were not many people of any age of whom he could say that.

Pliny wanted always to be seen as a civilised man. He tried to be humane in his application of the law, including the law on the freeing of slaves. Like Statius and Spartacus he even won a place in the favour of the Church. He left behind in his letters one of the first independent accounts of Christianity: and the use of torture on two deaconesses to gather his evidence does not seem to have been held against him. The Younger and Elder are enthroned today like thin-faced bishops on either side of the great Duomo door in their home town, local heroes caged against the pigeons, casting their eyes with disapproval on the tourists and beggars below.

Piazza del Duomo, Como

Thirty years on from those Galbani ghost days here, I had a second experience of conjuring the spirit of Pliny the Younger. In the year 2000 I was at last undergoing some exotic chemotherapy for my cancer. Nero had been revealed as a tumour of one of the smaller pink fishes in the body's pond, the pancreas, 'all flesh' in Greek, a delicacy apparently much prized by cannibals. This pain-bringer was no longer certain to kill me, merely likely to do so. There was now some possibility of escape.

The treatment was an accelerating cycle of normality, semi-madness, delirium and normality again – with gaps between these stages at first but gradually a continuous circle of effect following cause. There was neither sharp pain nor battle pictures of the earlier kind. Every edge was blurred. By my fifth cycle the useful time that I had once called my 'lucidity hours' was reduced to a few mornings a month.

My hospital nurses had plans for those mornings. I was to imagine scenes from my past, the happier the better. Arranging my personal history, like arranging my books and papers, was no longer designed only to make life complete and death almost reasonable. The memories would help me get well, just like the American chemicals that were coursing through my veins, the yellow bags of liquid that the sisters treated like Semtex. Old pleasures must enhance the will to live. I could not argue with that, or, indeed, argue much with anything.

To prepare myself for this promised good time, free from pain and the fear of pain, I sat in the sunshine in a garden chair. Each of my legs had to be individually identified in my head, selected as though from a rack of legs and hauled next to the other. They were like Volumes One and Two of a Victorian novel, separately comprehensible, better together.

I had 'a long tube of red hot hay' beside me on the grass; or, at least, those were the words written on my memory-jogging scrap of paper. The reference might have been to my right arm or my left foot or almost anything. My mouth was the most lucid thing about me, refreshed with chlorhexidine gluconate, a variety of green liquid wash, peppermint-flavoured according to the label, wire-brush flavoured as it seemed to me but still scouring and cleansing for a tongue like the element in an old kettle. I had taken my warfarin to thin the blood and my vitamin B capsule to stop my hand shaking. I was even able to chew a soft yellow lozenge called Nystatin which chases fungus away. New doctors were in charge now, American and British, pugnacious scientists instead of consultants and diplomats. I was hopeful and ready to remember.

The sun shone hot. The roses were burning red. Out came the mental pictures of family holidays, of weddings and christenings and boat trips on the Thames, fixed photographic images but full of light like the colour slides that my father used to keep in blue plastic boxes and project on to our walls. Down, as though from some system of photo-files, came pictures of newspaper colleagues calling out deadlines and congratulating each other on successes whose nature was not clear at all.

This did not seem too hard. It was something like a bran-tub gamble at a fairground. I could not choose the subjects with much precision. Occasionally there was an unhappy picture and, like Athenodorus in the haunted house, I concentrated with modest success on keeping it away. But the most persistent picture was a scene very like the one I have just been writing. It was the scene of the young yogurt-buying classicist on the shores of Lake Como – and with him the ghost-finder and, with them both, another figure, unnamed, dressed in Roman style, not likely to have been Caesar, Spartacus or Pontius Pilate. It was the younger Pliny. It could have been no other. There was no sound from the image but Pliny was speaking to the yogurt man and the yogurt man was speaking to me. I never saw Pliny back in 1969. I did not see him in my chemo-fuelled rose garden three decades later. But I did see myself in Como seeing Pliny in Como.

Ten years later still, now again in Como, I cannot call up that figure from the ancient past, much as I would like to, much as I play with every idea of the fighter I have chosen to follow on his road. I can only call up my own recollecting of that past. I can only remember myself struggling – with deformed and distorted will – to make pictures disappear and appear. The Spartacus Road is not a ghost-hunt but I do have here the image of a ghost-hunt, an event of recollection that I have every reason to believe in.

A few months after those memory games in the garden, the chemical poisons and a surgeon's knife put an end to Nero. The source of so many violent pains and picture shows ended on a white slab the size of a dinner plate. He looked like whale blubber. There was the simplest photograph of him in my hospital file, a print not a negative, needing no one to hold up any dark transparent corners to the light.

Pliny has two other stories from the spectral world in his letters. The first is that of a giant female Spirit of Africa which appears twice before a Roman general, predicting both his success and his death. The second is of an ethereal hair-cutter, a ghost who sheared the locks of two of his own freed slaves. He wants his correspondent to weigh up carefully the case for believing in ghosts and for not believing in them. He wants a balanced argument but also a choice. He wants the application of human reason and a firm statement, based on the evidence, for one view over the other.

Before that he has another piece of advice from Como. He argues the case for continuing in health the disciplines we have learnt when we are diseased. If in sickness we dream not of lust and slandering our enemies but of lakes and springs, that is how we should behave when we are well. If we prosper against a cancer death sentence (as I did) while imagining the imaginings of the ancient past, we should not abandon that aim, however hard in the cold times of health and sanity it may seem.

Via Roma, Tivoli

No one now knows why the northward march of the slave army, its liberty march as some saw it, stalled, stopped and slid back in the direction it had come. Perhaps the marchers realised that Rome's forces on the other side of the Alps, from Thrace to the Pyrenees, were as likely to defeat them as were those in Italy. Roman rule was rapidly tightening over the mountains of Spartacus' own homeland. Perhaps they felt they had not finished here yet, preferring warm rape and wine to the rock and ice which were the alternative most apparent.

There was much proper vengeance still to be taken on cowering farmers, their caves of alcohol, their daughters, wives and spinning-rooms. Terror is a drug just like freedom. Its fighters wanted more of what they had come to enjoy, the flashing eyes of those about to die, the hope-drained pleading of mistresses and masters before the sword struck.

The army held men of increasingly divided views. There were those who refused any longer to live by Roman rules and those who saw and accepted no rules at all. Hardly any army has ever been united in where it should go and what it should do. Most armies are not asked for an opinion. Perhaps the slaves had some sort of vote. Many later writers thought and hoped that the stories of this democracy were true.

The commanders wanted fresh slaves to join their fight. There were more recruits on the Roman road south than there ever would have been on the herdsmen's paths into the northward hills. The case for staying together, for avoiding the fate of Crixus on Mount Garganus, was clear enough. The case for constant movement, for seeking ever fresh ground for pressing men and pillaging supplies, was no

less potent. Soon the army of Capua, Metapontum and Modena was back deep into Italian countryside, doing its business in undefended places.

What did Spartacus himself want? What did the others of the original Capua escapers want? Forcing prisoners to play gladiator improved morale. Everything that built their strength had a purpose. They might plan attacks on farms or armies. If they were mad enough they might attack Rome itself, only fifteen miles from here at Tibur. This Apennine hillside town was the perfect place from which to assault the capital. If they were more measured in their ambitions they would wait and hope to grow stronger still.

Via di Villa Adriana, Tivoli

Meanwhile, the people of Tibur could only watch, wait, listen, talk and get on with their lives. They had leisure time to think about Spartacus but no intelligence of what he might do next. Tibur was the Capua of middle Italy. The name of Rome's luxury suburb came from its Greek founder Tiburtus, grandson of Amphiaraus, the prophet at Thebes and most reluctant of the seven attackers, the one whose arrow flew back to its quiver, who knew that his war would end in catastrophe and that he alone would survive. Tibur's people had preferred peace ever since, offering rural villas and water gardens to Romans who wanted a country place closer to the Forum than Campania. There was always the noise of crashing foam in a town built, long before Rome, at the place where the Anio collapses in the plain for its last stretch into the Tiber river. This was a little paradise that soothed sleepless city minds. Matters that seemed so garish in Rome, multi-coloured in blood and gold, became soft and grey among the whispering spray until only a thin wisp was left as a reminder. Or so its property agents said.

But, even here, anxiety about the slave army was hard to avoid. How mad, how measured were the men on their southward march from the Alps? Some of them, it was said, had the discipline of legionaries, learnt by marching in chains, ankle to ankle, neck to neck, in rhythms that recurred and recurred with every step. Some had never marched further than from clerical office to kitchen, a routine that now made their muscles seem new every day. Why had they not just left over the Alps? In Italy they were free but not free, like prisoners who had exchanged one set of walls for another, like wild animals who had escaped their wooden boxes but were now pacing back and forth in a larger cage. Tibur was in that same cage. That was the problem for the heirs of Tiburtus now.

Life had not yet changed here in any serious way as a result of the revolt. The wine still came from its makers, the corn from the ports. The road from the capital was no more than usually packed with the tired and troubled. Italy was large and the slave army was small. The seventy who had left the school of Lentulus Batiatus, those that had survived both their own successes and those of Gellius Publicola, were leading 70,000, or so one rumour ran. But many millions of slaves were still working, in mines and kitchens, quarries and bedrooms, behind bars and behind desks, for the avoidance of punishment and pain or, if not that, for the best human hopes of another day alive.

The sounds of the river winds in Tibur were ceaseless. They were proof of something beyond the fears of any man's mind. They were as calming as the hum of bees and as meaningless as the din of others' thoughts. They mingled with the sound of bells that has always pealed from deep down in the caverns of the Anio, as otherworldly to the hearer on earth as it is reassuring to his ear.

To most of those living between Como and Tibur the marching men were still nothing. Only to those who stood in their way had they suddenly become everything, every sort of pain, thought and fear, until the thinkers themselves had become nothing. Some had escaped from the army's path, and had told people who had told other people who had told people in Tibur, told stories of rolling horror, of what happened when a hundred men-of-rage hit a house of ten men, twenty women, slaves who pleaded to join them, slaves who simply pleaded.

There are things that people see which stay always in their original colours, not dead tones of flesh but the last blue or green of an eye, not one dark sex forced upon another but the chalked-in-purple pattern of a stare. Some memories, some memories of memories, are bright and solid for ever. Some fade to black and white. Some last only in words, like prodigies, like diamond swords of moon and rain in the sky. Some disappear for ever in spray. It has always been the art of Tibur to make as many anxieties as possible disappear – under high and heavy white stars like those hanging now over its falls.

Statius described a villa here, one of his brightest pieces of praise for bricks and mortar, blurring the lines between what the builder sees and what the artist sees. His is an imagination in which a flooded river is held back by a man, where the leaves of a tree are jumbled with the heavens and where flying waters and a painting of the waters are the same. A mansion floats on waves of glass.

The poet's client, the politician owner of the house which once stretched along both banks here, was a poet himself and a convert to the life of an Epicurean. None of the poems of Manlius Vopiscus survives. But we have pieces of his marble columns, sections of the brickwork which held up his hillside and Statius' description of river nymphs flowing to cool his dining rooms. As Frontinus the water-man complained, there were always wealthy men who thought that public pipes were there to be tapped for private pleasure.

Hercules, a favourite subject for Statius, was the presiding deity at Tibur. His statues often stood throughout Campania in the name of his bellicose title, Hercules Victor. But here he was Hercules the haggler, god of market-traders and cattle-herders, devourer of leftovers, the god to whom anything could be offered and everything omnivorously accepted, a semi-divinity slipping in and out of the water clouds.

Horace praised Tibur too. A few years after his Journey to Brundisium, the poet was given his own house near here as an imperial reward for loyalty and fine words. A few years after that, when Augustus had defeated Mark Antony (he of the 'solid gold piss-pot': how far that was from those wonderful anti-materialist Spartacus virtues, explained Pliny the Elder), seven decades of civil wars were finally over and Horace began to mention Tibur more and more, his beloved land with its 'orchards watered by restless rivulets'. Archaeologists and tourism entrepreneurs have expended enormous effort in not quite establishing where this was. Piranesi drew a map that mocked them for their pains. But anyone can read what Horace wrote, his description of himself composing like a waterside bee and of Tibur itself as '*supinum*', leaning backwards, not the keenest city for the young and ambitious, a bit laid back in the modern sense perhaps.

'Laid back' was always fine here, except in one of the worst of those Italian war years before the benefits of permanent imperial rule had begun. To be *supinum* was to take something of a risk when a slave army was marching from one end of Italy to the other, with an interest (pausing or passing?) in the country's capital only fifteen miles away.

Via Roma, Tivoli

Some inhabitants of Tibur lived here all the time. Some came for holidays. Some had built their own villas. Others had acquired property through political connections. All were concerned about the route which Spartacus might take. But for anyone with a country house for which he had not fully paid there were already new problems as a result of the rebellion.

In the previous decade there had been many examples of state assets turning up, after only tiny payments if any payment at all, in the hands of those deemed useful to the top man at the time. Most of those assets, from fashionable street addresses to vast country farms, had been taken from enemies of that same temporary top man. Like the dukes of Bedford after Henry VIII had 'dissolved' the monasteries, the recipients of this legal largesse were nervous for a while that their gains might be removed. But not for long. Like Russian oligarchs after Boris Yeltsin's dissolution of communist party businesses, many men in proud possession of pretty villas bought by loyalty rather than cash had grown quickly used to so satisfying a state of affairs.

It was only ten years since the brief but bloody dictatorship of the last Roman leader to have 'proscribed' his opponents and put their assets up for sale. Lucius Cornelius Sulla, lover of Campania and promoter of its Hercules cults, had been leader of the aristocratic faction in a civil war against his commoner rival Gaius Marius. These warlords had spent their early lives struggling against Rome's rivals at home and abroad and their latter years fighting each other. Both were now gone, Marius, the big man who brought the poor and even a few slaves into the Roman army, dead for thirteen years and Sulla, the lucky man who feared the power of all lower orders, dead for five. While few of the original owners of proscribed properties were likely now to claim their Tibur villas back, the Roman state, reeling from the costs of war on three fronts, had recently begun to remember the debts that might be collected for the Treasury.

The official mover of the bill to collect the outstanding payments was Gnaeus Cornelius Lentulus, the consul of that year whose army had been so conspicuously unable to repeat the success of his colleague Publicola on Mount Garganus, and whose defeated troops were gradually dribbling back home to disgrace. The mover of the motion behind the scenes is likely to have been Pompey, the soldier-politician who had twice married into the family of Sulla and whom the Dictator had called his 'young butcher'. For five years he had been away from Italy, suppressing the revolt against Roman rule in Spain and freelancing fiercely for his own supremacy.

Lentulus and Publicola were both friends of Pompey, a link which ensured that their defeat by Spartacus cost them only their consular commands, nothing more than temporary disgrace. Lentulus had been working to refill the Roman coffers by collecting unpaid debts. He could also be relied upon to win votes for his master. He was a man far too useful to suffer long for merely losing a battle against slaves.

Another supporter of Sulla had risen rather more slowly to be one of the praetors of 72 BC, the rank immediately below that of consul. Marcus Licinius Crassus had done greater service and paid a higher price than anything achieved or suffered by Pompey. He had lost both his father and his brother to the enmity of Marius. According to Appian, the father killed his son first and then himself, in the best old Roman way when there was no other way out. After seeing his father's severed head on the speakers' rostra in the Forum, Crassus had spent years in Spanish exile, with three friends and ten slaves, some of the time in the back of a cave, and had returned, in his early thirties, to win decisive battles for Sulla in Italy, the last and most crucial in 82 BC at Rome's Colline Gate.

The constitution which Sulla put in place after that victory, with only the most token powers for those outside the Senatorial elite, was the one under which Rome faced the threat from Spartacus. Prospects for a new Sulla were still excellent. If a Pompey wished to emulate the military and political supremacy of his predecessor, there was not so very much to stop him. Any other man, Marcus Crassus or Julius Caesar, had also to act in the knowledge of what was possible for Pompey.

Money and military prestige were the prime currencies. In Rome, Crassus was amassing unprecedented wealth from property, investment, land and slaves. In Spain, against the last, stubborn survivors of Marius' faction, Pompey the Great was winning mostly military glory. The move by Lentulus to make the owners of proscribed property pay their bills may not have been directly aimed at Crassus but it was a warning shot.

There were many disputes about proscribed houses and land, some of them reaching the courts and making great rhetorical reputations for those who won the cases. Crassus was directly accused of adding a name to the proscription lists to get a farm in the south of Italy that he coveted. One of

Cicero's first cases was to protect an heir whose property was coveted by one of Sulla's aides.

Horace had a friend with a house here, Lucius Munatius Plancus, the chancer whose memorial near that of his enemy Cicero was almost part of our Spartacus Road at Formiae. Plancus had arranged proscription for his own brother, Plotius, so that he could get his property, and Horace's seventh ode is dedicated to the plunderer. It is one of his most loving hymns to Tibur: 'its groves and orchards made soft by rapid streams: *lucus et uda Mobilibus pomaria rivis*'.

It is his delight and duty, Horace tells Plancus, to praise their holiday home over more famous beauty spots: this is 'some talk of Alexander and some of Hercules' with Tibur as the 'British grenadier'. He says how much he is looking forward to seeing his friend here, and gives no hint of poor Plotius' fate, hunted down as a friend of Caesar's killers and captured because his perfume betrayed his hiding place. Pliny the Elder thought that any man who wore perfume deserved anything he got, indeed that the death of perfume-wearers justified proscription in itself.

Does a decent Roman wear perfume? This sounds just the right sort of conversation topic for an evening here at any time over the high Roman centuries. Alternatively, the men at their Tibur dinner could take another favourite issue for old Pliny: why all the undiscovered gold and silver of Italy, which surely had to exist somewhere in so wonderful a country, was best left under the ground, flavouring the grapes and removing the moral hazards of its discovery.

In 72 BC, beset by financial and political demands to secure its very safety, the Roman state decided that it needed more money faster than even some new enthusiasm for mining could provide. It wanted a bigger share of the proscription proceeds that had so pleasurably and profitably changed hands. Even if the army of Spartacus were to bypass Rome this time, and bypass Tibur on its way to somewhere else (who knew where?), there was much that summer to disturb the peace-seekers on the Anio's spray-drenched banks.

Piazza del Risorgimento, Picentino

The army of Spartacus avoided Rome and spared Tibur too. It returned to the southern hills and plains where it had begun, stronger than it had ever been in every respect bar that of a strategy.

The Roman Senate responded by removing military command from Pompey's juniors, the two defeated consuls, and giving it to Pompey's rival, Marcus Licinius Crassus. The job was not one that could now be easily refused, even by a politician who had willingly exchanged the routines of soldiering for the then most radical forms of capitalism. The threat was real. The opportunity for glory was greater than anyone could have imagined a year before.

Crassus had the personal resources for taking on the task. Thanks to city property, industrial farming and an innovative employment agency with thousands of specially trained slaves on its books, Crassus had the money to recruit and finance his own legions. In a sneer at the cash-squandering Pompey ('why did anyone call him "the Great"?') he said that no one should ever be considered rich unless he could pay for an army of his own. At a time when most aristocrats avoided business, when property deals were for the countryside not the town and a gentleman's slaves were for himself and not for hire, Crassus had no competitors in meeting the 'private army' criterion of wealth, the one that he himself had set.

He also had a pressing political motive. Pompey's war in Spain was almost over. Soon he would be home, with an inevitable demand for the consulship in 70 and the threat of civil war if he did not get it. Crassus needed to be certain that he was the second consul that year. Victory over Spartacus was his best chance of ensuring that.

He raised six new legions, bearing most of the cost himself. Army veterans, with small farms to defend, were enthusiastic recruits to the ranks. Distinguished men of Rome also joined the city's benefactor in what, this time, with new legions and leadership, with 45,000 men in the field, would surely be a sharp success. Crassus quickly ordered one of his junior officers, a man called Mummius and known in no other context but this, to take 8,000 men southwards on a scouting expedition.

Crassus was famed as a man of strict, unfussy character. His law-court speeches were practical and plain. His money-lending practices were demanding on repayment day but, by the standards of his time, not extortionate in their rates of interest. His personal Greek philosopher was no Epicurean but an austere follower of Aristotle. He kept careful hold on his plans. When a soldier asked him what time he was going to break camp, he replied, 'Are you afraid you will not hear the trumpet?', a story told in Frontinus' rules on keeping essential secrecy.

Crassus' orders to watch Spartacus, to follow him but on no account to engage in even a skirmish, were unlikely to have been unclear. Mummius ignored them nonetheless. There was the lure of glory and the sense still, perhaps, that a slave army needed no more attention than that of a young legate. The result was another rout of Roman forces, somewhere in these low wine-and-chestnut-growing hills, another battle that Roman historians have not wanted to record in any detail, a defeat that spurred the commander to delve deep in the ancient army manuals of discipline.

Sallust's account of this time has vanished except for the tiniest pieces. But we can pick up the Spartacus Road now with a guide who had studied Sallust closely. It is only thanks to Plutarch, the father of biography, that we know of Spartacus' priestess wife, the one who so intrigued Carlo the Capuan in Rome, the Thracian bacchante who saw the snakes coiled around her husband's head as he slept in the slave market. It is Plutarch who reports the first signs of Rome taking Spartacus seriously after the defeats of Varinius and Cossinius, and tells us of the battle of Mutina.

So far my green-backed classroom copy of Plutarch has stayed in the book bag. It has remained unread because its main subject is not Spartacus but Crassus. Plutarch's purpose in telling us of the warrior slave was to illuminate the Roman politician, businessman and general. His popular *Lives of Great Men* has long been studied and admired. If we want to draw the character of Spartacus from the biographer's account of him, we need always to keep Crassus in mind too. Each adversary defined the other, as in so much of the political caricaturing, in newspaper profiles and cartoons, that Plutarch pioneered.

This father of all biographers was a Greek who lived a long life under the rule of emperors in Rome, from Nero in his childhood in the 50s to Hadrian at his death around 120. A contemporary of Pliny the letter-writer and Statius the poet, younger than Appian the historian, older than Frontinus the man of water and military tricks, he shared with all of them the need to adapt as writers and thinkers to an age when freedom was variously and unpredictably constrained.

His family came from central Greece close to ancient Thebes, from Chaeronea, a name once known for world-shaking battles between Greek states but, in Plutarch's day, a place of Roman students, travelling artists and business-men adventurers. He did much of his writing during his priestly career at nearby Delphi whose prophets had once guided great wars but who now advised on wedding dates and marital infidelity. Delphi's centre was the *omphalos* rock, recognised in the Greek world as the smooth round navel of the whole world. Delphi's 'freedom wall', on the side of Apollo's temple, had been the place where former slaves from everywhere had once come to record their freedom. But in the first century AD a priest at Delphi had become a tourist guide more than a political one, a diminution in status which did not stop it being a desirable and respected position for a proud family man with a passion to interpret the not so distant past.

Plutarch admired Roman power. That was wise. The Romans admired Greek art and philosophy. That was their equal wisdom. But Plutarch was dissatisfied with the official conceit that Greeks made bronzes breathe in imitation of life while Romans used the metal to kill people. Plutarch was a fine prose stylist and lived in a vast museum of art, but he did not think that aesthetics were the highest aims of man. He had hardly more respect for marble statues than his contem-porary Frontinus the water-man. He wanted to make men come to life in his words. Through words he could show that the Greeks and Romans each had their great political and military figures, had always had them, similar, subtly different but in many ways equal. He formed the plan of matching par-allel lives of Greeks and Romans, choosing pairs whose virtues and failings illuminated those of the other. It was a transforming idea.

He began at the beginning of history. Theseus, cousin of Hercules and mythical founder of Athens, was matched with Romulus, founder of Rome. Both men fell out with their fellow citizens in the end, showing, as so many later journalists and biographers loved to show, that there was no gratitude in any public life and that even the finest political careers end in failure.

The life of Alexander the Great paralleled that of Julius Caesar. Alexander of Macedon was the one man who might have altered the balance between Greece and Rome. But he had conquered eastward and Italy had been spared to strike another day. These were Plutarch's two longest Lives. Pompey shares his life with the failed Spartan king Agesilaus, a local bogeyman of Delphi and Chaeronea. Brutus, killer of Caesar, stands beside Dion, tyrannicide of Syracuse. The Roman dictator Sulla and the Spartan king Lysander were paired as talented generals who had both ravaged Athens and who had both come to bad ends.

Plutarch compares Crassus to Nicias, one of the Athenian commanders in the great war with Sparta in the golden age of Greece. Both men were exceptionally rich for their time, Nicias from silver mines where chained slaves died in underground water, Crassus from proscription, property speculation and the skilful use of his personal fire service. Plutarch considers Crassus' methods the more reprehensible. Both spent heavily on bribes to their publics, Crassus the more uselessly squandering his resources, as Plutarch sees it. Both were unfortunate in treading the stage in the age of greater stars. Nicias was a religious obsessive while Crassus had no care for religion at all. Crassus was violent and tyrannical while Nicias was timid and cautious to equal excess. Nicias was famous as a peace-maker, a worthy title which Crassus could not claim. Making peace with slaves was not an option, winning it not much of an achievement.

With skilfully manipulated strokes, Plutarch takes us through Crassus' life to the point of his campaign against

Spartacus. Like his literary successors, he showed how the child was father to the man. An avaricious plutocrat from a family of avaricious plutocrats is a less powerful story than that of a poor boy from a proud beginning. Crassus' family had a modest home and, even after acquiring his colossal wealth, the general maintained a modest household, in a marriage to the wife of his dead brother, entertaining generously but without luxury. If he pursued women, it was only for their money; his reputation for mere financial pursuit had to save him on one occasion from the capital charge of violating a Vestal virgin. Plutarch has this prominently in his story.

Crassus had known exile and hardship after the deaths of his father and brother in the first phase of Roman proscription and terror. But his was a more comfortable retreat from the thuggish grip of Marius than that of many, a hideout in a Spanish cave with an interior like a secret temple and two maidservants sent in by his protector to meet his young male requirements. Food and sex, essential for life itself, have to be brought appropriately into any profile of a life.

Plutarch does not pretend that his selection of events is sanctified by the discipline of history. He writes how 'excellence or baseness', the character question with which he is so concerned, comes out not always in conspicuous acts but just as often in a single word, an incautious comment or a joke.

He thinks like a painter, comparing his attention to the 'little things' of life with an artist's preference for the revealing detail in a face.

He likes any kind of rhetorical contrast. In creating the profiles of others, he is always putting himself on show too. He is Plutarch the public performer, defender of both sides, pleader for Caesar as well as for Alexander, for Nicias as well as for Crassus. He was born within a few years of Statius and it is not hard to imagine him declaiming at the same literary spectaculars, circling, lightening, darkening, dazzling, giving cause to decide between his parallel subjects but leaving the final decision for those looking on. It is easy to imagine him in a modern newspaper office, edging his article this way and that, showing balance in both sententiousness and sentence because balance is what must always seem to be there.

Crassus is a man defined by contrasts and parallels. He gained his money by politics and he saved it for political use. He lent his tame philosopher a coat for their shared outings and reclaimed it when the trip was over. He lent fiercely but fairly. When he fought against slaves, he did so with a special understanding of slaves: he had invented a whole new Roman business of training clever Greeks to be architects and accountants and hiring these 'living tools' to those who could not be bothered to improve their tools themselves. All pieces of the past are selected to explain pieces of the future.

Plutarch's Crassus becomes more substantial because the Roman is not compared only with Nicias of Athens, his parallel life, but with the Greek slave against whom he earned such a part of his reputation. When compared with Nicias the hesitant Athenian who lost both control of his people and the turning-point battles of the war with Sparta, even Crassus gets the author's vote, grudgingly and on points. But Plutarch disapproves deeply of Crassus, his obsessive acquisition of wealth most of all. He cannot approve of Spartacus either; but whenever he can make the slave-leader look good and the Roman leader bad he does so.

His Spartacus needs to be a big figure. The gladiator had done so much damage to the might of Rome. He could not be a mere nothing. He had to have not only great bodily strength but 'a great spirit', to be 'more intelligent and nobler than his fate and more Greek than his Thracian background might suggest'. When he first escapes from Capua, he finds new weapons and rejects his gladiatorial arms as 'barbaric': the cluck-cluck approval of the Delphi priest comes louder than the relief of the freed fighter. Plutarch, no enthusiast for Rome's favourite spectator sport, is the prime source of the 'great hero Spartacus', the one whom the likes of Symmachus so wanted to spit out and forget and which later writers so much wished to glorify.

From virtually the moment of Plutarch's death, this version of the classical verities, Athens vs Rome, hero vs hero, became the authorised version of the classical age. The balance shifted between the two but stayed between the two. The process began immediately with Aulus Gellius, an early collector of the literary scrapbooks we call his *Attic Nights*. It continued past the fall of Rome and survived into the Renaissance and into Shakespeare and beyond, with Spartacus just a tiny part of the whole, forgotten by those who wanted to forget it but recreated in passion by those who wanted to remember.

In 71 BC, the defeat of Mummius' misguided forces added another victory to the slave army's battle standards. Crassus, Plutarch tells us, gave the young man a rough reception and his runaway troops a rougher one. When he handed out new weapons he made the soldiers solemnly pledge that this time they would hold them to their deaths.

Some of the men who had thrown away their weapons may

have been survivors of the defeats suffered earlier by the armies of Pompey's friends. There was 'an effeminacy and laxity' among those men of Lentulus and Publicola, says Plutarch. The dangers of a viral defeatism entering the bloodstream of his army were too great. Five hundred soldiers were divided into fifty groups of ten. From each group of ten, one was chosen by lot to be clubbed to death by his colleagues.

Decimation was a disgusting act which Plutarch, writing for his respectable readership, could mention but did not elucidate. The smashing of friend by friend was a sight that the gladiators would have often seen. It was what they might have once done themselves on any day. This decimation was a spectacle for the whole army to watch, enough spectators to fill the mightiest amphitheatre in this region of amphitheatres.

In normal circumstances, a standard gladiator show, a common reward and inspiration for soldiers, would have been enough to boost morale. Showing the 'good deaths' of netmen and pikemen to the troops was a tradition. Showing the shameful deaths of fellow Romans was a revival of a more ancient history. But sometimes a revival is the most potent show to put on any stage. Plutarch had no criticism of this act. It made another powerful parallel within his parallel lives.

The army of Spartacus, maybe recognising the benefit of self-slaughter to Roman morale, moved away from Crassus. It may have suffered a defeat first, losing some 6,000 men as Appian reports. Its next direction was back down south towards the Straits of Messina, new territory where it could recruit and regroup.

IX

REGGIO CALABRIA
to BUCCINO~VOLCEI

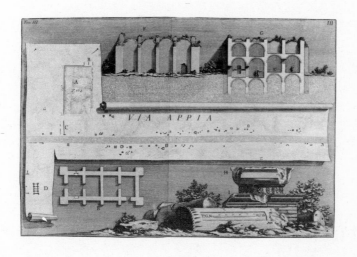

Santa Trada di Cannitello, Reggio Calabria

The second half of the film is in shining clarity compared to the first. It is on the same DVD, courtesy of Carlo from Cracow, but on wide-screen TV courtesy of a fortress hotel overlooking the sea towards Sicily. The blue skies are brighter, the terracottas warmer, the dimple on Kirk Douglas's chin looks deep enough to hold a cocktail olive or a piece of popcorn – and there are olives here to test that theory, Calabrian home-cinema snacks in a shallow pot.

There are already a few points that were not quite clear on Carlo's back-alley sofa. The gladiators in the arena wear strange top-knots in their hair, little tails borrowed as though from some Comanche tribe. Batiatus tells his new recruits to wear them with pride as a symbol of their special status as spectacular killers and men-about-to-die. It hardly matters: but none of our ancient Spartacus Road guides ever mentions gladiatorial hairstyles. Perhaps there was a hairdresser on the set who needed something to do.

Snatches of Roman politics appear from time to time, as though snipped at random from a children's history book. Carlo from Capua might properly have queried the Senate House in which poor Glaber (renamed Glabrus) reports his Vesuvian disaster. The place where the senators deliberated in the 70s BC was a rectangle, similar in shape and size to the one on the same site that survives for tourist trips today. In the film it is shaped in a semi-circle as if the speakers were themselves arena fighters. But this has a certain cinematic purpose. The wretched Glabrus looks ripe for his *coup de grâce*.

Only to a reader fresh from Plutarch is the character of Crassus himself so jarring. It is as though every sentence in the Life has been rewritten by the script-writers with an added 'not'. Laurence Olivier's Crassus lives in a vast colonnaded mansion instead of the modest family home that Plutarch describes. He is sexually voracious, both towards Varinia from Britannia and towards the Greek slave Antoninus. This DVD version contains what the sleeve-note describes as the originally censored 'oysters and snails' scene in which Olivier attempts to probe Tony Curtis's proclivities in a sunken bath. This Marcus Crassus is uniquely ambitious to be a dictator himself, declaring states of emergency in which he can become sole ruler of the Roman world. The original model for this portrayal was playing on a stage where others, much more ruthless and talented, wanted it much, much more.

On the balcony outside my bedroom cinema the light is fading over the Messina Straits. Sicily is almost as black as the sea. The prosecco is flat and abandoned in the glass. Just imagine for a moment. What if Crassus were to be seeing this? The film is as good a portrait as the general could ever have made for himself, as good as any that Pliny made of his own life with all his subtle literary skills. If Marcus Licinius Crassus, son of an obscure Italian mother, dutiful husband of his brother's widow, moderately successful rival of Pompey and Caesar, were to come through this hotel-room door he would be legitimately prouder than he ever was in life.

We might not know at first who he was. At the ghostly sight of the great man in the entrance hall, no one today, not even this follower of the Spartacus Road, would recognise him. A bit of reputed baldness in the ancient sources would hardly be enough to differentiate the richest Roman from any returning contemporary. I might readily identify his *bête noire*

Pompey from his chubby round adolescent butcher's face and kiss-curl fringe modelled on the busts of Alexander the Great. But Sulla's other butcher has no certain portrait that has survived, no image that lasted much beyond his death.

For Crassus to see himself onscreen as the absolute symbol of Rome, the Hollywood summation of all that was most Roman, would satisfy his steeliest dreams. How extraordinary for him to see immortalised the years when he, Marcus Licinius Crassus, was at the heart of the action, when that other man, Pompey, was looking on jealously from Spain and when Julius Caesar was a sinister kid who barely makes it to the main credits.

Even as a patriot he would have loved it. Rome never loses. The strangest aspect of watching Kirk Douglas uninterrupted from beginning to end is that he is never shown winning anything except his woman. He occupies an abandoned camp at the foot of Mount Vesuvius in his first weeks of freedom but, after that, nothing. There is barely even a reference to his winning a battle, although Spartacus himself won maybe nine. The DVD contains the original cinema trailer and in this promotional footage Crassus does say that Rome is under threat for its very existence as a result of the rebellion. But he never says it in the film itself.

If Plutarch were to walk in through this same hotel door he too would have applauded what he saw on the screen – even if he cavilled about its facts. This is a film portrait with a firm but subtle moral purpose. Crassus represents an authoritarian state that is running out of control, the obsessive anti-communism of Cold War. Crassus is a bad American but still an American. He represents a state that needs to be tough in a dangerous world, but chastened too from time to time. The superpower's internal opponents, while threatening, must not be so successful as to suggest they might win. There should be a pretty love story to keep the common crowd happy. Plutarch would have gone along with that approach, balanced, cautious, realistic about power and responsibility, squeezing excellent entertainment from compromise.

Plutarch, like Pliny, is one of those ancients whom we can begin, however perilously, to think we know. Even more than Florus and his racy tabloid versions of history, he has the whiff of the newspaper office about him. His profiles of great Greeks and Romans broke ground that has been trampled ever since. His essays and talks seem today like the output of a moderately conservative columnist, smart, entertaining, not too deep or difficult, supremely well informed, not too fixed in any philosophical position, always with enough room to backtrack and trim. His prodigious quantity of output would satisfy the most demanding employer.

Moderation in all things, the motto of his Delphi shrine, was Plutarch's personal philosophy too. Some old men, like that obstinate buffer the elder Pliny, might be opposed to guitar music, male toiletries and foreign fashion on principle. Plutarch was not like that. He just did not see why well-brought-up men should want to become guitarists, to manufacture perfumes or to live as fashion designers.

Plutarch had nothing against people admiring celebrities of art and style. But why should they want to become these celebrities themselves? If someone said that so-and-so was an excellent piper, the right answer from Plutarch was that he must be a worthless man: 'otherwise he would not have been so good a piper'. Such severity of argument sustained our modern columnists for decades until its collapse in our time of celebrity-culture-for-all. Now there is only the occasional grumpy Plutarchan left to moan.

The names of 227 books by Plutarch survive and the texts of 128 of them, from *On Not being Angry* to *Whether Sea*

Animals are Wiser than Land Animals. He wrote pages of advice to young politicians and young brides, of the kind that has since graced many a newspaper feature page. He attacked ill will in rival writers and portrayed himself with huge success as the wise man with the big heart, the one who wanted his words to make a difference and to do good.

Humanity was not consistent about the treatment of slaves or about anything else much. So neither need Plutarch be. Aulus Gellius records in his *Attic Nights* how one of Plutarch's slaves, upset at being flogged on his master's orders, asked whether this punishment did not violate his newly published diatribe against anger. Plutarch had replied that his eyes were not blazing, his voice was not loud, so how did the slave even think he was angry. Ridiculous? Well, it was worth a thousand words, worth an argument. The overseer should continue with his whip while he and his slave worked out who was right. There is no columnist's story like an old columnist's story and this one reads as though it has raised a wry smile on many a Greek evening.

Plutarch wrote about how Epicurus was wrong about death. The theory defied common sense. Plutarch was suspicious of all dogmatism. He showed much common sense of his own, although he never, even for his own time, reached the highest ranks of thinkers. In the view of Aulus Gellius' cleverest friends, like the single-testicled, sharp-tongued philosopher Favorinus, Plutarch was not quite clever enough, not from the highest drawer of the mind. Favorinus was a destructive academic sceptic, Plutarch a pick-and-mix populist. It is not too hard to hear the disdain of the old Oxbridge don for the best-selling young colleague who writes columns for the papers and appears on daytime TV.

Plutarch, Aulus Gellius and Favorinus all wrote many books but none from the smartest of them has survived. The first two could spot a good story. Favorinus did not do that so well. He made a good story himself. He was a famed sexual athlete and adulterer whose deformity gave him both the access of a eunuch and the enthusiasm of the afflicted. He was famed too for falling out with the Emperor Hadrian and surviving. His writings were (at length) on perception and on the theory known (but not needing to be known about) as the Cataleptic Fantasy. He wrote, with ingenuity as well as length, on whether suspension of judgement led necessarily to a failure to act. But neither his prolixity nor his subtlety long outlived him.

It was Plutarch who had the last word. He identified the kind of story that other people wanted to repeat. He tells how Pythagoras worked out the height of Hercules by translating his shoe-size into the answer 'six foot three inches tall'. The key was the number of Herculean footsteps around the Olympic running track and for anyone in the Tibur temple, or any other temple to Hercules, this gave a good idea of what size of superhero was there to be worshipped.

Aulus Gellius had the same sense for trivia. He tells us how to deal with bookshop boasters, the kind that pretend to know their Sallust when they cannot tell one failed Roman general from another. He describes the famed 'Campanian pride' of Capua. He was the first to tell us about Archytas and his self-propelling dove – all of these items surprisingly useful on the Spartacus Road.

Via Chianalea, Scilla

The Korean woman looks sadder than before. She thought she had already found the place to which Spartacus had retreated. She has her map on which that 'best defensive line' has been drawn, from the same map book as before, the same set of nets piled upon nets, motorway service stations beneath the crossed swords of battles, lakes, long ago drained, in which churches now sit. She now thinks she has been misled. There is a better answer here.

The Scilla peninsula stretches like a Yale key into the Messina Straits. In front of us is its highest part, a flat-topped fortress. Beyond that are lower jagged teeth of different sizes. The houses of fishermen hang from the cliffs below.

We have picked up our conversation as though we have been travelling together since Capua. In one sense we have done precisely that. I have not thought of her since that glimpse in the cave of the archangel at Garganus. She is a companion only of a very uncertain sort. But on the Spartacus Road that makes her almost a marching partner.

She wears the same coral-red dress. Her hair seems flatter and streaked, like that of an exotic deer. But maybe I had not noticed enough before. Her husband has returned home, she

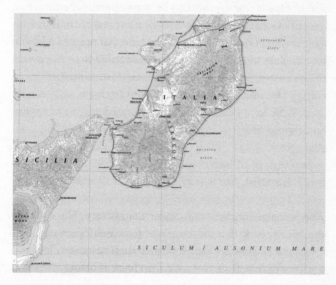

says briskly. She has stayed in order to cross over into Sicily, to see one last 'great historical events' site, the ruined walls of Motya where in the time of Plato and Archytas the Greeks used the world's first military catapult.

She also wants to finish the Spartacus story. She has sat in caves named after Spartacus, stood on top of hills named after Crassus and his aides. She has pondered the possibility of there being real military remains of Rome's struggle with its slaves. But were they Roman traps for rebel slaves or Renaissance traps for tourists? She is thinking sadly that, like all the caves of Odysseus and rocks of the Sirens, they have been named to deceive the unwary.

Plutarch says that Spartacus wanted to cross the Messina Straits from here to start a Third Slave War in the place where the previous two had succeeded for a while so well. That, at least, seems highly likely. In Sicily the charismatic commander Eunus had kept his forces united, had taken the cities of Enna and Taormina, had inspired emulators, and had looked for some time as though he might administer as well as terrorise. Only five miles away from here were still the Romans' great Sicilian farms where hundreds of thousands of slaves worked in the grimmest conditions, still the most willing and able rebel recruits.

In Sicily in 71 BC any slave of the Romans digging irrigation trenches or planting corn could find the lead shot left from those wars of 135 and 104 BC, bullets fired from slings and etched with good-luck messages for the sender and evil words for their targets, lead decorated with lightning bolts and scorpions. Victory under Herakles! Victory under Athenion! Thirty years on, and sixty years on, there seemed an opportunity for the size of revolt that this time could make a difference.

Spartacus' transport ships were to be those of the Cilicians, a tribe which had its homeland in the mountains of what is now south-eastern Turkey but which maintained its greatest power at sea. Among these rulers of the waves were former citizens of many countries who had fallen between the cracks of rising Rome and decaying Greece. The Cilicians were known as 'pirates', men who fell the wrong side of what constituted legitimacy in the ancient world, unpredictable people who might do deals with slave armies as well as slave traders, enemies as well as friends of Rome. The essence of piracy was to be mobile, not necessarily as strong as neighbouring forces but quicker to strike and retreat, to make a pact and break a pact. Occasionally pirates attacked others' ships, boarding with cutlasses in what came to be their successors' favourite roles; most often they raided unprotected land, taking whatever they could steal to whichever part of their inhospitable homeland could hide it best until it could be sold.

Plutarch describes how the Cilicians negotiated and received a downpayment of gifts from Spartacus. But, whatever pact was made, they failed to keep it. It might not have reflected well on Spartacus' reputation if they had. Even transporting the 2,000 men mentioned in Plutarch's account would have been

a massive task. More than ten times that number would have had to be left behind in Italy, to be taken across later if Crassus had allowed them any 'later'. To have abandoned the bulk of his forces in order to return later with greater force would have been an act of revolutionary ruthlessness. It would have certainly changed Arthur Koestler's view of the story. It did not happen.

Did Crassus himself pay the pirates to sail away? Some writers have thought so. There were informal links between Romans and Cilicians of the sort that always exist between long-standing enemies. Crassus' father had fought them. So too had both the father and grandfather of Mark Antony. Pirate-hunting could be a family business. In the year before the break-out from Capua, Marcus Antonius Creticus, the jovial incompetent father of Shakespeare's future hero, had fought a typically desultory pirate war to a typically messy pirate peace. He had been about as successful as the first Romans sent on land against Spartacus but probably more respectful to his prey: pirates were beyond the pale of civilisation but not as far beyond as gladiators.

The Cilicians may have done a deal with Crassus for more money. They were slave-traders who both fought Romans and met their demands for slaves. They cared for neither group. More likely, though, they looked at Spartacus' prospects and had second thoughts. Stronger than any kind of back-channel promise was the nervous view that the pirates must have taken of Crassus' legions, now heading fast into the foot of Italy. The art of piracy was to profit by the projection of force into the places which armies left behind – not to carry out rescue operations under approaching fire.

In the early months of 71 BC Crassus did not attempt to drive Spartacus directly into the sea. He drew a line and then he stopped. He had some knowledge of the terrain. This was where he had stolen the villa that had estranged him from Sulla. He hoped to besiege his adversaries behind a wall from where he could dispirit, starve and defeat them with the minimum cost to his own men and reputation. Where exactly was that line? My Korean friend had thought that she knew – and has become seriously disappointed. She has now come to Scilla instead. Yet this place too, this thin key of land, once home to Homer's six-headed monster, once the killing partner of the whirlpool Charybdis, seems still not where she had hoped to be.

She is not the first to feel dissatisfied here. Scilla and Charybdis have been a disappointment for as long as tourists have taken any kind of classical trail. There are caves where sailors have imagined the six-at-a-time devourers of Odysseus' sailors. Some have heard moaning noises from deeper in the rocks. But in modern times, and probably in Spartacus' time, it has not been a strait of sucking whirlpools, merely a four-mile stretch of water which a slave army without transport could not possibly cross.

Today its greatest pride is a massive modern mural of Christ the sun-seeker, with shoulder-length blond hair, golden-belted white gown, a colossus rising to the heavens from the Scilla rock with a guard of five white gulls. The monsters here are the ones which the fishermen of Chianalea catch, the Stella Gorgon (*Astropartus mediterraneus*), the golden sea-horse (*Hippocampus antiquorum*) and the *rana pesatrice* which hides its thin blue eyes in the sand of the seabed and which visitors, except on menus, may easily avoid.

Plutarch says nothing of Scilla. He tells how Crassus' soldiers, somewhere around here, hacked a trench from coast to coast, five yards deep and five yards wide and some thirty-five miles long. This description has suggested two much grander possibilities for the Spartacus Road. Both coastlines undulate vigorously in this lowest part of Italy, creating a bruised and swollen toe on which two routes for the wall can easily be found. The first route, and the one closest to thirty-five miles long – runs east to west across from Thurii on the Gulf of Tarentum. The German scholar Theodor Mommsen, historian of Rome and tireless collector of classical inscriptions in these parts, declared confidently that this was the line of Crassus' rampart.

Many successors, thinking that Plutarch and Mommsen made a powerful combination and recalling much longer trench lines in later wars, have agreed. Other scholars and promoters of local tourism suggested a slightly shorter line, between the next two indented bays to the south, running eastwards along the mountainous ridge from the town of Locris. My Korean friend, with her own national experience of sales promotion and long divisive earthworks, has very reasonably pursued these thoughts.

This idea of Spartacus, pinned behind an ancient equivalent of the Western Front, has a high appeal to those who want the biggest possible figure for future histories. Our current alternative, imprisonment in a tiny refugee camp like Scilla and prey to the whim of bandits scarcely more respectable than himself, seemed no fate for a hero. Spartacus was a man considered worthy of a kingdom. Behind either of the long walls conjectured for Crassus, the slave leader would have been lord over hundreds of square miles, with his own ports, new possibilities of acquiring or even building ships, and plenteous food for his fighters, their families and their pack-animals. Like Eunus in Sicily, he would have been a slave king.

But the mathematics of the Korean classroom has dissuaded my critical friend. She has with her the work of modern historians with an equally realistic view of numbers. She scribbles tiny figures, multiplies, divides, squares and cubes and sighs. The quantity of earth to be moved for the long walls would have been vast. Even the shorter and easier of the proposed routes would have matched the greatest spectaculars of the ancient world. Either would have challenged even the ancient pharaohs, digging without constraint of time, and certainly every engineer for whom time did matter, at least until the Napoleonic Wars. Crassus could not have wasted such time. He had an impatient Senate in Rome and two rivals for glory determined to exploit his delay. He did not have enough men to build or defend such a long siegework. A short trench across this slim Scilla promontory seems much the likeliest course.

Wherever the lines were drawn, Spartacus was careless in choosing his camp and slow to recognise the danger of being besieged. Perhaps he trusted in a Cilician rescue too long. He ordered rafts to be made, earthenware jars lashed to logs with straps of hide, futile for the winter currents of the Messina Straits. There was no need to imagine the mythical monsters of Homer, the Scylla with her bloody teeth, the Charybdis who sucked down those who evaded Scylla's jaws. The reality was quite rough enough. Florus enjoys the impending doom, 'the casks bound together with twigs'. One of the tiny fragments of Sallust suggests that he too saw the pathetic drama of a desperate army tying barrels under beams of wood.

There is the first sense, here on this rugged, narrow rock, of eventual defeat. The slave army was two years old. It had had time to lose some of its rage but neither time nor leadership to replace the missing anger with other motivation. Its weapons of wicker, made by basket weavers, had to stand against Roman bronze, made in the finest armouries of the Republic. Its stock of provisions, along with its morale, was low and falling. Cold damp rose from the ground and fell from the skies. Across the straits in Sicily there was a Roman governor, Gaius Verres, who was cracking down on the slightest sign of sympathetic revolts. There were crucifixions to discourage any slave who might have heard of Spartacus and wish to join him.

On Scilla the slaves had to escape by land. They tested the Roman line, burning brushwood, making sallies at what seemed to be the weaker points. Crassus' fresh and decimated legions held firm. Spartacus took a Roman prisoner and crucified him to create terror on both sides of the wall. For the Romans, there can have been nothing more impossibly alien than the flogging of a fellow citizen and soldier by slaves, the binding of his arms to the wooden crossbar, the hauling of the bar into the sky and the screams as he lost and found breath for days until he died. For the slaves there was the intimation of what fate could await them if the wall could not be breached and their war was over.

Their morale was sufficient for one last effort, a night-time break-out under cover of cold and snow when the Romans were off guard. It is Appian, the source most hostile to Spartacus, who tells of the crucifixion. Sallust, Plutarch and Frontinus all note the feat of escape. Only a third of Spartacus' forces struggled across the bridge of human corpses, dead cattle and earth that they had thrown across the Roman trench. But that was enough for the siege of Scilla to be lifted. Crassus could not afford to risk attack from the rear. According to one of Sallust's fragments, the slaves escaped to Mount Sila, the high ground immediately behind us as we look way from the sea. That is enough to persuade my Korean friend that this time she is certainly in the right place – in as much as there is any certainty to be had on this journey.

Plutarch's long walls are just an aggrandising of the battle scene. This Theban journalist of the old school is once again making his adversaries worthy of each other. Neither man-bites-slave nor slave-bites-man is much of a story. Both were commonplace. Flawed Roman (weakened by impatience and excess of wealth) faces masterly gladiator (strengthened by Greek heritage). That is a tale to remember.

Florus wants his story too. He turns Spartacus into a Roman. This slave does not breathe fire or wear fake regalia. He forces some of his prisoners to fight in gladiatorial contests, just as the Romans did. He crucifies other prisoners for the best punitive and theatrical effect, just as the Romans did. He is as vengeful. He is a brave military leader, fighting in the front line just where the best Roman generals fought.

The Korean woman has her Florus and her Plutarch now. Behind her bifocal lenses her eyes move quickly up and down, from page to marbled pediment, from ancient to modern and back. We idly discuss the two writers' methods and aims. Where did the slaves break through? Perhaps it was on the cliff edge where now stands the bronze statue of a naked man wrestling a swordfish, left knee bent back, mouth screaming effort at the sky. Or by the *Mitologico Scilla*, a bare-breasted woman in stone, with one head of her own and three belonging to killer dogs, the version of Homer's monster preferred by Roman art-collectors and poets. Or by the town's vivid war memorial to twentieth-century wars, a soldier holding open his enemy's eyes so as not only to punch them out but to be seen by him punching them out, seen in the kneeling man's last living act.

Piazza San Rocco, Scilla

I thought that we might later perhaps have dinner, discuss our trips, what happened next, what happens next. She had never been to Gargano, she said. Plutarch describes how Crassus had panicked and asked for reinforcements from

Macedonia. Was this so? He describes a battle by a lake whose waters were sometimes sweet and sometimes bitter. This could be by the sea somewhere – or at one of the mountain lakes which survived in Italy for another 1,900 years before being drained for farming. Scholars, combining the arts of Greek and Latin with ruler and compass, have decided on what was once the Lago di Palo, near Buccino, satisfyingly close to where the rebellion began.

There is a museum near by in Reggio with not only common objects from Republican times but two of the world's finest Greek sculptures, seen only by the few who pass by here. There is much more to speculate about Spartacus, many possibilities from which we can choose. We make a half-plan to meet later. When 'later' comes she has gone.

Piazza de Nava, Reggio

The arm that stretched from the sand and weeds of the seabed was Herculean in stature, a little longer than life-size though not by enough to reassure its finder that it had not been once from a real life. This is the part of Italy famed for exotic murder. Anyone on a scuba-diving expedition in the 1970s might reasonably have suspected the worst. Once grasped by the diver, the hand was clearly of metal, not flesh but bronze. A long body was attached and a luxuriant bearded head. Beside it, after a little more searching, was another, the statues known here now as Man A and Man B, in terms still reminiscent of Mafia trial witnesses or pathological killers whose real names must for some reason not be made known.

Both figures are of fighters from the heroic age whose left arms would once have had a shield and whose right held a spear. Even without their weapons, still somewhere in transit, these are dangerous men, held alone in a cold, white basement room under the Piazza de Nava, to protect them as much, it seems, from gangland rivals as from future accidents like that which 2,000 years ago hurled them to the bottom of the sea.

Their identities have defied all assaults by scholars. Man A is the younger, the more relaxed in pose but also the more ready to spring and strike. He has wide-open, white-bone eyes, a mouth that is set as though taking a breath, five sharp white teeth, gleaming cheekbones above the well-brushed curls of his facial hair.

Man B has the older wearier look, his mouth more closed, his beard less coiffed. One of his eyes is missing, open only to the hollow of his head. If his spear had been with him, instead of somewhere snagging nets, the grooves on his hand and shoulder show that it would have slanted obliquely, 'at ease'.

Both have the closely observed thighs, the tight, almost feminine buttocks, the impossible waists, massive chests and shoulders that are still for some the ideal male physique. There are many body-builders who seem much less alive than these extraordinary works of sculpture, each vein and muscle first carved on a clay core in wax, next transferred to plaster moulds, before being finally given their bronze permanence.

Yet few bronze statues of the Greek classical age have survived. The first Roman collectors appreciated them although Horace was an influential voice that deplored the national obsession with the spectacles of plunder. Later there were better uses for scarce metal: if a man needs a wheelbarrow or a cannon, and no one is prepared to pay him the premium for art, gardening and the gun win every time. These two have lasted because they were lost, probably cast off from a ship in trouble on the coastline that guided Greek art to Rome, bound for connoisseurs of spectacular plunder like Piso at Herculaneum, Pliny at Como or even the Emperors Hadrian or Nero.

Their origins were perhaps the shrines of Olympia, where sport and religion attracted a host of memorial statuary, or Plutarch's workplace at Delphi. Epic bodies like these stood there alongside the heads of poets and philosophers, ideals of beauty next to the realism of intellect, a stone library of all Greece. Estimates of the bronzes' date vary from the fifth century BC to the first. Time is truly nothing with works as ominous and luminous as these. One of the latest theories is that they came from Argos. Chemical analysis of mineral contents suggests an original home in the city that sent the Seven against Thebes and proudly commemorated them in its temples.

These are the statues that Statius never saw although they may have represented two of his *Thebaid* killers, two archetypes of his terrible, irrational, ineradicable enemies of life. Man B is said to be Amphiaraus, the old prophet who entered the war knowing the catastrophe it would bring. Man A would then be Tydeus, the instigator, the champion of sport and war, the chewer of his enemy's skull.

Via Stefano Brun, Buccino-Volcei

When the slave army arrived here, the rings of hills around Volcei had still not recovered from the burnings of the previous year. The grass was still black, the buildings charred, the air damp with the cold scent of ash. Sulphur bubbled into pools from deep beneath the earth and competed with the air. Only the icy lake was sweeter, swollen with fresh winter streams which every year flowed fiercely into the brackish, bitter pools of the summer.

The Germans were in the vanguard, making camp between the waterside and the town. Plutarch gives their leaders names, Castus and Gaius Cannicus. The main army followed closely behind, carefully manoeuvring through the high circles of ground. The landscape was hard to read. It seemed laid in rolls, in circles, like pottery plates made by children or like the relics, ancient even then, scattered around by lost peoples who had lived here before. Each day there was some new centre. From each small peak the best place to fight appeared to change.

Spartacus knew some of the ground. Crassus' scouts, scouring through the same deceptive hills, knew more. The Romans could not know their enemies' intentions. Would there be the thrust north against Rome that many still feared or an escape over the mountains to the east? Did the slaves know themselves? Either choice was possible or none. Our ancient histories, even read here in this place of the battle-grounds, allow a familiarly restricted truth for these final chapters. Sallust and Plutarch report disagreements between the two parts of the slave army: modern critics have been more doubtful.

Crassus' own priority was the clearest. He had to crush the slaves quickly and without assistance. He had the problem of Pompey to consider, the great man imminently returning from Spain, eager to add the head of Spartacus to his other laurels and to humiliate his Roman rival. From the east there was news of another returning Roman army, from Macedonia and led by Marcus Lucullus, the brother of one of Pompey's many enemies in the Senate. The banker was in danger of becoming a bit player in a bigger game.

Crassus found the Germans by the lakeside first. He sent a detachment of his men to gain the highest ground above them. But when the battle began it quickly became chaotic. Spartacus himself arrived with his own vanguard forces. Confusion in the sulphurous oakwoods and olive groves around the Palo lake was no use to the Roman general. Crassus withdrew to take stock, dividing his forces so that the Germans should be

317

blocked from the path to Rome, the necessity that was absolute, and that Spartacus' army might be caught before it escaped east, if that was what it intended to do.

Two reliable Roman officers were sent to keep a good eye on – and a safe distance from – the Thracian gladiator. Crassus himself pursued the Germans, sending forces again to the highest ground and ordering the troops' helmets to be bound with cloth to stop the reflection of the sun. This stratagem again was foiled – this time by two Gallic women sacrificing on the hills and sounding the alarm. Crassus immediately feigned a cavalry retreat, drawing his opponents between the two wings of his army. This was a tactic of the old Roman training ground but one no less satisfying when it worked. There were no prizes for military originality here, except in words that would not be written for two hundred years.

Some 12,000 slaves died in the battle by the bitter-sweet lake, all but two of them, Plutarch approvingly notes, with wounds in their fronts and not their backs. This was the 'hardest of all battles that Crassus ever fought'. It was his first clear victory of the campaign. Inside the commander's tent there was now the first proof of Roman honour restored. The Germans had kept five eagle standards, one for each of the legions they had conquered in their campaigns from Metapontum to the Alps. These were the symbols of power lost by Cassius Longinus, Lentulus and Publicola, Varinius, Cossinius and Glaber. All were back with Crassus.

Beyond the canvas of the victorious command posts, the memories of the immediate past were less easy to efface. It was extraordinary to any civilised Roman that this threat from within, not a vast foreign force, had left such a legacy of abandonment and destruction. For miles around this had become a landscape fit for Statius' worst nightmares of the future, smoke on the lakes, polluted fields, rivers choked with bodies, terrified inhabitants. History, archaeology and imagination produce together the same dark picture. Twice ravaged in the Third Slave War, the lands around Volcei did not even begin to recover until the rule of Augustus. No dated objects have been found for the next forty years. The little farms became latifundia, a word first used in the time of Pliny for giant, sparsely populated tracts.

Today the lands are lakeless. Lago di Palo kept its waters till two hundred years ago when it was drained to produce fertile farmland and fewer mosquitoes. Some of the brown-topped hills have villages where few but their inhabitants ever go. There are highland streets where every house is window-less, every door open to the wild dogs and the magpies. The sulphur streams fuel thermal baths for German tourists. Buccino is 'twinned with Corinth' and keeps its old Roman name beside its new Italian one. Buccino-Volcei is a twisted stack of houses, churches and archaeologists' netting, strapped perilously around its ancient mountain peak.

Spartacus' men, according to Plutarch, were undaunted by the defeat of their German vanguard. They surprised part of the Roman scouting party, forced it to flee and wounded Gnaeus Tremelius Scrofa, one of Crassus' officers. Plutarch says that this defeat of the scouts was the decisive blow that the slaves laid upon their own bodies. It made them think that they could truly achieve anything. 'This success was the ruin of Spartacus' army, the point at which mere runaway slaves came to think too highly of themselves, no longer seeing honour in constant retreat and no longer prepared to obey their leaders.'

This is Plutarch at his journalistic best. Overconfidence followed by catastrophe was always a strong theme, one loved by the tragic playwrights and lively in any sort of newspaper story too. The motive of the writer is more on show here than that of his subjects. It is hard to believe that the slaves felt genuinely invincible at this desperate point. Perhaps Spartacus knew now that Lucullus was approaching him from Brundisium and that his escape route was blocked. Perhaps he was simply ready for one decisive encounter with Crassus.

The ancient historians describe such aspects of that last battle as made sense for their purposes, how Spartacus kills his horse and fights in the front line on the ground, how he is left alone among his dead comrades, defending himself to the end, how he is wounded, fights down on one knee, how his body is never found amid the mass of the slaughtered. To Appian this was a truly 'epic' end, well worthy of the ancient poetic models in his mind. Florus describes Spartacus' place in the front line as that of 'a true general', with a comparison implied between the less heroic Romans and a man who must surely have been something of a hero to have threatened Rome as much as he had. Koestler has him fall to a 'short, hard terrible blow between his eyes' and his last sight that of Crassus' own eyes, their brows 'slightly raised'. Whatever the truth of anything that the writers would think or say, the war was over.

Via Camere, Raito, Vietri sul Mare

The news of the victory spread fast. It was received with the simplest relief in places which Spartacus had passed by on his two-year campaign, pleasant places that he might have not passed by if he had been allowed to continue it, in Tibur, in Puteoli, in Pompeii, in the pottery factories of Vietri here above the port of Salernum. Normal life had continued throughout the revolt – but with unwanted and unwonted questions. Could any slave be trusted? How could owners decide? How normal was a life when the Gallic gardener, the German bodyguard, even the Greek maid, had an alternative to what and where they were?

While Spartacus was alive and at large, there had been new security measures, new costs in money and in security of mind. Visitors still climbed Mount Tifata to see the two-handled cup from Troy, the elephant's head and the fast-expanding temple of Diana. Sabbio's cloak factory in Capua kept up its profits: military suppliers fared well from the financing of new legions by the richest man in Rome. But wage-earners were needed to take herds across the mountains now that slaves could not be trusted quite so much.

To the politicians, and to the historians who followed them, what mattered most was whether Crassus won the credit in Rome, or Pompey, or whether the up-and-coming Caesar could gain some advantage at the expense of them both. Around the bays of Naples what mattered much more was that their way of life was secure, their prospects improved, a peculiar fear of premature, unpredictable death removed, the memories of Nola, Nuceria and Metaponto avenged and allowed to fade.

The leisure industries of philosophical study had continued without hindrance while the slave war went on. The fashionable Epicureans were not supposed to fear death at all. But the revolt had heightened fears of death even among those who told themselves they knew better. There had been all the greater need to repeat as a mantra the message that 'Death is not to be feared'. Students chanted the words together. This instruction came second in the master's four-step plan by which they pledged to live their lives, just one step below 'God should not concern us'.

Like much ancient learning this was learning by rote. Epicurus had not encouraged disciples to modify his work only to learn it by heart. It was the repetition that produced the beneficial effects. During the Spartacus revolt the schools continued to offer *otium* to those whose daily lives denied them its peace. The bay below Vesuvius did not close its universities just because of what had begun two years before on the mountain's heights. Abandoning the fear of death, always easier to follow in logic than in living, was never more elusive than in the past few years. Epicurus had insisted both that his arguments were philosophi-cally sound and that the result of understanding his arguments was a better life. Times of intense danger made the attainment of calm more desirable but also, it seemed, more difficult.

Any disciple – then or later, even now – had first to work his way through Epicurus' theories and accept their force. One: fear is nothing but the feeling induced by future harm. Two: only what we can perceive can be a harm. Three: death is nothing to us because it cannot be perceived. After death every bit of a man dissolved into atoms. There was then no perception, no harm and therefore no reason for fear. The teachings of

Epicurus were supposed to be a design for life, not merely a classroom exercise. A student who did not follow the master, or try to, was no student at all. This was not a creed that could be left at the school door.

Gladiatorial games had also continued in the arena towns throughout the revolt. There was an added thrill from the watching of trained killers whose colleagues, in different places not so far away, were killing their potential audiences, not just educating and entertaining them. The arenas had become comforting places of pretence too, places where normality could be staged, where gladiators had their allotted place and knew it. On the theatrical sands a slave-leader could be brought to his knees every afternoon. What the slave armies were doing to the women and men of Botromagno could be forgotten for a few hours.

No one knows the purpose of that cartoon outline of Spartacus from the priest's house at Pompeii. Maybe it was advertising a character not a man. Perhaps it was a way of saying that a new player would take the starring role each day, that here could be as many understudies as were needed, until the script itself became dull. Even when Spartacus was gone, he could continue to be killed each afternoon for as long as necessary, until he had become yesterday's bogeyman. For a troubled Epicurean in the stands, theatre was a welcome relief from reality, a pleasure, the sort of pursuit that fell below his master's highest standards of quiet peace but was perhaps part of the means to achieve it. Cicero's closest friend Atticus, a wealthy Epicurean of this time, even had his own gladiatorial school.

But the games also brought problems to an Epicurean. The spectator could see the speed of death, the moment of dying, the last gasp, the sudden dissolution of a life, all the evidence of why the end of a life should not be feared. But he could also see the bodies, the flames and jaws of animals around them, and it was hard for him sometimes not to see himself, to imagine himself as dead and torn apart, even if not by the lion of the day, then by rot and worms and crows.

If he believed that the headless corpse on the sand was still conscious in some way, he was in serious need of extra tuition. If he decided that the dead body had wishes and demands like the dead in the dramas of the Greeks, he needed to go back to grade one of the Epicurean school. But those were not the only fears he might find at the arena. He might stare at a corpse and imagine his own corpse; he might imagine what he himself would look like as a dead man. These were fears of death that it was hard to destroy by logic. Ridding himself of those terrors was a higher-grade task. The answer from school was only to work harder, to learn the mantras, to repeat the slogans and apply the arguments as before.

At the end would surely come the blessed imperturbable state that the master called '*ataraxia*'. Epicurus, despite the reputation that has since attached to his name, did not seek to intensify or lengthen his own pleasures. He was not famed personally for excess of food, drink or sex. The highest pleasure for him was that produced by the absence of pain. That in itself was ambition enough.

In the arena there was much to inspire the Epicurean on the journey towards the *ataraxia* that he sought. There was much exquisite human pleasure there, even if the master himself had seemed not to want that. There was the clearest pain to be avoided. There was also the useful reminder that everything, in life and its arts, in soldiery and in sport, had its due time, that, however spectacular the show might be, one did not want it to go on for ever. Theatre showed the shape of a life, a beginning, a middle and an end, a place where death need not be sought but hardly feared.

Abandoning the fear of death did not mean embracing it or

bring it upon oneself. Acts of suicide were no part of the Epicurean programme. It was the traditional old Romans, their minds crippled by irrational terrors, who slit their wrists and slumped into their warm baths. Such was the superiority they saw for themselves in their luxurious gardens here, comforted and inspired by the busts they kept of their great thinkers from the past. Epicureans were unique among philosophers in their veneration of sculpture. Looking and imitating were their paths to the true good.

The games did not solve every argument about whether harm was brought by death, a harm that, if it existed, could be legitimately feared. The common kind of fighters in the ring had few pleasures to live for and much pain to endure. So for them, most clearly for them, death was not a harm. The rich, the politicians? They could look after their own peculiar concerns. But what about the common spectator in the cheap seats, the man with the happy home, the loving wife and young children? After he was dead, he would miss these pleasures. Surely he would be harmed by the loss of them?

No, said the teacher. A good Epicurean might be harmed if his wife and children were taken away from him. But he could not be harmed if it was he who died and left them. In that case, there would be no 'he' left to desire. There would be no unsatisfied desire to be felt. Only the living can be harmed by pain or fear of pain. There are many things to be feared but death is not one of them. Remove the fear of death and the pupil can concentrate freely on avoiding pain, enhancing pleasure and the rest of the master's precepts.

This did not sound right to most Romans, especially to those untrained to argue against it. It has not sounded right to later students, even to those taught specifically to pull apart its chains of reason. Of course, we fear death. In the Italian-Greek towns from Vietri to Vesuvius, many who knew of the Epicurean doctrines distrusted them. Their arena was a place not of mystic contemplation but of tradition, a school for swordsmanship, a place for strengthening shared values not for healing the anxieties of the individual. A man like Crassus was less concerned with the theory of whether non-existence before birth was the same as non-existence after death, fascinating though a talk about this might be at the end of a pleasurable dinner. His anxiety was the harm that the holding of such beliefs might do for the interests of Rome, its institutions and its leadership.

Far from wanting to take their citizens' minds away from death, the city's elders wanted to keep them there. Romans defined themselves by the memories of what their dead had achieved. They lived among the images of their ancestors so that they should better emulate their achievements. They worshipped their gods because their gods had helped their ancestors. A great civilisation could not be built on maximum pleasure and minimum pain. That was fine for days of *otium* at Tivoli or on the bay of Naples, but not for the *negotium* that had uniquely created Rome.

Cicero understood and argued this with vigour. He divided his time between philosophy and politics. He was more open-minded than most and saw the benefits in understanding what he did not agree with. All critical thought was Roman discipline of a kind. All thinking was like drill and ditch-digging in its way. An officer who could use his mind for abstraction as well as action was a better officer. An educated soldier was part of a club to which the barbarian could not belong. Yet, for all that, some directions of thought were more desirable than others. Avoidance of pain and the search for pleasure, whatever the intellectual rigour attached, were not the best basis for a political handbook.

Cicero had trained hard and worked hard for his success, and saw that effort as a virtue in itself. He was a *novus homo*, a New Man in society. He was self-made in an age when that was a disadvantage. Like Horace, he lacked the masks of his own meritorious ancestors, the images of death in solid form, masks of gold or wood that the best Roman families could keep, adapt and polish as versatile examples and warnings. Cicero had Greek statues for his dining room but no wax masks for his family funerals. Unlike Horace, the proud Epicurean son of a freedman, he cared about his lack. Cicero, always insecure, saw Rome's success as others striving as he had done, and successful Roman philosophy as encouraging them to do so.

His political art was in finding the fine lines in public life, cajoling the powerful, keeping Pompey away from Caesar when he could, edging away from every imminent catastrophe of dictatorship and civil war. Did he believe gladiatorial games to be 'cruel and inhumane'? He had considered the question and did not want to make up his mind. At the end of Spartacus'

327

revolt, Cicero was on his way to gaining his consulship and ensuring his family's future masks of respectability. But his own enduring fame was from his intellect, in the law courts and in the translation of Greek thought to Rome.

His work on this subject of pleasure and pain is famous in unexpected places. Page 36 of my travelling edition of *De finibus*, known in English as *The Ends of Goods and Evils*, begins with the words '*lorem ipsum*', a familiar sight but not from any previous thinking about Cicero and Epicurus. *Lorem* is not itself a Latin word but it does begin some of the most reproduced Latin of modern times. It forms the start of the dummy-text that designers of newspapers and books around the world use to fill the space between their pictures. '*Dolorem*' is the word Cicero uses for pain; the '*do-*' is left behind on page 35; and the '*lorem*' of page 36 begins miles of international lay-outs for pages, most of which will never exist in any other form. If all the texts of the ancient world were slowly and systematically to decay, Cicero's thoughts on the seeking of pain for pleasant purposes, a 'trivial example' from the gymnasium, would be the last to be lost. Understanding the passage would be like deciphering Sallust's account of the Spartacus war from the relics of the bookbinder's knife.

CICERO DE FINIBUS

lorem ipsum quia dolor sit amet, consectetur, adipisci velit, sed quia nonnumquam eiusmodi tempora incidunt ut labore et dolore magnam aliquam quaerat voluptatem. Ut enim ad minima veniam, quis nostrum exercitationem ullam corporis suscipit laboriosam, nisi ut aliquid ex ea commodi consequatur?

Cicero was happy to explain the tenets of Epicurus. It was a dangerous philosophy for his dangerous times, but it was better to know one's enemy than to be ignorant of his strengths. He also wanted to refute the Epicureans, not just to reject them as bad for Rome but to confront them on their own terms, to prove that their reasoning was wrong. Criticising them for their rejection of public duties was insufficient. He sought the weakest parts of their argument and attempted to use those to bring down the whole.

With his best courtroom instinct, he went hard for the man himself. Epicurus had claimed that in his last days in his Athens garden, unable to urinate and collapsing from kidney stones, he had relieved his agonies by recalling his most pleasurable philosophical discussions of the past. Ten years ago, my hospital nurse was acting herself like a secret Epicurean, suggesting deliberate distractions from chemotherapy in the memory of happy times in Italy. Cicero mocks all this as absurd, enjoying the absurdity of the old Greek soothing his bladder with a compilation of his greatest philosophical hits. His *ataraxia*, his so carefully acquired calm, would have made him a dull companion for a Naples holiday as well as a socially useless misfit. The man was a humbug as well as an aimless example to youth.

Epicurus had even made a will, Cicero objected, and not just a simple will but a complex legal ploy for ensuring that his school survived after his death. How could someone who saw only nothingness after death plan so obsessively for his legacy? The making of wills, says Cicero, was for ordinary men the equivalent of erecting statues, building memorial tombs, seeking favourable mentions in the history books. It was a central act of civilised life, of seeing beyond one's own life, as Epicurus, by his simple actions rather than his fancy words, had comprehensively proved. For a philosopher whose essence was the unification of his thought and his life, a prosecution for hypocrisy was the most damning indictment of all.

This debate went on over many books, many dialogues set in country homes and gardens by the bay of Naples. Later writers argued that the complete Epicurean exercise was futile:

fear of death was fused deep in the human psyche; it differentiated us from animals; to remove it would be to remove our humanity. There were soon those who believed, in bewilderingly different ways, that there was an immortal soul that survived our deaths, that some part of those Christians forced to fight and die in the arena ended at the right hand of God. For 2,000 years, critics of Epicurus would become both bolder and more subtle than Cicero, and there would be some equally well-armed defenders of the doctrine too. For a while, in Oxford days, I followed closely both sides and cheerfully called myself an Epicurean when the question was asked.

Via Stefano Brun, Buccino-Volcei

In the rolls of hills around Volcei, Crassus divided his victorious forces and sought out every survivor. He knew that he

was not entitled to a triumphal procession by chariot through Rome, the traditional honour for those who defeated foreign foes. He would have an *ovatio* instead, a pedestrian parade suitable for those whose victories, as Aulus Gellius puts it, were 'bloodless' and 'without dust'. The best official reward he could arrange was a triumpher's laurel crown on his ovation day rather than the common one of myrtle leaves, a distinction which, while significant in Roman eyes, was modest in scale beside his sense of achievement in bringing the Spartacus rebellion to an end. But he had other plans too by which his glory should be remembered.

X

SORRENTO to ROME

Trav Punto Capo, Sorrento

What we do not know cannot harm us. That part of the Epicurean phrasebook has survived cheerfully into English. An important line of battle against Epicurus is held by those who deny that this proverb is true, who say that what we do not know can harm us a great deal, that harms do not have to be perceived in order to be harmful. If an individual can be harmed by something he knows nothing about, he can in theory be harmed by death. Therefore, he should be allowed to fear death. Therefore, Epicurus was wrong.

Suggestions for these 'unperceived harms' have included hidden disease, brain damage that leaves a boxer content with his lot but half the man he used to be; or hostile reviews that damage ticket sales without the actors or producers being aware of them; or happy children in the Balkans whose lives would have been transformed if they had been born as Italians. But nothing much of that was part of the Roman debate. Epicurus' populist opponents stressed the difficulty of combining Epicurean theory with civilised life and work. How could life be tolerable if everyone were pursuing their personal pleasure and avoiding personal pain? It would be chaos. Who would pay for the gladiatorial games?

Bolder defenders of Epicurus responded by trying to re-interpret the master's life and work – to bring them closer to the demands of ordinary life. They pointed out that the man who has achieved *ataraxia*, while mentally organised for burial, was not thereby a lazy parasite. He could still enjoy his life, for many years ahead, and others could gain enjoyment from him.

Why had Epicurus made his will? His aim was to please his friends at the time. He was not betraying obsessive anxiety about his future. The will was complex because he needed to ensure that the laws of Athens would protect his students. Without it his students might have been evicted from the school on his death. Many of them lacked the native rights of the city and would, without his efforts for their present calm, have been fearful legitimately and in a respectable Epicurean way.

Philodemus, the Epicurean teacher whose works are buried at Herculaneum, recognised especially the danger to the argument of requiring consistency and perfection. Excessive love, fear or anger, actions outside the limits of blessed *ataraxia*, inevitably happened from time to time. We might call them blips. He called them 'pangs' or 'bites'. One could make one's will with the best aim of present pleasure and preventing pain; one could dream of a happy future for friends or children quietly spending one's money; one could wail at the possibility that the terms were not proof against city bailiffs or greedy husbands of one's daughters. The central aim had simply to be a return, as quickly as possible, to the true path. Epicureanism was a doctrine of human health as well as philosophical theory. Its proof was in how it improved the life of each of its followers, each one of whom, individually, when finally death came, was utterly and absolutely vulnerable, a 'city without walls'.

The teachings of Epicurus made lives better. They gave succour to the depressed, to those tired of struggle, to the childless, to all who looked around for reasons to go on living and failed. Live for the present. Gather ye rosebuds. '*Carpe diem*', in Horace's contribution. Seize the day. These too became proverbial reassurances, made always against the deep-seated public sense that, while beneficial in many ways, they were not wholly true or good.

There were fresh arguments from time to time. What was the difference between the future after death and the past before birth? The individual had perception of neither. The world after we are dead, however civilisations may rise or fall, was surely no more to us than the ancient customs of the first king of Argos. Since no one fears an earlier birth, why should anyone fear a future death? This became a potent tenet for the poet Lucretius, the first writer to set down Epicureanism sympathetically and systematically in a language other than Greek. But Lucretius changed the setting. The example of the past that the Latin poet chose was not Argos, the city that sent the Seven against Thebes, but the cities of Italy ravaged by more recent war.

Of all those met, however briefly, on this Spartacus Road, Lucretius is the writer whose name comes with the blankest picture of himself attached. His art is all there is, and it is art in the cause of philosophy. Some of his most beautiful words, '*Suave mari magno . . .*', were written by the window of a room in Pompeii: 'Sweet it is, when the winds stir up the waters on the wide sea, to stare from dry land upon the troubles of others'. But archaeology has added nothing about their writer. He remains merely the man whose language most mocks man's fear of the gods, the poet who first stripped the mystery from thunder, rain and death. In 71 BC, the high days of Crassus, he was just beginning *De rerum natura*, the hymn to Epicurean philosophy whose power so long preserved the doctrine of the Naples schools when generals and emperors would have destroyed it.

Capo Sorrento

One hundred and fifty years later a much lesser poet and local businessman, Pollius Felix, was polishing his own Epicurean lines here at his sprawling villa at the tip of Sorrento's cape,

the type of pleasure dome that got his philosophy a bad name. He had built twin temples to Hercules and Poseidon, twin pools of rough and calm, urban colonnades and country gardens, windows with views of Vesuvius and Ischia, sweet freshwater gullies mingling with the salt. Statius describes the scene in his usual spectacular way. Where there used to be a hill, there is level ground. Where there are wooded heights, there was once not even land. Where once the sunshine shone through dust, there is now a colonnade fit for Corinth. Green marble mimics grass. There are vineyards, with no unkind mention of Sorrento's 'noble vinegar', the notorious ancient wine of which my priest in Formia warned. At night this palace swims in its own glassy waters. It is itself a '*spectulatrix*'.

Its owner has retired from public life. He has experimented with different philosophies. He has made mistakes. But he has now reached *ataraxia*. He is '*paratum abire*', ready to depart from life without a care. He is also carefully choosing his metres, maybe under Statius' gentle tutorship, in order to spread further the thoughts of his final philosophical master.

Statius had not been keen to visit this pleasure dome. He had to be pressed to cross the bay from Naples after one of his stadium performances and would have preferred to be back on the Via Appia, the queen of roads, returning to Rome. But Pollius was pressing. He was probably bored, a likely state of mind for even the most accomplished Epicurean who still remembered his public past.

A traveller on the Spartacus Road has unwittingly passed through other sites where Pollius wrote his poetry. The lord of Capo Sorrento had houses in Tarentum and Tivoli as well as here. He collected statues that the great Greeks had ordered to come alive, 'iussum est quod vivere'. He had a study with busts of rulers and writers. He too would have liked to own Man A and Man B from Reggio. Of how he acquired his money there is no record, only, thanks to Statius, of how he spent it.

A visit today to the home here of Pollius Felix requires a short walk from the centre of the town, beyond the big hotels and bars, where Pavarotti's Sorrento songs have taken on Statius' former role, and away to the low cape on the southern side. The narrow way is dark behind high walls until there appears the same double view of mountain and islands, the high arch into the shaded rock-pool, the square brick pillars where the bath-houses stood, the pedestals for the twin temples. The ground plan seems precisely as Statius, our arts and architecture correspondent for the occasion, describes. We can assume some legitimate exaggeration of the fixtures and fittings. There is now some graffiti added by later dwellers. There are no surviving words by the original owner, not in the libraries here or anywhere.

Some members of the slave army escaped after their defeat. Pompey's legions found the largest group, some 5,000, and marched over them with short, stabbing swords as though it were just another day in Spain. A letter from their commander arrived at the Senate saying, in Plutarch's words, that 'although Crassus had defeated the gladiators in battle it was Pompey who had exterminated the war at its roots'.

There were also smaller bands of fugitives. Appian describes four separate squadrons which Crassus despatched against those who evaded death on the battlefield. There were said to be a few survivors still sheltering inland from Thurii twenty years later. The Emperor Augustus had the childhood name of Thurinus, possibly from the actions his father Octavius had taken against these remnants of the revolt.

A few may have killed themselves, or each other, though we have no record of that. In peaceful times, when untimely deaths might create problems for theatrical producers, suicides by gladiators – by a sponge-stick down a throat or a neck between the spokes of a cart-wheel – were rare enough to be remarked upon. But at this time a few suicides would not have been noted, might not have been noticed. Slaves trained to kill could be inventive in self-destruction, as Symmachus later found.

In earlier days the mass of slaves captured by Crassus would have gone back to their masters. They would have been branded, given new work in the quarries or the mines, made in other ways to pay the cost of their absence. From the town of Polla, a few miles from the decisive battlefield of the Spartacus war, there survives a stone plaque erected by a Roman magistrate who had built the 321-mile road from

Reggio to Capua some sixty years before. He boasts of restoring 917 runaways to their Italian owners after the first of the slave wars in Sicily. The commissioner at Polla was a man of precise numerical detail, in men, road mileage and the needs of the economy.

Alternatively, the captives could have been stood on their blocks and sold for the state treasury – or for the private accounts of Crassus and his officers. From Mount Tifata, by Diana's temple in sight of the Capuan amphitheatre, there is a proud slave-trader's gravestone, a memorial to a man called Publilius Satyr, with a vigorous portrayal of how his business was done. On the left is the seller, very clearly the seller, dressed in the Greek style, his left arm waving high in Greek enthusiasm, his right arm back to balance his weight, his whole body leaning towards his wares, his back leg pushing forward to force the purchase. On the right is the buyer, very much the buyer, in Roman toga, with lowered right arm lightly disparaging the offered object, with left arm on hip as though he would rather be somewhere else, leaning backwards away from the deal. Between them, staring forward, arms away from his body and hanging down, naked except for a loincloth, raised on his sale-block, is the little man for sale.

This may not even be a slave-dealer's memorial at all. It may just be that of a man who wanted his picture in death to be accompanied by some ordinary scene of everyday life. Selling slaves was as much a part of living as baking bread or cutting corn. A sale of the prisoners would have been possible, acceptable, not an abnormal choice if it had been made. Some punishment of the leaders was probably inevitable. At the end of earlier slave wars there had been crucifixions as well as imprisonment and sale. Crassus could have been expected to do the same, to crucify a few as a warning and to sell the rest to defray expenses.

Instead, Crassus had a true showman's plans for the slaves against whom he had intended to risk a little and had ended by risking so much. Only the most fitting finale would suffice. In the words of Orosius, pupil of St Augustine and horrified describer of the day when Romans had to fight in the arena before an audience of slaves, the whole story of Spartacus had been one of horrors. The slave war had been 'not a mere spectacle reserved for the sight of a few but the cause of universal fear'. At its ending 6,000 men had to be crucified between Capua and Rome along the 115-mile course of the Appian Way. That was to be his great spectacular.

For the Romans this was much more trouble than a slave market. Mass crucifixion was a rare and complex feat of punishment, the cutting of the trees, the marshalling of the condemned, the marching of conveniently sized groups to their allotted place. Spartacus was already dead. No one had seen him die. The people of Rome, and their slaves, would see the remains of his army die. Crucifixion was normally considered too slow a punishment for an official entertainment. This was to be an exception. Nothing on such a scale had been seen before. The first crosses were raised here where the Via Appia passed by the Colosseum of Capua – where there now stands also the brick arch built by Hadrian and the park where the Vespa-drivers play cards, confuse visitors and argue. The rest of the line stretched ahead out towards the Volturnus river, planks and poles, telegraphing and amplifying the commander's message.

A core argument for the Epicureans was that death is quick, that the moment of dying is quickly past. Philodemus says that the atoms of the body are so tiny and ready to spring apart that insensibility comes at extraordinary speed. Separation is their natural state. Fear of pain is wholly legitimate, indeed natural, for animals as well as men. But any severe pain cannot last; and any lesser pain can easily be borne.

All disciples knew that the process of dying had been hard for Epicurus himself. But the master had endured the severity in his own ways, through memories and images of pleasure. His moment of death had been as quick as all moments when it came. Someone had become nothing. That was the nature of all things. The uniquely human failure was fear of death. Seventeen centuries on, William Drummond elegantly agreed: 'Now although Death were an extreme Paine, sith it comes in an Instant, what can it bee? Naye, though it were most painefull, long continuing, and terrible uglie, why should wee feare it?'

But for any Epicureans beside the Appian Way such logic must have struggled against sights and sounds. Death by crucifixion did come in an instant – but it was only one of a million instants. Outside the schools of theory, these deaths had no half-brothers called sleep. In the training schools for

the arena the commonest fear was dying too soon. On the cross the fear was of dying too late. In the theatre of life there was some argument, not decisive but reasonable and serious, for dying in Act Four rather than Act One. On the cross a death in Act One was best by far.

The 6,000 crosses, one every thirty or forty yards past the white rock of Terracina, through Formia, through the marshes of Foro Appio, up to the sacred lakes of Ariccia and on to Rome, were a theatre of pain for Crassus, an exhibit, part entertainment, part education, a warning that there should never be another slave war. There was perhaps a certain pleasure for the general in feeling so little while others felt so much. Maybe the local philosophers had a point and pleasure and pain were really all there was – but only a passing point, a debating point for the hours after a victory dinner.

For those hanging up high above the 'queen of roads' (or tied to little more than gateposts when the wood supplies had run low) there was fear and pain beyond the boundaries of dispute. For slave-labourers and slave-teachers, swordsmen and herdsmen, veterans of Vesuvius or new recruits from the Volcei farms, there were only the inner sounds of dissolving self. There was no sense of time forward or back, no thought, no memory of rape or wine, no theatrical acts, no division of the hours except the uncertain swings of night and day, the darkness that fell over the sun and the shattering lights under the moon, the ice cold that came in the afternoon, the heat of the dew. That is some of the very little of what is known of a crucifixion.

For as long as the men were alive there was feeling followed by fainting. Chins were choked from respite to respite, eyes swivelled but not as fast as the swirling of the dust in the men's minds. Then the crows found the eyes, first with feathers beating, then with pecking and pecking and the systematic pursuit of blindness. Then the bigger and smaller birds.

Almost everything could be seen by those below who wanted to see. Most of the rest could be imagined. There never was another slave war. Once the last corpses had rotted from their ropes, the crosses had been burnt, there were only the wariest mentions that there had ever been this slave war.

The Epicureans of Campania could not – and did not – stop their arguments. Pain and death could always for them be separated by clear light and theory. The master had known it and proved it. If the two fears came back together in the darkness of night, they were phantasms, fantasies. But surely, said the critics, a death like these 6,000 deaths could be feared. Muddled thinking, the Epicureans would reply. The dying are not the true teachers. Logic is loosened by pain, its messages dissolved by the very subject it confronts. The debates of philosophers continued with shouts and shrugs. Most people in Capua were meanwhile well pleased.

Via Appia, Porta Capena, Rome

This is the end of the Spartacus Road, a place of picnics and broken columns not so very far from where it began. What happens next? What happened next? Which way for its inhabitants, for poets and gladiators, for Rome itself? There are many questions left, only a few that can be answered before the last walk to the forum.

What happened to Crassus? After his victory he emulated the dictator Sulla and 'dedicated one-tenth of his fortune to Hercules', an act of uncertain financial significance or sacrifice, and moved on. He briefly joined his rivals in ruling the Republic, led an army to the Euphrates, was defeated, humiliated and executed there. His Persian conquerors cut off his head, filled it with molten gold and used it as a theatrical prop in a Greek tragedy that they liked to perform. Some of his soldiers were transported as slaves to the far-eastern borders of the Persian Empire, possibly the first Europeans that a Chinese or travelling Korean ever saw. A daughter-in-law of Crassus, Caecilia Metella, has the finest surviving tomb of all those here on this street of tombs, finely carved with ox skulls and flowers.

To Capua? It became a colony for men to whom Julius Caesar owed a debt of service. Caesar purchased his own Capuan gladiator school to promote his future career. After his assassination the city again survived and prospered in its own peculiar way until Rome, and all the Italian cities, fell to powerful outsiders from Germany, Gaul and the new lands of Islam. Symmachus' concerns about why and how Rome weakened – through excess of Christianity, greed, old age or civil strife – are still raised anxiously by those who think themselves its successors today.

To Carlo from Capua and Carlo from Cracow? To my own fellow-travelling Koreans? Those questions are of more immediate matters and are harder. A beribboned busload of men looking very like the first Carlo, brightly uniformed centurions, sphinxes and gladiators, has just passed by on its way back to Rome, perhaps from a wedding party in the suburbs. There is no reason to imagine changes in the DVD markets of Modena or that Korean Air Lines failed to bring its passenger home.

The Spartacus Road itself? The Via Appia is still celebrated here where the line of the 6,000 crosses ended. In the near distance is the grove of the Golden Bough, the church where St Peter saw the risen Christ and the tomb where an emperor's foreign secretary, a former slave, once embalmed his wife among statues of herself as Roman goddesses, in marble, clay and bronze. Priscilla's empty plinths are still inside the ruin. Statius wrote a spectacular poem about them.

Acknowledgements

To the books that came on the road: *Appian, The Civil Wars*, Penguin Classics, 1996; *Cicero, On Ends*, Loeb Classical Library, 1931; *Claudian, Poems*, Loeb, 1922; *Florus, Epitome of Roman History*, Loeb, 1929; *Frontinus, Stratagems, Aqueducts of Rome*, Loeb, 1925; *Giovagnoli Raphael, Spartacus*, Albin Michel, Paris, 1920; *Horace, Satires 1*, Aris and Phillips Classical Texts, 1993, *Opera*, Oxford Classical Texts; Koestler, Arthur, *The Gladiators*, Vintage Classics, 1999; *Livy, History of Rome*, Loeb, 1929; *Pliny, Letters*, Loeb, 1969; *Plutarch, Lives*, Loeb, Vol 3, 1916; *Statius, Silvae and Thebaid*, Loeb, 1928 and 2003.

To other books: *An Iron Age and Roman Republican Settlement on Botromagno, Gravina di Puglia*, Alastair Small, British School at Rome, 1992; *Archytas of Tarentum, Pythagorean, Philosopher and Mathematician King*, Carl A. Huffman, CUP, 2005; *Aulus Gellius*, Leofranc Holford-Strevens, Duckworth, 1988; *Ausonius, Poems*, Loeb, 1919; *Barrington Atlas of the Greek and Roman World*, Richard J. A. Talbert (ed), Princeton, 2000; *Cowper, William, Poetical Works*, Edinburgh, 1864; *Drummond, William, Poems and Prose*, Scottish Academic Press, 1976; *Epicurus on Freedom*, Tim O'Keefe, CUP 2005; *Facing Death, Epicurus and his Critics*, James Warren, OUP 2004; *Horace, Odes Bk III, A Commentary*, R. G. M. Nisbet and Niall Rudd, OUP, 2004; *Marcus Crassus and the Late Roman Republic*, Allen Mason

347

Ward, University of Missouri Press, 1977; *Sallust, The Histories*, Clarendon Press, Oxford, 1994; *Statius, Silvae 5*, Bruce Gibson (ed), OUP, 2006. *Symmachus, A Political Biography*, Cristiana Sogno, Ann Arbor, 2006; *Symmachus, Letters*, J. P. Callu (ed), Paris, 1972–82; *Thinking Tools, Agricultural Slavery between Evidence and Models*, Ulrike Roth, Institute of Classical Studies, 2008; *Troy between Greece and Rome*, Andrew Erskine, Oxford, 2001.

To Sally Emerson, as ever; to Robert Wolff of Houston, Chris Russell, Martyn Caplin, Daniel Hochhauser and Bill Lees of London, masters of medicine; to Belinda Theis; to all Italian hosts, particularly the Raito Hotel in Salerno and the Tramontano in Sorrento, no better places to write about Epicurus; to William Goodacre of Tastes of Italy; to Peter Brown and Trinity College, Oxford; to Mary Beard, Christopher Kelly and Malcolm Schofield of Cambridge, who read the text; to Paul Webb; to Martin Redfern and Annabel Wright at HarperCollins; to Maureen Allen and Roz Dineen at the *TLS*; to my peerless agent, Ed Victor, and to my daughter and son, Anna and Michael Stothard, without whom this book would not be as it is and to whom it is dedicated.

List of Illustrations

While every effort has been made to trace the owners of copyright material reproduced herein, the publishers would like to apologise for any omissions and would be pleased to incorporate missing acknowledgements in future editions.